Amigas del Señor
Methodist Monastery

Beth Blodgett, (Sister Alegría)
Prairie Naoma Cutting (Sister Confianza)

Quaker Abbey Press, LLC

Amigas del Señor: Methodist Monastery
Beth Blodgett (Sister Alegría) Prairie Naoma Cutting (Sister Confianza)

Copyright 2010, Quaker Abbey Press, LLC,
4819 SE 70,
Portland, OR 97206

Editors: Rosalie V. Grafe, Cliff N. Hansen, Tim Harnett
Front cover: Adapted from *Très Riches Heures du Duc de Berry,*
Photos: Beth Blodgett, Prairie Naoma Cutting, April Cutting,
Rosalie V. Grafe

ISBN 978-0-9820035-1-0

For CIP, contact Library of Congress

All profits from the print version of *Amigas del Señor: Methodist Monastery* go to support the work of the monastery and sisters of Amigas del Señor

I am not called to be successful, I am called to be faithful.

Teresa of Calcutta

Think about who are the big men today, and who are the little guys; who are the rich and who are the poor; who are the bosses and who are the underlings. In each one of those situations, to which group do you belong? To which group does your church belong? Make it your business always to take the part of those who suffer, not of those who cause suffering.

Justo L. González
Tres Mases en la Escuela de Patronos ©
1997 (Author's translation)

TABLE OF CONTENTS

LIST OF ILLUSTRATIONS

FOREWORD

Amigas del Senor: Methodist Monastery, recounts the trials, successes, and mishaps of two women who have embarked upon the
daunting task of establishing a monastery in a foreign country.
Two years ago Beth Blodgett (Hermana Alegría) and Prairie
Naomi Cutting (Hermana Confianza) emigrated to Honduras,
one of the poorest countries in the world, with the intention
of living in voluntary poverty and offering medical assistance
among the poor. They have experienced all the difficulties that
face immigrants, becoming accustomed to a new language,
strange food, and a different culture. Gaining acceptance and
trust among the local population, and learning how to make
even the scant living characteristic of the people around them
have presented constant challenges. Their mission and pur-
pose are not always understood, either by the people they have
come to serve or by the people they have left behind in the
United States.

Hermanas Alegria and Confianza are struggling to lead a
monastic life according to the spirit of the age-old traditions
based on a life lived in common nurtured by daily prayer together, scripture reading (lectio divina), material poverty, and
meaningful work. The sisters make decisions according to
the Quaker model, by prayer and discernment together. Their
venture is unique sinceit began, not in the usual way as a foundation from an established monastery, but anew under the
sponsorship of a Methodist community.

This first-hand account of the experiences of these coura-
geous women during the past four years makes for fascinating
reading. One can laugh, or at least smile, at their misadventures.
There are sad moments, too, as they encounter ignorance, pov-

erty, and lack of medical and legal assistance for those who need it most. Their decision to live in voluntary poverty can lead the readers to assess their own attitudes toward possessions and abundance. Everyone can learn something from this story of a tenuous beginning which will certainly bear fruit in future and unknown ways.

Sister Alberta Dieker, O.S.B. (Order of St. Benedict)
Queen of Angels Monastery
840 South Main Street
Mt. Angel, Oregon 97362

Author of *A Tree Rooted in Faith: A History of Queen of Angels Monastery.*

AUTHORS' PREFACE

These letters are your invitation to travel with us as we
founded and then lived the first few years of Amigas del Señor Methodist Monastery.

There is an old saying in monastic circles: "Everyone wants
to live with the monks, but no one wants to take the vows."
Here is your opportunity to "live with" the nuns during these
exciting years.

We often ask ourselves, "What kind of nuns are we?" Usually this is a rhetorical question to which the obvious answer is
"Not very good ones." But we also ask ourselves this question
in earnest. We are United Methodists (officially members and
everything). Our governance is Quaker (Society of Friends as
learned at Multnomah Monthly Meeting of the Religious Soci
ety of Friends). Yet we are very traditional as monasteries go.
We travel two by two. That's how Jesus sent out the disciples.
We wear habits; live in material poverty;and schedule our days
around prayer. We live closely with the Creation.

Both of us come from "liberal Christian backgrounds." The
"conservative" Christian vocabulary, used by our friends and
neighbors here in Honduras, has taken some getting used to.
Now we use it too, as it takes on new meaning for us. That
[earlier]discomfort has resulted in omission of most of the
spiritual journey in these letters.

This is not the book that we would write if we were to start
one today. We will not go back and re-write with hindsight to
clean up our act. This is what happened as it seemed to us at
the time. Transparency takes courage, but you already know
that we have that. Transparency also takes humility. We are trying to grow into that.

ACKNOWLEDGEMENTS

We remind ourselves that we are here talking about the book, not the monastery. All of those who have supported us in any way with the monastery, obviously, also helped with the book. They are too many to name and the type of support highly varied. Thank you to everyone.

Several friends suggested (persistently and vigorously) that we write a book. We hope that publishing this series of letters fulfills that vision.

We are grateful to Linda Sullivan who suggested and arranged to have our letters included in the online communication of the Oregon-Idaho Conference of the United Methodist Church. How fabulous to have someone in a large bureaucracy with eyes to see and ears to hear.

We thank God who told Rosalie to say "Yes," to us. Thank you, Reader, for sharing in our lives.

Dios le bendiga,
Sister Alegría
Sister Confianza

Amigas del Señor
Methodist Monastery

THE LETTERS

Beth—New Ministry in Honduras—January 16, 2006

My first trip to Honduras was in May, 1999—a medical mission trip. My first few trips were to a clinic founded by the Carolina Honduras Health Foundation in Limón, Colón, Honduras.

As I learned more Spanish, more tropical medicine and more about the communities served, my interest grew. My focus, as a pediatrician, had been in both disease prevention and health promotion. It was soon obvious that the public health center was better for me than the fast and furious urgent care atmosphere of the usual medical mission setting.

Having grown up on a small dairy farm in Wisconsin, I thought that I knew about farmers. I was wrong.

For the first time in my life, I met farmers who were skinny (too skinny), farmers' wives who were skinny (too skinny), and farmers' children who were stunted! (Note: the sexist language is deliberate; it represents the actuality in Honduras.) Farmers' families are without an adequate diet. Impossible, but true.

More visits—about twenty months total over six years—more conversations, more mutual teaching with the health care professionals in the public health clinic,more experiential learning. A three-week stint at ECHO (Educational Concerns for Hunger Organization, a Christian organization devoted to helping train helpers for third world agricultural work).

Fifty percent of Hondurans are under the age of eighteen. It is not rare for fourteen-year-old girls to marry and start families (or to start families without getting married). Honduras needs pediatricians.

Vitamin A deficiency (which causes night blindness) is so

common that public health personnel administer the vitamin to infants with their immunizations. The nation's public health budget is a small fraction of what is needed. Clinics routinely run out of important medications like antibiotics and asthma medicines. In Honduras, I have treated patients with deficiencies of niacin, riboflavin, iron, and Vitamin B12. (In the twenty-first century!)

On my parents' family farm, we raised crops for a nutritious diet fit for royalty. I learned that tropical farmers (even subsistence farmers) could also produce a well-balanced (although less elegant) diet—if they knew how.

All of these thoughts are of the practical, physical world. But what went on deeper was, of course, of greater importance. I have spent, and continue to spend, a lot of time with Friends (Quakers) and participated in the Discernment processes—two or more Friends sitting together in silence to listen for a commonly understood direction to go.

In the mid 1990s, I began seriously to wonder if I had a monastic vocation. Completely lacking experience to help with this discernment, I read many authors: Theresa of Avila, Brother Lawrence, Francis of Assisi, Mother Teresa of Calcutta, Julian of Norwich, Elizabeth Fry, John Woolman and, of course, the famous Anonymous who wrote *Cloud of Uunknowing*. (Very good authors, I recommend them all.)

The year 2000 was the first year I paid no income taxes. My convictions to not support violence (either organized or disorganized) convinced me to reduce my income below the taxable level. The discipline of that practice was good training for what came next.

It has become clear that my routine need for spiritual practice (prayer, worship, meditation, choose your own word) is higher than it may be for others. My summers included several weeks at campgrounds in Oregon: Suttle Lake, Latgawa, Wallowa Lake and Camp Magruder. This fed me.

Don't ever forget, the greatest bargain you'll ever have is

being a camp volunteer, especially if it is a kids' camp. The pay is great, but none of it is in money. I spent one November at St. Brigid of Kildare Monastery, a United Methodist Benedictine monastery for women in St. Joseph, Minnesota. As I understand it, this is the first (and only) United Methodist Monastery for both women and men.

Everything happens for a reason. Every experience builds on the previous experiences. In October, 2003, I was practically handed four acres of land in the Limón region of Honduras. In 2004, I had some fruit trees planted there. In 2005, most of those trees had survived and I experimented with some vegetables. (The okra, oh, the okra.) These elements form the background for this story. For more, see: http://www.mission-resources.unitingchurch.org.au/?page_id=30

We are feeling our way a bit since then. There will be an experimental farm——about half an acre. There will be volunteer health work. There will be music; there will be prayer; there will be connection to the public school.

Prairie is a Sojourner. That term in monastic tradition means one who makes a commitment (in this case, one year) to be a part of the monastery, but without a life-long plan of living there. I am looking forward to this year. Exciting stuff, an answer to prayer. We will be *Amigas del Señor* —Female Friends of the Lord.

Beth—Two Weeks and Counting—January 18, 2006

The next step is a very big one. On February first, Prairie Cutting and I leave for Honduras, leaving Oregon by Greyhound; we will be taking buses all the way to Limón.

Our first Honduran stop will be in La Ceiba, where we will join Gloria Borgman's medical mission team who will be based there for their outreach to El Pino and the Region of San Francisco. We'll spend the weekend with them before they dig in with their high-energy health care and we take the bus to Limón.

For the first time, we will not be staying with friends in Limón. We have rented a tiny house from an aunt of Gloria Lacayo's. Yes, about one-third of the town is related to Gloria. Aunt can mean almost any relative only slightly older than you—people that we would call cousins several times removed.

Profa Licha is delightful. She is a retired teacher. She is one of the three founders of the junior high—all elementary teachers who saw a need. They just started it, with the community donating building materials and work. When the government inspected and approved it five years later, the school became official. Now it is staffed with teachers trained to teach junior high.

Prairie and I will be founding a Methodist monastery for women. I had to make the hard decision whether to have it be Quaker or Methodist. The Methodist church is active on the north coast of Honduras and we have strong connections with it. It will be strongly influenced by Quaker tradition. Our name is *Amigas del Señor*. That means Female Friends of the Lord.

We have four acres of land in the neighborhood of Limoncito. It is on the road to La Fortuna (population about 300). We are about two miles from the center of Limoncito (where the elementary school is). The folks who live further up the road where we will live are part of La Fortuna. So, we will soon know as neighbors, more people who are from a different neighborhood than we are officially in.

We have some fruit and nut trees planted. The buildings are still in the dream stage. If today were a really high-confidence day, I would say planning stage. We expect to live in town for a few months at least.

Prairie has completed a bachelor's degree with a major in music, and speaks Spanish. (She is very modest about her Spanish, so it is hard to know how good it is.) I think she'll be able to help me with my grammar and I'll be able to help her with the vocabulary useful to our work.

I am very grateful for her.

So far, we are right on schedule in the preparations for this trip. I am looking forward to climbing on that bus, taking a big sigh, and then a nap!

Prairie—January, 2006

As many of you know, I leave February first to volunteer for a year in Honduras. I will be going with pediatrician Beth Blodgett of Portland, Oregon to the town of Limón (population 3,800) on the northeastern Caribbean coast. We will be doing health work with the local clinic where Beth has volunteered over the last few years, as well as doing some experimental farming and gardening, trying to grow foods that will provide much-needed nutrients for ourselves and the local community. Beth's dream is to start a small monastic community in the United Methodist and Quaker traditions. She has purchased about four acres of land on a mountain several miles inland from Limón. We will be moving there as soon as we get some buildings built (sleeping and living quarters, a kitchen, and a composting toilet) and have another couple of women to join us.

Beth—The Beginning of the Journey—February 1, 2006

Monasticism has the tradition of personal poverty. Most monastic orders let it go by the wayside very early in their life. That is, as soon as they have wealth, they want to hang on to it too. After all, think about all the good you can do with material wealth.

Prairie and I leave tomorrow morning via Greyhound. Sometimes people ask me why we are traveling by bus. My answer is that we don't want to hitchhike.

We travel by bus because that is how our neighbors in Honduras travel. That is to say, we poor people travel by bus. It is what is available to us. On the north coast of Honduras six to ten percent of households have a motor vehicle. Over half of those are working vehicles, like a pickup truck that must earn its keep. People who have motor vehicles as luxury items (meaning they aren't working vehicles) are few and we all understand that those folks are rich. We travel by bus. It is a very good lesson in patience. It is a very good lesson in self-importance. Sometimes people tell me that they wouldn't travel by bus. They don't even suspect that they are bragging about how rich they are. It will take many days to get to La Ceiba, where we will spend almost a week, then on to Limón.

Last week, I had lunch with friends before I went to the bus station in Portland to buy the second-lap tickets. I needed to use the bathroom and promptly. So, I went looking for it. One must enter the ticket-only part of the bus station to use the bathrooms. The guard refused me entrance. I explained that I was about to buy a ticket, but that I really needed to use the bathroom first. She told me to buy the ticket and then she would let me in. (I don't think that she would have, since it wasn't going to be a ticket for that day). I told her that I couldn't wait that long and asked where the closest public restroom was. The Amtrak [train] station. So I went there. I am an experienced Amtrak traveler, so I knew that would be okay. If I had not been, I would have been in trouble. Of course, if I were used to being poor, I would have known better and not showed up at a Greyhound station with a full bladder. These details aren't so interesting when they are about our own country, the challenges faced by our own poor. But this is part of the experience of being poor.

Greyhound Bus Station, Portland, Oregon

When you send us letters, they may take two weeks or a month to arrive. Mail arrives in Limón once a week. Then the messenger tracks down the recipient to tell her that she has a letter at the post office. Then we walk to the post office to claim our letter. If the postmaster knows the addressee, he may entrust them with letters for other people in their neighborhood or circle of acquaintances. One signs to register acceptance of a letter for oneself or one's friends. If the postman is not there, his wife will give you a letter if she really knows you. If not, she will deny that anything arrived for you. Responsibility is a terrible thing to accept, you know. Postage (this week) is eighty-four cents to mail a letter of an ounce or less from the U.S. to Honduras.

Prairie's address is:
[1]Sor Prairie Cutting
Limón, Colón
Honduras
Mine is tougher, what titles to use?
Beth Blodgett
Limón, Colón. Honduras

---

1. Sor is the title for a religious sister (nun). We later decided not to use this title.

Beth—*The Road to Tepic, Nayarit, Mexico*—*February 6, 2006*

Our trip is going along smoothly. We stayed overnight in Phoenix. The bus from Los Angeles to Phoenix broke down just east of San Bernadino, California. So, we just sat on the freeway, waiting for another bus to arrive. The second bus worked just fine. We left Phoenix on the Greyhound at nine AM on Friday, February third. Prairie noticed some purple cacti. I thought that I had mis-heard her. But, sure enough, purple cacti—sort of delicate versions of prickly pear. I had never even heard of purple cacti before.

We arrived at Nogales, Arizona just before noon and left Nogales, Mexico just over an hour later in a Cruzero bus. (Cruzero has a business relationship with Greyhound.) We went through immigration. and paid forty-one dollars for the privilege. Last time I passed this way, no one asked for my passport or my money.

As I understand it, Mexico is getting more serious about its borders, both in terms of international issues and in terms of changing the reputation of the border guards for corruption. We went to the office, to fill out papers, then to the cashier (in a different building) to pay our fee, then back to the office where our passports were waiting for us. The lady who accepted the fee wanted an ID card. I told her that the Immigration Office had our passports. Then she asked for another ID card. When I told her that it (my driver's license) was inside my money belt, around my waist, under my dress, she didn't need it any longer. It was not a place for undressing. We had planned on getting only to Hermosillo that day. But when the bus arrived, we reconsidered.

We ate *mole* [a sauce] for the first time. We liked it. We bought tickets for an overnight first class bus all the way to Tepic, Nayarit, Mexico. People are very proud of their states. We see a lot of billboards, encouraging state loyalty. As an example, they buy things that have been grown and/or manufactured in this state.

We arrived here about three PM, after a chilling ride. No, not scary. Hardly anything scary ever happens. The bus was a first class bus with air conditioning. We were just cold. We have changed into our blue dresses. We knew that the Greyhound, way up north, would be cold, so we started out wearing long pants. Now, we put on the long-sleeved blouses over our dresses and use a sheet for Prairie and a Nepalese prayer shawl for me to stay warm enough in the bus.

Traveling overnight is tiring. We were very grateful to arrive. Our chosen hotel wasn't ready for us, so we walked around town a little before checking in. We were permitted to put our luggage behind the desk, so we were free to walk out into our first truly hot afternoon. By the time we got to the Central Square, Prairie had the pink cheeks sign—signifying heat exhaustion. We quickly found a place that sold huge fruit drinks. I had pineapple-coconut and she had limeade. That solved our heat-dehydration problem and, as the sun began to go lower in the sky, we were cooler.

I take my day of rest very seriously. When Prairie turned off the light in our hotel room at nine PM, I was already asleep. We agreed to sleep later the next morning, thinking that if either of us were still asleep, that would signify we needed the sleep.

Prairie and I had discussed a lot of our travel options in the evening—tired minds don't do very well at finding solutions. But, fresh in the morning, it seemed wise to take this whole day off from traveling. After all, our hardest work is planning out the travel, choosing hotels, figuring out how to get from the bus station to the hotel—so, today we are resting.

We took music to the park, as the hotel doesn't seem the place to sing or play. One doesn't know the musical taste of one's neighbors, after all. It is a comfortable, sunny day. We are comfortable in our short sleeves and sun hats.

After we went to the tourist office for advice, we visited the grass cross, a location associated with many miracles. From there, we went to a city park with lots of different children's activities available. The zoo was tiny but had a lot of Mexican birds and animals. We did a lot of walking. Walking felt very good to our poor legs deprived of exercise for the last few days. For lunch, we went to a seafood place. Delicious.

The tourist office had some interesting things to say about tourist season, etc. When we looked over our *Let's Go Mexico* book and our map, we decided on the next leg of our trip. Our Spanish was useful. Sometimes it was hard to remember the vocabulary. Together we did better than either of us would alone. And, yes, people ask me if Prairie is my daughter.

Beth—A Long Bus Ride to Tejuantepec
February 6–7, 2006

Last Sunday (two days ago) as we were reading our travel guide, walking around Tepic and asking questions, we had to face hard reality. The tourist season is still strong along the coast and the prices are high. Also, the roads are narrow, so buses don't get very far in a given period of time. We decided on a cross-country route.

We left our hotel in Tepic at 5:55 AM yesterday. By 6:05 we were sitting in a bus to go to Guadalajara. Guadalajara was just a pass-through point to get to Mexico City. We arrived there about 6:30 PM. We crossed a time zone, so it didn't really take that much riding time, but it was dusk and rush hour.

Rush hour in Mexico City lasts until nine PM, we are told. This made us not want to take the Metro. (I did the Metro last time alone, but not during rush hour and not with as heavy luggage as we have this time.) Prairie carries a big heavy duffle and a blue cloth shopping bag. I carry her backpack on my back, pull my little carry-on, and carry a blue cloth shopping bag. This is too much for the Metro. Our route would have had us change lines—climbing up and down stairs. When we ride the buses, we check-in the big duffle and my carry-on. That still gives us plenty of access to stuff that we may want as we travel.

So, we arrived at the North bus station, went right to the money-changing place and then to the taxi-ticket-selling booth. As soon as we had our taxi ticket (seventy-five pesos for one to four people with the same destination), a very nice porter-type man offered to take our heavy luggage and lead us to the taxi stand. It was the best ten peso (one dollar) tip we ever invested. The taxi ride through Mexico City during rush hour made us glad we were in the backseat without responsibilities and the driver was doing the hard work. The ride to the East bus station was a long one. (I know we're headed south, but our bus leaves from the East station, go figure.)

This time we didn't want a porter. We wanted the slower pace that allowed us to notice where we were going. We checked out a few bus companies, including the one that I used last year. I was kind of disappointed that they had nothing for us. We bought our tickets for an eight PM bus a few minutes before seven. Then we split up. I stood in line for the luggage check-in while Prairie cruised the bus station for food.

I stood in that line for thirty-five minutes to learn that I was in the wrong one. So, Mexican-style, I just cut across to the front of the correct one. We had some very nice fajitas, finishing them just in time to board our bus for Tejuantepec. Our bus arrived just about seven AM.

When we travel all day and all night, we cover the distance that we would by traveling three days, daytime-only. It does leave us tired, though.

When we got to Tejuantepec, we took a taxi to the hotel recommended by our travel book. They accepted us even though it was before nine AM. We were very ready for a good breakfast. After clean-up, we went to a local restaurant for a good solid Mexican breakfast. I had scrambled eggs with onions and Prairie had huevos rancheros. Then with tortillas, and refried beans on the side and an order of fresh watermelon, we had so much we couldn't even finish it all.

Then we walked around town. Our legs really needed the exercise. There are fabulous little moto-taxis. They have a wooden platform behind the driver, with extra wheels—and sturdy railings. Of course one stands up on this platform behind the driver. We walked and walked, then took this cool little taxi back to the center of town. This is a very windy place. I can even see some trees re-shaped by the strong wind. It was a bit dusty riding into the wind standing behind the moto driver. Four pesos each—our frivolity for the day.

This town has a lot of old churches. We have visited some of them. The stained glass windows and icons are frustrating. I don't know how to read them. Crucifixion scenes with a brown-skinned Jesus seemed surprising at first. It didn't seem appropriate to take pictures in those churches.

We walked through the market and I bought a small mango (Prairie didn't want one) and some little fruits—very sweet—called little *zapotes*. But they are not at all like what we call zapotes in Honduras. They have big seeds, there isn't a lot of flesh to the fruit, but what there is, is very nice.

Our next leg of the journey will commence in the wee hours. We'll go to bed very early and then get up to catch the three AM bus to Tapachula. From there we will catch a bus to cross the border into Guatemala—to Quezaltenago— also called *Xela* (pronounced *shela*). It is not exactly on the route to La Ceiba, but Autumn, Prairie´s sister, is there right now doing an international studies program and we will visit her.

Our night traveling has proven to be very efficient. We'll stay overnight in Quezaltenago, before crossing the rest of Guatemala.

Beth—An Interesting Travel Day Gets Beth and Prairie to Quezaltenago—February 7–9, 2006

On Tuesday, we played tourist a bit in Tejuantepec, including eating lunch at a local food stand. Then at 1:30 PM we went to bed, setting the alarm for 1:35 AM Wednesday. We had a bus to catch, of course. We went to sleep easily—remember we had ridden a bus all night the night before.

At 1:35 AM we got up. Nothing like sleeping the clock around to restore one. At 1:50 we had a taxi to the bus station. At two we were listening to the bus station person tell us that the three AM bus we learned about the day before did not exist. We would have to take a short-hop bus, then another; then we could go to Tapachula.

By 2:05 we were on our way to the first stop. At 2:45 we were on our second bus of the morning, scheduled to go to Tapachula, a sort of bottleneck on the bus route from the U.S. to Honduras. Tapachula had a huge hurricane and flood last October and was damaged badly. We were told that the bus would take eight hours to get there—since the book said six hours, we figured there was still a lot of flood damage. Well, there was. We saw the classic look of the broadened, flattened riverbeds from a big flood. We saw bridges out; we had a detour; we saw a lot of bridge and road construction. And we saw some work in river-course control being done.

The ride actually only took seven hours. The bus wasn't very crowded, so we were able to separate, put our feet up just a bit, and snooze.

I won't tell you every detail of our travel day, but you should know that we traveled in nine different public transportation vehicles. I'll count them out for you: regular taxi, local bus, long-haul bus, regular taxi, *colectivo* bus (a tiny bus designed to hold about fourteen people that usually carries twenty), then walk across the border, then colectivo taxi (six adults, one toddler and the driver in an ordinary car), another local bus, a first-class bus, a regular taxi. This got us to Quezaltenago at five PM.

We were pretty happy to arrive.

Now, to Quezaltenago. It means "Place of the Quetzal." Quetzal is the name of the national bird; it has long green tail feathers. Quetzal is also the name of the currency in Guatemala. It is the second largest city in Guatemala and is off the beaten track. It was winter when we were there. At about 5,500 feet elevation, it gets cool at night—even when in daytime it's shirt-sleeve weather.

We went from sardines in terrible heat—having to take a rest, water and food break in the middle of our border-crossing hike—to mountain coolness. (Well, cold, actually.) The views on the mountain ride, from the Mexico-Guatemala border to Quezaltenago, were spectacular.

When we arrived in town, both hotels on our wish list were full. We had come to this place to visit Autumn, Prairie's sister, who is doing a university-based international studies program here. Her hostess took us in. We were very grateful. She put two cots into Autumn's little bedroom. She made us a beautiful dinner and was a very gracious hostess.

Tomorrow we leave town at 5:15 in a first class bus to Guatemala City. From there across the border to Copán. It should be a less interesting travel day than yesterday—at least we hope so. More next week.

Beth—Copán. and the Arrival in La Ceiba
February 13–14, 2006

When we were walking around town looking for a place to have a meal, one of the food vendors recognized us as *monjas*—religious women.

We stayed overnight in Ruinas de Copán. We had arrived after the closing of the park but took a nice walk in the twilight. It was good to stretch our legs and get a bit of a feel for the place. It is apparently just the end of the dry season as the area is not as green and lush as I remember it. We got a hotel easily—Los Gemalos (the twins), but we had the painful experience of finding out why. As the Doña was showing us the way, we passed an obviously empty suite and she asked us if we would like better accommodations, closer to the bathrooms.

We stayed with what we had reserved, but before we were done signing in, a local-looking couple asked for a room. She told them that she was sorry but she had no rooms. At the same time, Prairie looked at the hotel register—only foreigners. Ah well, another bubble burst.

From Copán, we took a first-class bus to San Pedro Sula. We watched a silly movie—in English—en route. At San Pedro Sula, we used the bus terminal bathroom (not at all first class) and got directions to the bus that would take us to La Ceiba. We stopped to purchase fruit along the five-block walk. I had an orange (possibly the best I have ever eaten) and Prairie had a banana. At the bus station, a bus to La Ceiba was just pulling out. We bought tickets for the next bus and found water. Prairie bought a meal without knowing what the entree was. It had rice, beans, tortillas and cabbage salad. The entrée was *chuleta*—pork chop. One meal was just right for the two of us.

As we were eating, we noticed that the bus was loading. No, announcement. So, we packed up the rest of our meal and boarded the bus. We finished our food on board.

We had called Doña Marina the evening before from Copán. She apologized for not being able to accept us. She had fallen and broken her arm in November and it has not healed properly. Her doctor says that she has osteoporosis and that is why it doesn't heal well. So far, no treatment has been very helpful for her recovery. Right now, she is receiving injections of vitamins. So, we went to Doña Thelma's house instead. I had stayed with her last November; it also felt like home.

Sunday morning we went to church at Zion. Well, the whole place was locked up tight and the walls had been sandblasted, building materials all over the ground, a huge mess. Fortunately, Juan, Gina, and kids had not yet left the parsonage for services.[2] It was raining just a bit. They gave us a ride to a neighborhood called *La Isla* (the island). There is a little Meth-

2 Pastor Jaun Simpson has been a valuable ally to me since 1989. He has since moved to Rooten. We miss him.

odist church in La Isla (very charming and with much better acoustics) where the worship service was held.

We experienced a cold front. We were told that it was the same one that hit New York. Can that be? Cold fronts here always mean rain. So the day before, we too had rain. We enjoyed our lazy afternoon that Sunday. Yesterday, we got up, got ready to go and made our list of all of the things to do while we were still in town and began doing them.

One of the things was putting Prairie's name on my savings account. Yes, so far, the monastery is theoretical and the finances are in my name. But it seems wise for us not to be dependent upon one person for having access to the cash.

Big forms to fill out. It was quite a stitch. Banks (here) need to know a lot of stuff that seem to me none of their business. The banker (a young woman) directed all of the questions about Prairie to me (as Prairie said—as though she doesn't understand Spanish). The questions included things like what her income is—zero. What her occupation is—monja. What her training is—musician. What her educational level is—bachelor's degree. These are all pretty unbelievable to the banker. We are in a country where only a few of the most gifted are considered musicians and they certainly don't get university degrees. The banker seemed to use all of her professional control to keep from asking, "Why are you willing to have this person have access to your bank account?" She also had a hard time with our address: Loma Alta, Limoncito, Limón, Colón. It should have reference to some landmark, especially a business. There aren't any businesses near our place.

But remember, it is a rainy day. We are each wearing a hat, but they don't match. Prairie's is green. I am wearing a long-sleeved white blouse over my dress for warmth. Prairie is wearing a bright red water-resistant windbreaker. We hardly look like a matched set; still, the contrast to Friday evening in Copán is sharp.

I've made it to Honduras, after a rather interesting trip by bus—we made up the itinerary as we went along. I will give you a brief overview of the adventure so far:

Beth Blodgett, my travel partner, and I left Portland early on February first by Greyhound. We took an overnight bus to Phoenix, Arizona, going through the Willamette Valley, Southern Oregon, over the Siskyou mountains (where there was snow) and into Weed, California, where the scent of its namesake wafted through the air at the cabin-like bus station. In Sacramento, we changed buses and tried to sleep until LA— where we arrived about 6:30 AM and changed buses yet again to go on to Phoenix. I had never been to the Southwest before and was rather taken by the desert hills and cacti through which we passed. Just outside of San Bernadino, California, we had the only bus trouble of the whole trip when the Greyhound bus broke down and we were stuck at the side of the road for several hours. We arrived in Phoenix around six PM.

The next morning we left on *Cruzero*, Greyhound's Mexican partner line, and headed towards the border town of Nogales where we and the Mexican nationals did our respective duties at customs. Beth and I got our passports stamped and each paid the twenty dollar fee for a thirty-day visa. Our original plan had been to get as far as Hermosillo—but soon we realized we would arrive rather early in the day. When we arrived, we looked at the bus schedules, and decided to take another overnight bus which would get us to the city of Tepic. The bus was first-class service, which included too cold AC and cheesy Mexican movies. (In fact, the sound was so low we had to make up the dialogue ourselves.)

We arrived in Tepic about two PM and went to the hotel recommended by the travel book, *Let's Go Mexico*. We were able to walk around and enjoy the town and its Parque Central. We were told that Tepic has about 300,000 citizens. We decided to stay a second night and take Sunday as our day of rest, so we walked to the Parque de la Loma (Park on the Hill), where there was a children's amusement park and a mini-zoo. We enjoyed eating at local restaurants which included good Mexican food like chiles rellenos and mole, as well as interesting food at a seafood restaurant, including fried shrimp tacos.

After having talked with a friendly guy at the tourist office (who spoke some English and had himself visited Portland) we decided to forgo our original idea of following the western coastline. It would be too expensive in tourist season and would take too long. Only local buses go along the coast. Instead, we would take a bus to Mexico City, a taxi to the other bus station (they have one for each of the four directions), and another overnight bus to a town called Tehuantepec.

Mexico up to this point was mostly desert, brown and dry. It varied a little, with some parts being more covered in trees, and some in cacti. I saw saguaro for the first time, and large prickly-pear, both green and purple. With mountains and mesas in view, we stayed mostly to the west of the Sierra Madres. In some places we saw crops of various types, and orchards, and further south there were pineapple fields—spiky bushes that looked to me like large aloe-vera plants, or ornamental yucca. Once we got into the southernmost part of the country, Chiapas and the Isthmus of Tehuantepec, the terrain changed to more jungle-like green vegetation.

Tehuantepec was an interesting smaller town, which has a higher population of native peoples of predominantly Mayan descent. We were now in Chiapas where many women wore traditional dress. Apparently in the summer months every neighborhood holds a fair celebrating its traditions.

The highlight of the day was taking a ride in a *moto-carro* (or taxi) which is a three-wheeled motorcycle with a small platform with railings on back, in which we stood and felt the breeze in our hair; it made both of us smile. We went to bed in the middle of the afternoon, because we were to rise about two AM in order to catch the bus to the border and get into Guatemala the next day.

There was evidence of the major floods from last October, with widened rocky riverbeds, and temporary bridges where others had been washed out. A lot of work has already been done.

That Wednesday—when we left at two AM—was our most memorable travel day. We ended up taking nine different transport vehicles. We took a taxi to the bus station, a short bus trip to the next town, and then a good long ride to Tapachula, the biggest town near the Guatmalan border. There, we took a taxi to another bus station, and were informed we actually needed to take a colectivo to the border town of Talisman.

This collectivo had rather old seats. I was stuck in the back row with three other adults. Luckily, I was by the window, and was able to put my shoulder out to fit a little better. Unfortunately, I was sitting right on a metal bar (the edge of the seat), which left me sore and bruised for a day or two. This van seemed full when we got in, but the guy who solicited passengers kept squeezing them in till there were nearly twenty people in there. It was a twenty–minute ride to the border, but it felt like a century.

The day was hot and I was sweating and red in the face. As we got off the colectivo, we were accosted by four money-changing guys who were full of bad advice and worse exchange rates. We weren't thinking clearly enough to do otherwise. But we walked to Immigration, where I took off an extra shirt, and drank some water. Then we walked across the bridge to Guatemala, paid our entrance fee, and were able to get a bite to eat from a vendor selling chicken tamales. We asked around to find the best route to Xela [3], which included a colectivo taxi (a car filled to the brim with seven adults and a child) to a nearby town, where we caught a chicken bus (one of those repainted old American school buses) to San Marcos, then another bus

3 Quezaltenago

to Xela. We had to take one more taxi into the center of town to find a hotel. At higher elevations, on the last buses, the temperature cooled off so that I almost regretted having removed my outer shirt. It was pleasantly cool in Xela, but the hotels we tried were full. Luckily, I had the phone number for my sister Autumn's host family, and they were gracious enough to take us in for the two nights we were there.

We had a nice visit with Autumn, and got the chance to walk around the city, which is where I had studied Spanish for two weeks in 2004. I knew my way around, but it wasn't quite as romantic as my memories had made it seem. Friday we caught the five AM bus to Guatemala City, another bus to Chiquimula, a third bus to the border town of El Florido, and after crossing, a colectivo bus (I got to sit in the front seat this time) to Copán, Honduras. It seemed like a relaxing day of travel. We only spent the night in Copán, which is a small town, now and quite touristy (the proportion of gringos was big) because of the large Mayan ruins there. The next day it only took two buses to get through San Pedro Sula to La Ceiba, where we are now. Whew!

My impression of Honduras so far is that it is green, a bright green like spring. The rainy season is more or less over and we expect days to be hot, though it actually poured on us the last two days and has been rather chilly (in the sixties). We walked out on the old rotting pier, previously used by foreign banana companies, and looked north across the Caribbean—which was quite choppy that day.

On Sunday we attended the local Methodist church, which is in the British tradition and English-speaking. It was a good experience. The pastor referred to himself as being Creole; he's from Panama. He and his wife have four darling children, a son and three daughters, all under age nine, and the girls were most friendly to me.

We will be here a week doing errands and meeting some Methodist clinics and U.S. volunteers who are coming down, before going out to Limón next Monday to set up household.

Beth—Hard at Work in the Field—February 16–20, 2006

We have been running around doing errands all week. Some days by the end of the day, I am very tired. Some days, Prairie is.

We spent much of Wednesday with Eloyda in El Pino. I saw a few patients and we went over some general management stuff. We looked over some of the donated medical equipment from the U.S. These things seem so standard when you haven't worked in another country.

The cupboard is almost bare there, but the partnership with the public health center continues, which helps everybody. We just write a prescription and send the patient to the other clinic and they do the same if we have something they don't have. A medical team from South Dakota arrives tonight. When they leave, the pharmacy will be stuffed. The medical teams are very generous.

We have begun the realistic part of the financial management of our new project. First thing we must cast our bread upon the waters. Tuesday, we bought about ninety dollars worth of school notebooks, pencils, rulers and teachers' red pens. When they were all packed up, we got a taxi to the bus terminal to ship them to Juan Ramón Manaiza, my friend (now school superintendent) in Limón. He knows which little schools are the most impoverished. It is hard to imagine trying to learn to read—without the possibility of writing.

We got to the bus terminal and met the bus guys. They said that they would take them and that they wanted to be paid a hundred lempiras.[4] I called them robbers and tried to get a better price. Then another man came up, recognized me, and told me that Juana Nidia (the RN of Centro de Salud in Limón) was in the bus station. I was delighted, of course, and walked

4 Honduran currency

off to see her, leaving my boxes with the would-be robbers. I had called them robbers but was quite willing to leave them my valuable boxes.

Off I went to see Juana Nidia. It was good to see her. As always, she was busy; this time she was making one more report. Cooper, the head health promoter was there, too. (Cooper is the guy who gave me a ride on his motorcycle to the bus when I was still a little weak with malaria on a previous trip.) While we were still talking, the bus driver came and asked me what to do about the boxes. I paid him the hundred lempiras—the robber.

Our to do list was so long we wondered if we would ever get through it. But now it is hard to remember all of it.

We picked up our books from ECHO (Educational Concerns for Hunger Organization), and took them home and started reading. One really good booklet (in Spanish) about raising chickens for the smallholder is missing Section Four—in a six-section booklet. Unfortunately, all the copies were flawed. ECHO would send the missing section if they could find it. It is too bad for us, but worse for ECHO. We have almost the identical information in English. The presentation in Spanish was just less daunting. Somehow it seemed a little more do-able in Spanish

On Tuesday, we visited the Honduran Bible Society store. We bought about sixty-five dollars worth of books, including a great atlas of the Holy Land with maps from lots of different interesting times in the Bible—in Spanish, of course.

We took another taxi—this time home—with our books from that store, more we retrieved from the post office and the books that Juan has held for us since the end of October. Jyl Myers[5] and I had shipped them from Portland the first part of June. They arrived in a plastic bag, even though they had started in a cardboard box. They are why we needed an extra box.

---

5 Jyl traveled to Honduras with me three times. She continues to be both a friend and an Amigas volunteer.

Juan gave us the books in a backpack——a damaged backpack.

Prairie's sandals had not survived a few days of pounding the pavement. We took both the backpack and the sandals to a cobbler. He took a look and said that he could do the repairs. Yesterday afternoon, we picked them up. Good thing, too. Yesterday, as we were walking down a crowded street, Prairie stepped in a hole—a hole full of dirty water. So, she needed her sandals today. We soaked and washed her shoe, but it was far from dry this morning. Juan was delighted to receive the backpack again, repaired, no less.

The store we sought was one that might sell us a pancake turner. People turn tortillas with their hands. They use spoons for everything else. Once, when my friend Gloria made pancakes at her house, she made the batter thick enough so that she could turn it over with her fingers, tortilla-style. Solid.

Oh, and Wednesday was Prairie's birthday. We have been eating ice cream and drinking *licuados* (smoothie-like drinks) and Doña Thelma, our hostess, made a huge pineapple upside-down cake in her honor. We even sang "Happy Birthday."

Beth   Getting Settled—February 20–24, 2006

We spent a lovely weekend in La Ceiba where we met up with Gloria Borgman's team from the Dakotas. Eloyda and Charles, of the El Pino clinic, work with them. They closed the El Pino clinic for the week to serve more remote folks. We put in quite a week running around in La Ceiba. But we got all of our errands done, so we were content.

We were up early on Monday morning to catch the seven AM bus. Our taxi pulled into the bus station at about 6:40. The taxi driver honked the horn to attract the attention of the bus driver, who had been about to pull out! Then followed over half an hour of slowly driving through La Ceiba to pick up passengers, and then on the road.

We arrived in Limòn about 1:30 PM. Prairie snoozed in the

bus a little, but I had to look out to see the much beloved landscape. I know that I will be jaded by it soon, but this trip, it was still fresh and beautiful to my eyes. Also, of course, I had to enjoy the bus food. When we arrived, we went to Profa Licha's house to get the key. She walked us to our rental house. Three grade school boys carried luggage for us. We were very grateful and gave them each a seven lempiras tip.

The house was filthy. We were completely amazed and kept our polite Honduran smiles in place. It obviously had not been touched inside since I saw it in November. Of all the stuff the previous owners had left lying about, the frying pan was most useful.

The water is still out. The old mayor was not re-elected—probably because he couldn't get the municipal water back on before the November election. The new mayor says that the old mayor spent all the money so there is none left to fix the water system, but we have a pump. Our first task was to pump water and, of course, we had to prime the pump. There was a little sand in the water, but it settled out pretty well.

We went downtown to my friend Melba's tienda and bought eggs, bread, onions and other supplies. Back at home, we were able to wash up some cooking utensils and have dinner. Next day, we also had breakfast without going out again for shopping.

Tuesday morning we began cleaning in earnest. Scrubbing, washing laundry by hand and carrying water. As they say, "a good time was had by all." We felt very productive watching the house transform under our hands.

Then, more shopping, of course. There are two relatively large stores in town. We went to both of them. They are in opposite directions from our house. We bought all we could carry in one trip. Then, after a break, we went to the other store. We bought, among other things, a set of twin sheets, complete with pillowcases. The owners had left pillows; now we could use them. (The first night, we had put blouses on the pillows for makeshift pillowcases. That worked, too.)

That Tuesday, we also bought beans. We used the fast method for soaking them and served beans for dinner. One would starve without beans here. They were pretty good if I do say so myself (as the cook this time).

We were pretty eager to get to the post office since we were both expecting mail. In the late afternoon, we walked all the way to the post office. The postmaster was very happy to meet us. He filled us in about his health problems, of course, and gave Prairie her three letters. There weren't any for me. Sigh. Prairie shared, though.

We went to bed Tuesday night exhausted. My friends at Centro de Salud (the public health clinic) said the pharmacy is in pretty good shape, except there are no prenatal vitamins. The doctor is in Tegucigalpa because her mother is having surgery. There is a medical *brigada* at the gringo clinic, so they are not very busy. We made a date to work with them the coming Monday.

At the clinic, folks asked if Prairie understands Spanish. She is such a quiet soul, that everyone is delighted when she opens her mouth, demonstrating she understood everything and that she can speak Spanish, too.

Elizabeth agreed to teach us how to make corn tortillas the next afternoon. This sounded like a very good idea to us, so we planned for it.

Wednesday we did more cleaning, shopping and cooking (and, of course, water-carrying and laundry washing). Elizabeth didn't come, so about 6:30 PM we made cornbread. We used corn flour (instead of wheat flour) and cornmeal. We liked the results a lot. The house has a little electric stove, with a well-functioning oven (a great luxury). We were actually rather glad to have spent the afternoon puttering and waiting for Elizabeth as we needed a bit of a rest after our very active Tuesday.

We are very impressed at how well we are eating. We even

had cabbage soup for lunch one day.

Thursday morning, before we had left the house—but after we had carried water, washed the daily laundry, fixed, eaten and cleaned up breakfast—at about 8:30 AM Gloria stopped by on her way to work. (This is the Gloria who is the lab tech and lives in Limón.[6]) She told us that Oscar, her brother, was working at her place so it was a good time to get our box of stuff he had stored for us. We went right over. The sweet potatoes[7] had suffered pretty badly and the okra had died from the floods, too. He suggested that in a couple of weeks, we may have some sweet potatoes ready to eat. I am guessing less than half of what we would have had.

After catching up on news with Oscar, and making a date to go to the mountain with him on Tuesday, we carried our stuff back to our house with still plenty of time to catch the 9:30 AM bus. We got off at Chito's house. We expected to be making a date to go to the mountain. But no, he was ready to go right then.[8] We bought a few bags of water and some sweet bread in case we needed it. Off we went in his little rattletrap truck. It's a pretty fast trip by auto.

We hadn't worn slacks, since we hadn't expected to be going to the mountain. We paid the price in *chinchín* bites. (Don't ask. I don't know what they are called in English.) They are tiny little insects that sometimes draw a bit of blood. They itch a bit, but not like mosquito bites. We each got over thirty bites on our legs, mostly below the knees.

The area that serves as both garden and orchard is well grown up with weeds and ferns. We searched out some of the trees. Some looked good, some didn't. The almonds[9] looked smaller than when we planted them. The almond that Glo-

---

6 I had been in Limón from August to November, 2005.
7 Planted in August, 2005.
8 Chito sold me that land in 2003.
9 The word *almond* is used in Honduras to describe a different tree than the three we know of in the U.S. as the almond tree.

ria had planted at her place was three times as high—I guess almonds like sand. The books say that almonds don't grow in tropical climate. Ignore them. Books have their value, but didn't help much in this case.

We were there about two hours. A light rain refreshed us. We did more talking about where and how to build the monastery. Chito had a lot of experience. He is a very smart man. He went to first grade and after that, his parents insisted that he stay home and work for them. He does very well without formal education and uses his life education very well.

We stopped at his house on the way back to town. He lives next to his parents-in-law. He recommended Clemente, his father-in-law, for the contract to clean—meaning to chop all the weeds down in the garden area.

Clemente was home. So, after about fifteen minutes of joking and haggling, we agreed on a price. He'll start on Monday. He also gave us some green plátanos. Chito drove us home and we had fried green *plátanos*, sweet bread buns, and beans for a late lunch. We were happy to have a quiet afternoon.

Every day is interesting this week. I wish that I could just dictate and share it all with you. It is good to be here and good to have such a good start on our projects already. As you can tell, we are rapidly getting into pretty good physical shape. Prairie still has her cold, but has stopped taking a nap every day (when there is the opportunity). So we are moving rapidly back to normal.

We found lemongrass in the yard and are drinking lemongrass tea. It is considered a useful immunity booster in several traditional cultures. We drink it more than water—Prairie, to help treat her cold, and me, to keep from getting her cold. It also makes our five-gallon jug of purchased water last longer. This afternoon, we will refill the jug with pumped, filtered water, after adding a little bleach to make it safe.

Beth—Two-year-old Receives Treatment for Cancer

February 24–28, 2006

On Friday, we went to visit *Sor* Leonarda,[10] my friend and the closest thing to a pediatric social worker that we have in Limón. After we caught up on personal news, she told me the story of two-year-old Juan Mejía, diagnosed last fall with retinoblastoma (malignancy of the eye).

When I had left, Sor Leonarda was ready to take the mom and boy to Tegucigalpa for pediatric ophthalmology consultation and probable surgery. The child's upper eyelid had begun to swell, although the eyeball had not yet started to bulge. The family insisted that an uncle go along. The family clearly understands how easily the mom gets overwhelmed in the city. She had done okay (not well, mind you) here in her own town, but the big city—that's another story.

They all went by bus, of course. When they arrived at the big hospital, Mom was scared and wanted to leave but was not permitted to do so. The specialty clinic was very elegant, and by now mom was really scared. This was way too far out of her comfort zone. She herself was just a scared kid, although two-year-old Juan was her sixth child.

The doctor did a careful exam and talked to both the uncle and to Sor Leonarda. It was a grave situation. The hospital admitted the child as an emergency case. The poor mom was so frightened. The hospital had two patients on their hands now: Juan and mama.

The surgery went well. Radiation therapy was given. Some of Juan's hair fell out, but there was no evidence of tumor anywhere other than his right eye.

The costs rose and rose, far beyond the amount of money we had left with Sor. She is associated with a few organizations that help in cases like this and she got him signed up with Chil-

---

10 Sor Leonarda is no longer a religious sister. Her call to aid the Garifuna children led to "sewlaration"—an honorable discharge from her religious order. She has kept the title.

dren with Cancer. Juan now has a card that tells the health care providers in Teguz (Tegucigalpa) that his care will be paid for by that organization. This was a major accomplishment.

Sor has founded an *albergue* (means something between inn and refuge) for children who are orphans or otherwise without adequate adult care. Mom was scared Sor would take Juan away from her and put him in the albergue. Well, here is where knowing the culture was helpful. Sor used this fear to push mom to clean up her act. Sor just said, if you don't follow doctor's orders and be a good mom, I will take him.

Mom is now doing well at keeping young Juan in a more sanitary environment, cleaning his eye socket wound, and taking him in to Centro de Salud for nursing supervision of his progress. She is also baking *pan de coco* (cocomut bread) to earn money for the bus fare next time they go to Teguz. This is a complete reformation of this woman. Absolutely amazing.[11]

The specialist says that Juan should live to be a hundred and two if he gets good care. They will return in July to Teguz for him to be fitted with his first glass eye.

Beth— "Hi from Tocoa"—February 28–March 1, 2006

We had a very restful Sunday. We went walking along the beach to the mouth of Río Limón. Limón is situated between two rivers whose mouths are about a mile and a half apart. We walked along the beach, sat for a short un-programmed meeting (silent Quaker worship) on the beach, and then played in the water a bit. We experimented for the first time going swimming with our dresses on. It worked pretty well. If there is any current, though, the skirt acts like a sail. We will practice.

We had had such a busy week, with so many different topics that we were tired by late Saturday afternoon. Sunday was a great blessing. We had such a relaxed day that we actually

---

11 Mom's reform was short-lived. But the child is alive and still living with his mother.

stayed up until 9:15 PM—the latest yet.

Gradually, we are learning to live according to sun time, not clock time. The sun on a clear day rises by 5:30 AM—that is, I can write in my journal at 5:30 inside the house, but I can't read—not enough light. I haven't tried going outside for journal writing at that hour as our doors drag on the floor (even when we lift them), making a terrible racket. So, going outside before Prairie is awake is not a friendly action.

We usually do morning devotions at 6:30 AM. Our new copy of *The Upper Room* (a daily devotional) did not arrive, so we are using an old one from last year. I hope that the new one comes soon. I like the freshness and I like having reminders by the calendar day and date.

Monday, we worked at Centro de Salud. It was fortunately a pretty slow day. A medical group had been in town in January and had donated a lot of medicines. Fortunately, a lot were very useful ones, though some were unfamiliar to the nurses. So, after I saw my kids, I wrote out protocols for Biaxin and Cephalexine.. I also identified the amoxicillin (it was labeled by brand name, which was misunderstood). Prairie helped Warnita move furniture into the new office room. It is designed for counseling patients who come for the rapid AIDS test that we are now offering. Then they cut and folded gauze for bandages. They wrap the trimmed gauze in brown paper and Warnita sterilizes it with a pressure cooker. Nothing is easy here.

The old lady who sells oranges was there, so we not only got to eat a few, but we also had some to take home. It is a treat to have fresh fruit.

We went home for lunch and a rest and then returned for an in-service on the new antibiotics. I am very grateful to have them. We were out of anything useful for skin infections. At home, the mom opens the capsule of Cephalexin and pust the powder in food or broth for the little ones, but only we can treat those nasty skin infections and cellulitis. Warnita and I also made up a list of medicines to order through Eloyda (RN in El Pino). It is a long list.

We won't get another batch of medicines from the government until April.

Yesterday, we did a little grocery shopping. We opted for a quiet day at home for most of the day, but we had some tasks to do. The ants had invaded the Coleman cooler[12] where we kept most of the groceries (to protect them from the mouse—or mice—and the ants). Well, its seal was not tight enough to keep out the ants. (These ants bite.)

The ants also crawled up the shelf system where we keep the other groceries (like salt and oil) and the dishes. Ants everywhere. So, we had to clean everything out with strong dishwashing soap (solid soap, administered with a rough scrubber). Then we threw the groceries into the water to drown the few who escaped. We washed everything down a few more times. Then we put the cooler in a large tub of water. (Ants don't cross water, we are told.) Then we put the four plastic legs of the shelf system in plastic containers of water—three plastic and one empty sardine can. We still had a few ants, so we put a small puddle of honey on the bottom shelf. That attracted most of the stragglers and we got them.

So, our groceries now appeared to be safe. The ants were now crawling all over the stove, but so far, we just let them. Well, most of our groceries were safe. I had a four-pack of chocolate cookies in my bag. Because I forgot to put it back into the cooler the previous night, the next morning when I offered it to Prairie, it was missing half of a cookie due to a well-fed mouse. I was certain that the mouse was fatter than when we had arrived. Prairie says that mice don't usually take residence one at a time, but I wanted her to be wrong. We had some rat poison, but didn't want to use it. We didn't want to search the entire house (including the stored items of our hosts) to find a dead mouse-body when it died and started stinking. Hopefully, we would find the sticky paper type of trap

12 We never bought it to use as a cooler—it was just for storage.

on our next shopping expedition. We had scheduled a trip to the mountain with Oscar, Gloria´s brother, but we canceled it. We needed more regrouping time.

We caught the bus to Tocoa, then a second one to La Ceibita, a suburb, to meet with Randy, the Methodist pastor. He filled us in on the programs of the church and we filled him in about the monastery. He was very encouraging.

When the floods were here last fall, his neighborhood was spared. But since most of the people working in the palm-oil plantations, (which were flooded) were off-duty and without pay. The feeding program for poor children went from feeding 300 to 500 per day for almost three months. It was back to normal by the time of our visit.

After a tour of the church, the parsonage, and the building under construction, Randy gave us a ride into town. We needed to go to the post office. (Our local postmaster had no stamps.) He said that we would never find the way ourselves. When he moved to town, he said, he finally just took a taxi and asked to be taken to the post office. It is on the opposite side of the highway from the bus station and all major businesses. We bought all the stamps they had.

Beth—Setting Down Roots—March 1–7, 2006

So much has happened in the last week that I had to read the last letter I wrote to see where I left off. We were going to Tocoa, to look for mousetraps.. We bought two. The first night we put out the sticky-paper trap in a spot that was right on the mouse main drag. Gotcha! In the morning, there it was, fat, but no longer sassy. It was still alive. I hadn't slept well, because I had expected to hear some noise when it was trapped and have to get up to put it out of its misery.

When we got up, we had to take care of the mouse. Both of us are horrified by killing and by mice so it wasn't a very good job. I couldn't ask Prairie to do anything I wouldn't do myself, so I was the one who picked up the trap (complete with mouse) and took it outside. I brained the creature with a broken cement block. I am so inexperienced that the first blow wasn't sufficient. The second blow spattered blood on the unused part of the trap so we couldn't re-use it. Ick. But it is done.

We hadn't seen another mouse, nor had we seen mouse tracks (droppings). We were more careful about food storage and hadn't found any mouse-nibbled food.

Our shopping in Tocoa was really very successful. We bought a complete set of cooking pots because to get a useful variety of sizes and shapes, one must buy a set. We bought black,, as we hoped to have our solar oven in order relatively soon. They were all enamel pans, the most popular type of pan around here. We bought them in a store near the bus station and carried them home on the bus.

After another major kitchen rearranging, we found that two of the pots were so large we wouldn't be using them for just the two of us. We were able to put back into the storage box some of the items of our host family. That feels pretty good. We also bought a ladle, a slotted spoon and a scrub brush—little luxuries that would make life easier.

The ants were still a bit of a problem. We had left a pan of oil on the stove. Almost every day, we made fried green plátano. The surviving ants went for the cooking oil. We left the pan there as long as we could stand it. It was like some fabulous elementary school science project. The ants just kept coming and drowning, one after another. Finally, our housekeeping instincts over-rode our elementary school science curiosity and we threw out the oil and the thousands of dead ants. We still had one more green plátano and ate it boiled (not nearly so yummy).

When we arrived back in Limón on Wednesday afternoon, we were reminded that it was Ash Wednesday. The kids throw ashes at one another on Ash Wednesday. It is quite a mess. I have seen them use lime, too. It makes a better contrast on *Garifuna* (African-Caribbean) black skin. We were not obligated to join in, fortunately.

Thursday afternoon, Chito and Clemente showed up. Clemente had finished the contracted work of cleaning the garden and orchard area. This means that he chopped down all of the weeds and ferns so we could see what was there. He had overcharged us and was very eager to get his money.

We made a date to go to the mountain the very next morning. Chito drove the two of us and Clemente. Prairie was recording secretary, writing down the kinds of fruit trees and their locations. Some were still a mystery as, for example, the apple and the pear. These obviously meant a different fruit than we were used to calling by those names, but we didn't really know how they are known here.

We didn't take a bag of cow manure as there wasn't any that was dried. Wet cow manure is not something you want to carry on your back up a steep hill.

We planted three hills of yard-long beans and four hills of tropical pumpkins. The guys were pretty reluctant to encourage planting as we were almost a month late for the best planting time. The rains were pretty much over. But we had several soft gentle showers in the few days after the planting of these seeds and we were very optimistic.

Chito suggested Round-Up for the weeds, but I told him that I still didn't want to put poison on our land. He really thought that this was a mistake. Chito and Clemente recommended planting yuca, cassava, pineapple, and sugar cane. They were confident that those crops would "stick," meaning the planted material would survive and thrive in our soil. We would discuss it and decide later.

We talked about the terracing plan. It was too foreign for them. The A-frame Rosa[13] made last fall was rotten, so we took the plan home and made a new one. The next trip to the

13 Rosa (Helen) was my travel companion in 2005.

mountain would have Prairie and me going over Rosa's only-slightly-confusing outline. We spent an interesting afternoon on that craft project (me with machete chopping the poles, Prairie measuring, advising and tying the hard knots). Once we were clear about the lines, we would tell Clemente where to plant each fencepost tree. He would understand the plan as he saw it develop. But step by step....

Planting some crops would make the weeds easier to control. But, of course, we need to begin growing some food, too.

We put out the second mouse trap Sunday evening. Monday morning, no mouse. We left it out. No mouse when we got up at 4:30 AM yesterday for our trip to El Pino. More about El Pino next time.

Beth—Photos, Recorders, Sweet Potatoes—March 8–9, 2006

One of yesterday's activities was figuring out how to put pictures directly from our digital camera to an internet account. Well, we bought a cable that connects the camera and Prairie figured out how to do it. (I'm sure that by now, you can understand how grateful I am to have Prairie along.) So, she posted some new pictures. One is of her in front of an elegant meal—perhaps the best we have had so far. You see her sitting at the table with plates of food. Each plate has beans, white cheese, corn bread, and a salad made of cabbage, carrots and tomatoes,[14] dressed with vinegar.

We have this great vinegar, called *Rico* (which means rich, although the term is used for any food that is really delicious—whether it is rich by our standards or not). It has a little onion and a little garlic in it, something else, I just can't remember what. But it is the best vinegar that I have ever tasted. We were pretty happy to discover it.

---

14 We no longer buy such tomatoes—too costly. They didn't seem too costly then!

Our great dinner, Rico Included

We have learned two songs in Spanish. One is a call to worship, *Vengan, Todos Adoremos.* Another is a table grace. We could sing them both without the words or music by then. This may seem like a little thing, and it is, but it marked a nice milestone.

Oscar, Gloria's brother, has helped me in the sweet potato patch at Gloria's house. Oscar was the person we hired to plant and clean the sweet potato patch. We actually harvested a few of the potatoes on Monday, but many of those ready to be harvested had already been removed. The neighbor saw who took them, but we were not going to discuss it until we talked with Gloria. It was possible the person had her permission.

We took one huge white sweet potato home for dinner. Prairie decided to make oven fries. I did quite a bit of puttering around the house (getting ready for leaving the next morning for El Pino), while she wrestled the sweet potatoes—which had juice like liquid latex and were very hard to cut. Finally, when she was ready to put the pan of cut potatoes in the oven, she noticed her hands were black with the juice and sticky like tar. She used cooking oil to clean that up while I mixed up some ketchup from tomato paste, Rico vinegar, sugar and salt. We still had a carrot that we needed to eat before leaving the house for a few days. So, we had carrot salad (yes, with Rico vinegar) with oven-fried sweet potatoes with ketchup. We had a lovely, though unbalanced dinner, and left the house relatively free of accessible mouse-and-ant food.

Beth—A Trip to El Pino—March 8–9, 2006

For the trip to El Pino, we got up at 4:30 to catch the five AM bus, a direct one (faster than the usual). We lived pretty close to the bus line so we would have heard the bus horn if it had come early. The bus horns sound like train whistles. One doesn't miss them. It didn't come early; it didn't come late; it didn't come at all.

The sky was heavy with clouds, so we used a flashlight to get to the part of town with streetlights. Then we waited and watched the place slowly light up. We got out our *Upper Room* and did morning prayers while waiting for the bus. Our bus stop, by the way, is right next to the house of our lad with rheumatic heart disease. He is now looking great and even riding his bike to school every day! But back to our trip.

The six AM bus, the next scheduled, arrived ten minutes early. It only went as far as Tocoa, where we changed buses. We just had time to buy breakfast, which we ate on the bus. By then it was about eight AM. We had each eaten a hard boiled egg about 6:30 and we were ready for more.

We arrived in La Ceiba in the bus station just before eleven and caught the bus for El Pino right away. We had a light backpack with our personal stuff and a heavy box of medicines for the clinic nurse, Eloyda. She doesn't have a source for injectible penicillin and our Centro de Salud always has extra. She sends us medicines; we send her medicines. This helps everyone, especially the patients. Medicines going out of date before they are used are a waste we can't afford.

I went to buy some food while Prairie held our seats. The bus was pulling out when she told the driver to wait for her friend. I rushed back into the bus and we ate our lunch. It was early, but we wouldn't be able to carry food and our luggage from the bus stop to the clinic in El Pino.

Impulsively, I had bought three lunches—two big pieces of pizza and a fried chicken, cabbage salad and corn tortilla lunch. Prairie ate the chicken; I ate a piece of pizza. Then I put the extra food in my bag, feeling a bit foolish.

By 11:30 we were in El Pino. A bus preacher had gotten on the bus and gave a sermon as we rode. He wanted to tell about his prayer-induced cure of tuberculosis. He certainly looked very healthy. He got off right after we did and carried the heavy box to the clinic for us. He is a friend of Carlos, the pastor.

Eloyda had seen most of the patients, but was still there working, so we joined her. A medical team from South Dakota had just been on a visit. When teams leave medicines behind, she and I go over them together (when I can get in) to see about expiration dates, how to use medicines with which she is not familiar, etc. She was very happy to receive our box of medicines. Then she sent us two other boxes. Poor Prairie who is chief box-toter had imagined divesting ourselves of medical luggage and traveling light! It was all really useful stuff, of course.

We spent some time admiring the well-supplied clinic. Many medicines were there thanks to the generous visitors. Then we reviewed my order list. I had changed it a little bit, in response to what we learned from Eloyda. For example, we can order prenatal vitamins in bulk—wow, good news.

There was a visiting team doing construction and the leader of the Georgia group was there, Jim Thompson.[15] He and I had a conversation. I wanted to be sure that the medicine exchanges between Limón Centro de Salud and Clinica Metodista are not under the table. Of course, we now have official

15 Jim Thompson is the leader of a large outreach program in El Pino, sponsored by the North Georgia conference of the UMC.

blessing to continue.

The team invited us to lunch. Eloyda accepted and then finished her work before going to where the food was. The team had already gone back to work, leaving a ten-year-old girl supervising lunch. Of course, she couldn't protect it when the other children came and helped themselves. There was still Gatorade, but no food! We were thirsty, and Eloyda was hungry and thirsty, but we had that extra piece of pizza! All worked out well after all. (It was really good pizza, too.)

The day was full of good news. The container that the Georgia group shipped in early February had arrived. I was amazed. We had four boxes in the container—books and lightweight blue denim fabric. So, now we had six boxes. There was no way we could manage six boxes, a light backpack, an umbrella and two soft fabric bags to the bus stop. We did the obvious thing, we begged a lift from the foreigners with their nice vehicles. They weren't ready to return to the city. Good deal! We weren't either.

We needed to have a conversation with Carlos, the pastor, about our monastery. We had told him just a little bit about it by email. He was very enthused. He had wanted such an experience when he was a young adult, too (maybe nineteen). I can't guess his age now, maybe thirty? In fact, he thought of two young women in his congregation that may be very much interested. He listened carefully to our conversation about what we are doing. When he talked with the young women, he would be able to report it well. He wanted to have us accept his eleven-year-old daughter during the three-month school break so that Prairie could teach her music. I had to tell him no, although it was very gratifying to have him be so strong a supporter. He asked how else he could help. I told him that when we would come to El Pino, it would be better for us to stay there than in the big city. So far, when we stay in the big city we stay in the home of a wealthy family in a lovely neighborhood. It would be better to have more modest accommodations. He said we could stay.

So, it was quite a day. Medicines, monastic library, fabric, moral support, practical support. My cup runneth over.

Then the team returned to give us a ride home, they also invited us to dinner. Now that we are monjas, our job is follow our teacher, Jesus of Nazareth. We can find no documented case of him turning down a dinner invitation. (He did turn down a drink once, but dinner, never.) We accepted, with pleasure. Pizza Hut. Good food, nice folks. Very easy to be grateful today.

The weather was lovely, so we walked both ways from the house to downtown to dinner. It is about a mile. After all that bus riding and sedentary meetings, it felt pretty good to walk.

Beth—Heads Spinning, Contracts Signed, Mountain Consecrated March 9–14, 2006

My head is spinning. We just got back from a quick trip to the mountain with Mateo, who builds houses. Our friends have pushed us to have a wooden house built instead of the clay house that I had planned. They say there isn't any of that type of clay on our mountain and it would all have to be carried up there. Well, they obviously have their reasons for their advice— most of which probably wouldn't cross cultural boundaries.

Chito's nephew, Mateo happens to build houses and cut lumber. He comes recommended also by our friend, Warnita, who works at Centro de Salud. On Friday, Chito brought Mateo over to the house to introduce him. Then Mateo took us to see a building that he had constructed, *well constructed,* I might add (as if I knew anything about construction).

On Saturday, we took the bus to the dirt road and walked the hour to our mountain. I go faster going downhill and Prairie goes faster uphill, so this allows us to be patient with each other.

We checked on our yard-long beans and the pumpkin plants.

Most had come up and looked good. We walked around a little bit, noting that the fence really does need to be repaired. Then we walked back out. We were pooped. At least I was pooped. It was a hot day, too. We scooped water from the brook. We put one drop of chlorine bleach into just under two quarts of water (a quarter of the normal dose) and it smelled and tasted of chlorine. This meant that it was pure before the bleach. The next time we refilled our bottles, we didn't add any chlorine.

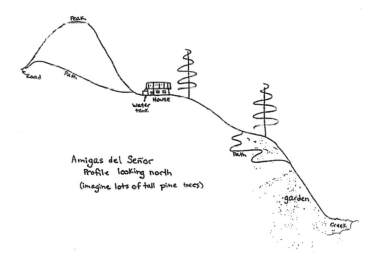

We consecrated the mountain

On Sunday, I started with mild malaria symptoms. I started the meds right away. Overwork is the trigger, but I didn't feel very sick. I rested a lot. On Monday morning, I washed the clothes (sitting down) while Prairie pumped and carried the water, made breakfast and washed dishes. Then we went to Centro de Salud for a morning's work. I lasted well. I did take a sedentary afternoon, of course.

Mateo was to pick us up at six AM, so we got up at five. He showed up about 6:30 and we all went up to the mountain. We walked from the truck to the site for the house. He had his big builder's tape measure and we measured off where the house will be. The house will be exactly the size of the building he had shown us—fourteen feet by twenty. It will be one room. We wanted two rooms of that size, but that would be too expensive right now.

We talked the whole thing over and were ready to make a contract. Prairie whipped out her notebook and I started writing, reading it aloud as I wrote. Mateo and I signed it. It is done. We would pay 41,500 lempiras plus the cost of the cement and the zinc for the roof. After we made an advance of 3,000 lempiras, ($158.52) we were in business. Mateo thought that it would be done in twenty days. He said that when he got a contract, he couldn't sleep until it was finished. Then he invited us over to his house, where he gave us each a soda pop. We also got to view his wife's fabulous free-standing kitchen, the perfect kitchen for Honduras. I felt a little envious.

So, by nine AM, we had a contract for a house to be built. We weren't so sure that we could be ready to move in so quickly.

A very exciting time. My head was spinning, or did I already say that?

Beth—The Day of the Sewing Machine—March 14, 2006

We have had a very busy last week. This is your second letter today. I couldn't wait to tell you about the house contract, so I didn't. Before that, I wrote from La Ceiba that we were to return here by bus, but after I wrote—and before we caught the bus—we went shopping for a treadle sewing machine. We returned to the *mercado* where we had seen a sewing machine on our first visit to La Ceiba. The expensive stores have "ambidextrous" sewing machines. (They can use electricity *and* treadle.) They also have zigzag. The last-mentioned cost twice as much. Poverty, remember.

So, we sprang for the Singer treadle version[16], as opposed to the slightly cheaper Chinese model (poverty, not destitution).

16 We now think that the Singer machine was also made in China.

They wrapped up the top part in cardboard and we hailed a cab. The machine has, of course, cast- iron legs. This is not a portable sewing machine.

The taxi driver took us to the bus station, where first we used the public restrooms. (We never forget our priorities.) The bus for Limón was nowhere to be seen. We were told that the 11:30 AM bus to Limón wasn't going that day and the one to Tocoa (which would get us halfway there) had just pulled out. A lady ran up the road on a short cut to intercept it for us. There were very few passengers—less than a dozen. The driver picked up the sewing machine and carried it the half-block to where the bus was waiting.

We got to Tocoa and there was no waiting bus to Limón. We were standing on the sidewalk next to our sewing machine when the folks told us that the next bus to Limón would be at 4:30 PM. (It was then just before three.) At least three different people opened conversations with me just to reassure me that the bus really would come at 4:30. We took turns staying with the sewing machine (I did mention, didn't I, that it is not portable?) and doing things like buying food, using the bathroom and other miscellaneous shopping.

Much to our surprise and delight, Prairie found a pair of inexpensive sandals. After exhausting the possibilities in La Ceiba, we were resigning ourselves to her getting flip-flops.[17]

At 4:20 PM, the bus rolled in. The bus guy put our sewing machine in the back, opening the hood of the vehicle afterwards—apparently, the engine needed a new belt. By five we were on the road again. Prairie had bought some tamales for us to have for dinner. Obviously, we weren't going to get home in time to fix the evening meal.

It was dark by the time we arrived in Limón. We got off the bus at our corner—a quarter of a mile from our house. We each seized one end of the sewing machine and started

---

17 These days, Prairie doesn't wear either sandals or shoes, only flip-flops or rubber boots (as needed).

carrying it. Soon, we stopped for me to rest. When we stopped the second time for a rest (well before half way home), a lady came up to us and offered assistance. She and her sister-in-law hoisted it onto their heads and carried it all the way home! This was no small feat, because one woman was four to five inches taller than the other one. They insisted that the sewing machine was not heavy—but they were happy to sit down and rest a bit before returning home.

Much to my delight, one of the women, the one who had called to us, was a woman who had been a patient of mine. Her *marido* (live-in, husband-like guy) had hurt her badly, inflicting a huge curvilinear gash on her forehead, up into the hairline. That had happened on a Saturday night. They came to Gloria's house for medical help early on Sunday morning. I was sick with malaria, but what could I do? So we all walked to Centro de Salud.

The patient was weak from loss of blood. Scalp wounds bleed a lot. The bleeding, however, helps to prevent infection. It was such a messy wound that it was hard to numb up. She had a difficulty lying still, because it hurt. I felt dreadful, thinking that I was doing a bad job. (I also felt dreadful, health-wise.) She seemed to feel faint even lying down. We took lots of breaks—sometimes for her sake and sometimes for my sake. Her women friends stood right with her, of course. There was a lot of swelling to her face and I did not expect a good result. I apologized for doing such a bad job and refused to accept payment (five lempiras—thirty cents—would have been the appropriate fee), because I thought she had enough troubles.

When she had called to us on the road, I didn't recognize her. She is really very pretty with the swelling gone. The wound healed into a nice tidy scar, much better than we had any right to expect. Her *merido* (partner) ran out of the house the night he hurt her and has not been seen in town since. A happy ending.

Our sewing machine reached our rental home with our

neighbors' help. We spent much of the next morning rearranging the stored items of our hosts so that we could put the sewing machine in front of the window and under the electric light in the tiny bedroom that we use for storage. We oiled it. The instruction booklet is omni-lingual. (No words, just line drawings.) We put oil on all of the spots indicated. We haven't even filled a bobbin yet, but we will as soon as we can catch our breath. The treadle sewing machine, including the cost of getting it home, was about one hundred dollars.

We are taking vitamin pills this week, with no vegetables or fruit to be had right now. Sigh. We still have a quarter head of cabbage. With spicy vinegar, it makes a nice salad to go with the beans and tortillas that Prairie made last night. Yes, we did get a tortilla-making lesson and supposedly we both can do it. But Prairie did it last night—solo.

I read to her. (We were very conscious of not wearing me out.) We did such a good job that I woke up ready to go about four AM today.

Beth—A Sedentary Week—March 14–21, 2006

I have just been released from self-imposed house arrest. Apparently, last Tuesday's outing to the mountain and then walking downtown for email access was just too much and my malaria got a little worse. I was so frustrated that I cried. This was probably not something Prairie was expecting. After all, I'm supposed to be the mature one. I cry very easily when I have malaria, even without being frustrated, like when a story touches me deeply. So, we just put our minds to a quick recovery. I ate as much as I could and as often as possible. (I did lose twenty-three pounds last time.) Prairie went out shopping every day except Sunday, looking for and finding foods that would tempt me. And they did. Melba gave Prairie some sour oranges. We made a drink with them. Delicious. It tasted like lemon-and-limeade with a little mandarin orange thrown in for good measure. I took my medicine, rested and ate frequently.

Prairie pumped the water, carried the water, did the shopping, did almost all of the cooking and hung up the clothes to dry. I washed clothes while sitting down (not even hanging them up as it is a high line and she is taller). I washed dishes sometimes and swept the floor, but mostly I read aloud while she did the household chores. Prairie made a chocolate cake called "Wacky Cake" on Saturday. That helped my appetite a lot. Delicious. No eggs or milk, just chocolate-flavored calories. Just what I needed.

The solar oven was delivered last week. We have puttered with it a bit. We put the aluminum foil reflecting surfaces in place and pasteurized a peanut-butter jar full of water. When we tried a larger (much larger—a big soup kettle) container of water, it didn't get hot enough. We have a lot of wind. Wind carries the heat away. We planned our next step: to put more insulation between the wood-constructed box (very sturdy and heavy) and the inner cardboard box with the aluminum foil reflectors. Next, to get some more cardboard. Nothing was to go quickly and smoothly, it seemed.

Prairie carried home a carton of books; now there was only one box left at Centro de Salud. Our education-book at that time was *Guns, Germs, and Steel,* by Jared Diamond. He is, in my opinion, the most important secular prophet of our time. We read to each other, especially when fixing dinner or washing dishes. (You know, that time of the evening when you might listen to the radio or have the television on.)

We have read our booklet on raising rabbits. Lots of laughs—they can have seven or more babies at a time—five litters a year! We decided, after reading all the details, that we were not ready to open this particular Pandora's box. Chickens first. The rabbit book was also part of our Spanish immersion. The booklet is in Spanish.

On the subject of the sewing machine, don't get me started.

It was really so different from an electric that I was dumb-founded. First, to fill a bobbin, you have to adjust stuff that is automatic on an electric. Then you have to call a young, strong woman to loosen the gears of the wheel. After she has done that, you have to turn the wheel by hand. If you try to use the pedal, the bobbin spins back and forth, instead of in the same direction.

Beth vs the sewing machine

Okay, finally, the bobbin is filled. Then you must try out sewing without thread to learn how to use the treadle. If you don't rock the treadle smoothly and quickly, the sewing goes forward and back and forward and back. It seemed to matter not at all if you had set the machine for sewing forward or for sewing backwards. If you happened to have malaria, you may find yourself crying with frustration. Prairie was better at the sewing than I was, but I kept at it.

Finally, I decided I had that part down enough to try sewing something. We had a big piece of sheeting material that needed to be hemmed on two edges. Measuring and cutting took two different days. Sewing scissors are on the way, but I did fine with my travel scissors.

Even with this new hard machine, I thought I could do it. No iron. No pins—the pins are supposed to arrive at the end of this month. But I thought I could turn over an edge and sew it down; then turn over that one again and start a hem. Great thinking. But to do it was another story.

By following our line-drawing manual, I threaded the machine. The thread broke, a little wire gizmo kept getting caught. We played with the tension (and are still trying to figure it out). Maybe this part of the process too, is related to smooth treadling. Any sharing of experience or practical advice would be appreciated.

The messenger from the post office came by yesterday to tell us that we have mail. Prairie will fetch it while I wait here in the air-conditioned internet place. We are still being very careful.

Yesterday, of course, was Monday, when we usually volunteer at Centro de Salud. Prairie went off by herself. When she got there, it was closed up. She was told that "We are celebrating tuberculosis." It is International Tuberculosis Day and they are hoping to raise awareness of tuberculosis. The junior high drum corps provided the rhythm section and the students marched. The Centro de Salud personnel also marched (including Prairie, of course) until they got to the *La Bodega* (a store) where they bought soda pop and cookies to serve at the city park at the end of the parade. So Prairie went across town carrying a box with seven two-liter bottles of soda. She helped serve. She is a real member of the community now.

Prairie—Buses, Roads, Local Villages—March 16, 2006

I'm overdue for an update! Time is flying here as Beth and I get settled into the routine of life in small-town Honduras and we begin preparations for the monastery.

Today I will tell you about my experience with transportation and the rules of the road, recounting the ride from La

Ceiba to Limón, plus a little about Limón itself.

When I was in Guatemala a year and a half ago, I was introduced to chicken buses. They are retired U.S. school buses that are used as public transportation, both within and between cities and towns. In Guatemala, the buses have been painted in brightly-colored designs, with the destination towns painted along the top where they used to say school bus. Honduras as a country seems not to have made quite the progress of other Central American nations in many aspects including manufacturing, business sense, and even a sense of pride about its products. (It is the original "banana republic" after all, and much of the land is still owned and operated by large fruit companies like Dole.)

Their buses show evidence of this as well. Many of them are still schoolbus yellow, with perhaps just the front end painted colorfully, and you can often still read the words school bus and the district where it came from. Rarely have the buses been painted in full color. Usually the destination is painted on the front or back end (or both), though it is not always correct if the bus is second or maybe third-hand. The buses are run by private contractors who own and operate one or more buses that will run between specified destinations.

For example, there is a company called "Miguel Antonio." The name is painted on the front window. It runs many of the buses that come through Limón. Other people or families might own and run a single bus. Each bus includes a driver and one or more people who take money and man the door. Some buses are local, and will pick up anyone who is standing by the road along the route, and drop people off wherever they wish. Other buses are *directo*, and will only stop at major towns and junctions along the way. There is a directo bus from Limón to La Ceiba that stops at Tocoa about half-way. It costs a little more but is faster.

The drivers' seemingly erratic ways of passing others and driving on all sides of the road require some explanation. Let me explain by using the example of our trip from La Ceiba.

This may also help you get a sense of the geography. We begin in La Ceiba at the bus terminal. There are buses lined up that go to all directions in the country. No schedule is posted. You either have to know what the timetable is for your destination or you must ask around. People who hang out at the station (employees perhaps, though you can't tell by their dress) know when buses leave for where. Luckily, Beth has been around enough to know more or less when the buses run.

We are catching the six AM direct bus to Limón. We find it, have one of the helpers put our big bags in the back, where there's little space for luggage, and then settle in to our slightly cramped bench seat. Sometime, when there are plenty of passengers, the bus pulls out, and slowly makes its way out of the city. Even the directo bus might stop a few times before getting out of town to pick up some stragglers along the route. The highway going east is paved, although there are no painted lines. Traffic mostly stays to the right, unless the vehicle wants to pass. In that case, it will sneak towards the left till it sees that there is space, and pass as many vehicles as it can before it is forced to move back over because of oncoming traffic. The road is wide enough to allow a car to pass even with oncoming traffic.

The trouble comes when there are people passing in both directions. For an inexperienced traveler, it can be frightening to watch the drivers go, but after a while you come to realize that they are experienced in this and know how to judge the space. Only rarely do you hear news of a car crash due to poor judgment. Sit back and relax.

During the first couple hours, the route to Limón stays between the coastline and the mountains. Then it turns south a bit towards Tocoa, the capital of its municipality of the same name.[18] This is now one of our big cities, where we can go shopping and use the internet more cheaply than in Limón.

---

18 A municipality is similar to a county in the U.S.

It has shops, restaurants, two hospitals—one private and one public—plus doctors, dentists, lawyers, and banks. A bit further east from Tocoa is the crossroads of Corocito, where you can turn to go north to Trujillo (the port capital of our *departamento,* or state, of Colón), or continue east. Continuing east we reach the town of Bonito Oriental, which is also bigger than Limón and good for shopping; it has plenty of commerce because it is another crossroads; a highway goes south from there to Olancho. Here the pavement ends. So we continue our last hour to Limón on a dirt-and-gravel road. We know we are definitely heading into the boonies now, because the drivers give up trying to stay on the right hand side of the road. Now they just try to avoid potholes (exacerbated by the hurricane-induced flooding last fall).

Just before arriving in Limón, we cross the Puente Rio Limoncito (Limoncito River Bridge). Every bridge is named, usually (not always) after the body of water it crosses over. There are a few houses grouped nearby. I knew that Limoncito is the address nearest the mountain property where the monastery is to be built, and that there is an elementary school there. Beth finally explained to me that the designation of Limoncito is not quite a village, but more like a township—an area of land, mostly rural but with some settlement groupings—and everyone living in that area has the address of Limoncito. In this case, it is an area west of the town of Limón, which is the municipality's capital and government center (the mayor of Limón is not just the mayor of the town but the whole municipality).

Beyond Limoncito to the south is the area of La Fortuna. We take the road to La Fortuna to get to the mountain property. So just another mile or two from the not-quite-center of Limoncito we come to *el desvío de Limón* (the detour to Limón). The road that continues east narrows and goes to Iriona and beyond into the wilds, perhaps all the way to the Mosquito Coast. We turn left, or north, and follow the road a few miles into the town proper of Limón, which is situated right on the Caribbean coast. Limón has a few streets going east-west and north-south. They are all dirt, and there are even a few barely-readable street signs designating First, Second, and Third. (I didn't notice them till days later.) Because it is off the main drag, and pretty far out, there isn't much going on in town, even though it's the municipal seat. There are two stores that sell dry goods—packaged foods and household items. One is called *La Bodega* and is run by Andres.

Beth and Andres in front of La Comercial

The other is referred to as *La Comercial* and is run by a husband and wife. The husband also is the head of a wood-working shop directly behind the store. He makes furniture. We had them make a solar oven for us, which just got finished to our satisfaction today. The price had gone higher than expected when they had to make a special trip to Tocoa to purchase the thick glass we wanted and get it cut to size. Oh well—now we begin experimenting with cooking foods using the sun.

There are many more little *tiendas*, (tiny storefronts that sell snacks and various other items), each one a little different. There is one that we sometimes go to for vegetables, another where we bought some plastic dipping pans, and yet another where we can get *rapadura* (molasses in a solid block). Also, just down the main drag from La Bodega is a tienda run by Melba, a friend of Beth's.

She often has vegetables, cheese, and eggs. Plus, she has a shaded porch in front with chairs where people often wait for buses.

On a different street there are a couple of places[19] where you can use satellite internet and make international phone calls. (I'm at one of them now.) Many people in Limón have relatives in the U.S. who they keep in contact with. For in-country calls, you can go to Andrés' place, where he has several wireless phones.

The western edge of town is bordered by a river. The post office is there (at the end of the road). It is a man's house, with a rusting metal sign set in front that says *Honducor*, an abbreviation for *Honduras correo*, (mail).

Beth—A Plea for Help With a Crisis
March 21 April 5, 2006

You are getting this because you are involved in some way with providing health care to Hondurans. So, here is your update. Not good news.

Background that is important: Most powerful positions in government are political appointments. In the public health department, the career health care providers do not have policy-making authority. When there is a presidential election, all the old political appointees are fired and then replaced by new political appointees. We had an election in November. The new administration (President Manuel Zalaya) took office in January, 2006.

Ninety percent of health care for eighty percent of Hondurans is provided by public health clinics and public health department hospitals. About fifteen percent of folks can just

19 Now only one.

buy their health care. About five percent can buy the services that they can't get at the public health department. A small percentage of the highly subsidized health care is provided by church-sponsored clinics, other non-profit clinics and mission trips. This is a small, but very important piece of the picture.

Normally, the public health facilities receive shipments of medicines three times a year. They place an order and then receive what there is available. Usually, they receive about sixty to ninety–five percent of what the demand will be by their patients. Some months they have everything, some months very little.

In the state of Colón, where we live, the last shipment received was August, 2005 Another shipment would have been due this January, but, with the change of administration, no one was surprised that it didn't come—but now it is April. Not only has the shipment not come, but there is not even news of it in Trujillo, the capitol.

Why am I aware of this now? That is two questions, why not sooner and why not later?

Why not sooner ? I am involved with two clinics in two different locations, both of which are sheltered from this mess. One is Clinica Metodista in El Pino, which is supported entirely by the United Methodist Church and does not depend upon government at all. It is well supplied, thanks to donors and visiting teams. The other is the public health clinic here in Limón. It, too, has received help, sometimes from visiting teams and sometimes from the donations that come through Rose City Park UMC to support my work here.

Why this week to be aware and not later? Two important conversations: Juana Nidia told me that there is no news of when the shipment may arrive in Trujillo. That would be the shipment for the entire state—every public health clinic and the two hospitals. No news now implies that it will be at least a month before the medicines arrive. The second conversation—equally disturbing—was with Warnita, the experienced auxiliary nurse. We were talking about the immunization campaign slated for the week of April twenty-fourth. We plan on me going along so I can do pediatric consults while the families are all gathered for immunizations. Warnita knows that we will need a lot of amoeba and worm medicine. We do not have enough. We (Prairie and I) have had glitch after glitch in getting money sent from the States and are lucky to have grocery money, let alone cash for buying medicines. The conversations continue. Warnita is resigned to us doing outreach clinics with inadequate medicines. But, she adds, the really bad part is that the hospitals with the sickest patients don't have medicines. This hit me hard.

So, we have a major human-caused disaster. You will not hear the Honduran government asking for international aid because it is the Honduran government that is responsible for the mess, after all. Needless to say, this new president is not earning a lot of points with health care providers.

I am asking for help. Immediate help. And lots of it. [Ed. note: This was April, 2006.] If you have contacts in Honduras who know how to order bulk medicines from Honduran pharmaceutical companies, wire them money and instructions to buy medicines to share with local public health clinics and hospitals. Trust them to know who needs what. They might choose differently than you would, but they will probably choose more wisely.

Secondly, if you have a clinic with a nice stockpile of medicines, authorize three-fourths of it to be shared with government clinics and hospitals. This is the rainy day for which you were saving.

What you can do there at home is to start gathering the medicines that you know need to be transported from there. These are especially: amoxicillin 500mg capsules, erythromycin 500mg tablets, and doxycycline 100mg capsules or tablets. These are staple antibiotics that health care providers here are skilled at using. They are also expensive to buy here and would break the monastery bank if we tried to buy them ourselves.

What the bulk purchase of medicines by local folks can do is provide treatment for asthma, amoebas, worms, scabies, pain and fever, allergies, certain infections, and simple high blood pressure. A large number of people can be served with a low cost-per-patient ratio for these problems. Diabetes medicine is in a higher cost range, but is very much needed—and cheaper here than there.

We do not know how long this crisis will last. I cannot forget that a child died in the last three years from intestinal parasites. I have treated two children in the last month with infected scabies. I could treat the skin infection, but couldn't treat the scabies. These patients will be back. Treating worms and treating scabies can be life saving. This sounds too absurd to be true, but it is! So, make your contacts. Get started.

Am I asking you to send money to me? No. Your Honduran counterparts (church and charitable connections) can do this work better than I can. They are mostly located in larger population centers, so they have better access to essentially everything. This is my part—telling you.

Prairie—Life in Limón—March 23, 2006

A friend just reminded me that I haven't actually told you anything about my life here yet. She asked, "Are you living in a tent, or what?" and I realized that some of you have more of an idea than others of what I'm doing here. So today, I will try to remove some of that mystery, and tell you a bit about life in Limón.

First of all, the reason Beth and I are here is to found a women's monastery. This has been a calling of Beth's, and I am joining her here this year because I am interested in the simple life she foresees, and in trying to better understand God and God's relationship with me and the world. I know I don't usually talk about God a lot, but having been raised in the United

Methodist Church, this discussion has always been a part of my life.

A couple of years ago, Beth purchased about four acres of mountainous land about five miles south of Limón. Part of our work right now is to make the plans for the monatery and get it built, so we can move there. Already a garden has been set up on a steep hillside above a creek. Numerous fruit trees were planted in the last year or two (including mangoes, avocados, and various citrus trees, as well as some other tropical fruits) and we have also planted a few beans and pumpkin seeds. Last week, we were able to make a contract for someone to build the small wood house for us. That is major progress, as before we came in February, all ideas and plans about actual buildings were still just dreams.

So we are currently living in a small rented house in the town of Limón. Much of our time is spent just living, which includes buying groceries and other household items, cooking, and cleaning. But we also work on our spiritual formation, as we read books (like a bible study on liberation theology), and other educational material. Currently we are reading together *Guns, Germs, and Steel*, a book that looks at human history by asking the question of why certain peoples were able to conquer others. The author, Jared Diamond, brings together the fields of archeology, anthropology, evolutionary biology, and history to try to explain those reasons. It is most interesting. We also have many books on gardening in the tropics, and on raising chickens, rabbits and honeybees. I am learning so much more than I'd never imagined I would!

But for you, the interesting part is probably how we are actually living. We've been in Limón for a month now, and it has been a sharp learning curve as I adjust. Luckily I came with an open mind and willing spirit.

The house where we are currently living is made of cement blocks and has a zinc roof. People who can afford the materials build houses like this, as they are pretty sturdy. The floor is tile. There is a main room with an electric stove and sink at one end, a small round table with plastic chairs in the middle, and a rocking chair and a bookshelf. Plus there is a bedroom with a twin and a double bed, another room where we store some of the owner's things—plus our new treadle sewing machine—and a bathroom. We were lucky that the house came furnished, as we didn't have anything when we first arrived. However, little by little, we are acquiring the things one needs for a household (pots and pans, plates, utensils, foam mattresses).

We do have electricity, although it sometimes will go out for no apparent reason. Since our stove is electric, this can be a bit tricky. Luckily, Beth knew we could buy a one-burner kerosene stove, for use when there was no power, which we bought, and were able to substitute for the electric one as needed.. Cooking is a challenge even with the electric stove. There is no refrigerator. We are learning that cooked foods like beans, rice, and soup, will last several days in their pots, as long as they are brought to a boil every so often. Fresh fruits and vegetables last a few days, and even cheese and a thick cream called *mantequilla crema* lasts a day or two. Perhaps the most disappointing thing is that we can never have a cold drink.

Within a couple days of moving in, we realized that mice were enjoying our food as much as we were. The owner had left a small Coleman cooler, so we put our dry goods in it (beans, flour, rice, dry milk). Within a few more days, we found that ants also enjoyed our food—primarily sweet things and oil. In fact, we had had a pan of oil that we used to fry *plátanos* [similar to plantain] sitting on the stove, and one morning, we saw that hundreds of ants had committed mass suicide in it. Beth knew that ants couldn't cross a barrier of water, so we now have our cooler set in a wash pan with a bit of water in the bottom. We keep condiments, some food items, and dishes on plastic shelves, and so we gathered some small plastic containers in which we placed the feet of the shelving unit with some water. These steps, along with a mousetrap and some Raid, have more or less freed us of those pests. (There is still one group of tiny ants that gets into some of the food, but they don't bite and are so small we don't worry about them.)

Another small animal that lives in our house is the gecko. I was startled when I first saw one, as they are new to me, but Beth reassured me that they are no household pest. In fact, the more there are the better, because geckos eat small insects. They crawl along the walls in a funny wiggly way, and make chirping sounds similar to some birds. I have seen dark colored ones, as well as ones that are a translucent pinkish-green, and they range from one to five inches long. They are kind of entertaining to watch, and we were saddened when one was caught on our sticky mouse trap.

Well, even though the house has a kitchen sink, toilet, and shower, there is no running water! Last September, during the floods from the hurricanes, the PVC pipes that brought water from the mountains broke. (The water system was originally installed about five years ago.) There was also a mayoral election in the fall and apparently the last mayor spent down the treasury so that the new mayor had no money to do the repair. People still seem to have some hope that the water will be restored soon. In the meantime, we are hauling buckets of water from a pump (*bomba*) in the back yard, for cooking, washing our clothes, and bathing. I have showered for most of my life, so learning to bathe without running water was a bit of a challenge, especially cleaning my thick hair. But I think I have gotten a system down that seems to work, and I use only about a gallon of water (a five-minute shower takes about ten gallons).

Hand-washing clothes is also new to me. We do it on our porch, using two plastic tubs and a washboard (in this case plastic), plus the solid cylinders of soap that are sold, and a scrub brush for hard stains. Some people have washing stations set up with a wooden counter and corrugated metal for a washboard, or they may have a *pila* made of cement. We wash a few clothes every day or two, so that there never gets to be too many at once. (For one thing, they all have to hang on the line, of which we don't have too much.)

In terms of drinking water, so far we have been purchasing five-gallon bottles of purified water. However, we are trying to switch to purifying our own water. This can be done by boiling it or adding a few drops of chlorine. (Actually, germs are killed at 150 degrees Fahrenheit, and we have a little device called a "WAPI" (Water Pasturization Indicator), that shows that this temperature has been reached—when some wax inside a plastic tube melts at just above that temperature.) The trick is, the water from our pump has sand in it and also seems to have a layer of some kind of oil that rises to the top.

From our porch, where we have hung a hammock, one can see the Caribbean Sea about 300 yards away across a soccer field. I am lulled to sleep at night by the sound of the ocean waves. The proximity of the ocean means that the ground is all sand here. This also means a lot of dust in the air. Also, the salt in the air often dirties my glasses and is known for corroding the metal roofs, window frames, and iron fences and window grates, very quickly. We are glad to know that the mountain property is far enough from the ocean (though it is still visible from there), that the salt won't be a problem, plus the ground is clay and rocky up there.

Besides the rumble of the sea, there is also the sound of chirping and buzzing insects and birds. I have watched hummingbirds come drink from the zinnias and papaya flowers in our yard, and iridescent green lizards with long tails dart among the dry grass. At night I have taken in the wonder of a sky filled with stars and a field filled with blinking fireflies. There is a certain wonder and beauty to this place, and I am learning all the time to appreciate it more and more.

Prairie—A Watery Couple of Weeks—April, 2006

Here's an update about our adventures (because life is always an adventure) the last couple of weeks.

Two Fridays ago, the clouds came rolling in from the Southeast. This meant rain. I had just been getting used to the heat and the glistening sweat that comes with it. The rain brought a cold front and we were actually comfortable in our short-sleeved dresses. At least one evening I put on a long-sleeved shirt and a couple of times I wore socks to bed to stay warm. For the next week and a half we had cloudy days and rain off and on.

The next morning, I pumped water as usual. Then a few hours later, I went to do it again, and the pump just stopped giving water. I kept pouring in water to prime it, but it just sucked it down instead of flowing out. I told Beth, and we immediately went over to our landlord Profa Licha's house to tell her about the problem. She didn't exactly believe us, and asked our neighbor to give us a bucket of water to prime it more, but still nothing happened. Finally, we paid our neighbor to bring us several buckets of water from their pump, while I told Profa that the pump still didn't work. She said she'd notify the repair man. He finally showed up late in the afternoon, just when it was starting to drizzle. We watched him do the repair, which was fascinating, since I didn't really know how pumps work. The handle is connected to a vertical rod that goes down nine inches or so into the shaft. At the bottom is attached a simple valve mechanism, plus a leather ring. Our problem was that the ring, which creates the suction that the pump uses to bring up water, had fallen apart. So the repairman, an older Garifuna[20] man who walked with a limp, cut us a new leather circle and put it back together with the rest of the mechanism. He checked that it worked, and then went on his way.

Grateful to have water again (how easy it is to forget what an essential resource it is and take it for granted), we went about making dinner. Just as we finished, the electricity went out! We could only assume it was related to the rainstorms, so

20 Black descendants of Carib, Arawak and West African cultures

we continued our evening by candle and flashlight and went to bed. The power stayed out for about forty-eight hours. That meant that we had to cook meals outside on our single kerosene burner and use flashlights at night. Also, when we went to work at the Centro de Salud on Monday, they were having to put their immunizations, which are kept in a freezer, into a small cooler with ice packs. (Luckily they weren't completely melted.) The rumor was that a couple of power poles had gone down. We heard a big cheer from town as the power returned Monday evening around six, just in time for dinner.

Tuesday we went to Tocoa to do some household shopping. It managed not to rain during our time there. We purchased items like a machete, some forks and spoons, more mousetraps, a padlock for our house on the mountain, some fertilizer for our garden plants, and a watermelon to take home. We also splurged a bit, and bought cheddar cheese and white bread rolls at a supermarket for a mid-morning snack. Cheddar is a rarity around here. Locally we can only get the salty white cheese, which is cut to size off a big round. We have been practicing ways to eat this cheese, as neither Beth nor I are particularly fond of its strong flavor. We like it baked in biscuits and served with tomatoes as a Caprese salad.

In Tocoa, we got tired by about eleven AM, and the bus to Limon wouldn't leave till 12:30 PM, so we had another snack break at a *licuado* stand near the bus station. (Licuados are Central America's version of a smoothie or milkshake.) They come either milk or orange juice-based, and with whatever combination of fruits and nuts or other elements you would like, mixed with ice to make a cold, thick, delicious treat. This time, Beth got an orange-mango combination, while I went for the milk-based banana-peanut. Tasty and filling. (Some of you may know that I didn't like bananas or peanuts until the last year or so.)

The rest of the week continued cool and drizzly. We did plenty of resting, as Beth was still recovering from her malaria relapse. At the end of the week, a group of student nurses from the U.S. came to town to work at Clinica Carolina, the Methodist-run clinic. (Which was how Beth first started coming here.) Beth had been in contact with their leader, Jenny, for several months, and had even arranged for a box of books with them that they could deliver to us. (We'd expected it to arrive before the boxes sent in the container that came to El Pino some weeks ago.) So on Friday, I walked down to the clinic to see if I could find Jenny and tell them that we were at their service. I also let her know that Beth was still suffering from malaria. When she heard that, Jenny got the team doctor and another nurse to do a house call. We all went back to our house in one of their air-conditioned vehicles. They all did a consulta for Beth, while she told them all about malaria, which none of them had much experience with. It was humorous to see the patient have more knowledge of the illness than the doctor. They asked her to come in the next day to do some tests.

So on Saturday, one of their drivers picked us up, along with our friend Gloria, who is the lab tech at Clinica Carolina, and we all went over there. Gloria tested Beth; no malaria showed up in her blood, but then again, she'd been on treatment doses of medicine. Beth helped the doctor with translating. I also helped do some translating with the student nurse who was doing intakes. It was an interesting way to meet people of the community. (Lots of colds, it seems.) We worked past our usual lunchtime, so Beth and I both got tired and hungry. We finally went home and took naps. Luckily, Sunday is our day of rest—which we took seriously.

On Monday, I joined Jenny and a few others from their group, as they went with Juana Nidia, the head nurse at Centro de Salud, to the elementary school to do fluoride treatments. We went to a whole bunch of classrooms, and gave a brief interactive presentation on foods that are good and bad for their teeth, as well as instructions on tooth-brushing. I did a fair amount of translating. Then we did the fluoride, which was some goopy stuff that we painted on the surfaces of their teeth. Some kids mouths were in pretty bad shape, with discoloration or even teeth all rotted out. The medical team had brought toothbrushes to hand out to everyone as well. We did about 200 kids and then returned on Wednesday to do a few classes we'd missed.

We were able to collect our books from Jenny, and she kindly is taking a batch of letters and postcards to put in the U.S. mail when she returns to the States today.

This weekend was more relaxed than some. The weather had finally warmed back up, so that it was almost too hot. So both Saturday and Sunday mornings we went down to the beach and played in the water. The Caribbean was a beautiful blue-green, just like you'd expect from a postcard, with gentle waves—refreshing but not chilly. We lolled in the waves and on the beach and fully appreciated our coastal location. It made a lovely ending to two weeks full of water.

Prairie—*Semana Santa y Pascua*
Holy Week and Easter—April, 2006

Two Sundays ago was Easter [*Pascua*], and before that was Holy Week, or *Semana Santa*. That week is practically a national holiday, and many people get it off from work and visit family. It included numerous adventures for us, so read on.

On Tuesday of Semana Santa, we had a mini-reunion with a fellow University of Puget Sound alum. Alice is teaching math at an international school in Tegucigalpa, and she was touring the North Coast for her Semana Santa break with a fellow teacher. They were here just for the afternoon and night, but we made the most of it. The three of us went swimming in the Caribbean, and Alice and I were sure to pose for a photo we can send to our alumni magazine. There was lots of chatting and comparing our divergent lives, as they live in the capital city, and here Beth and I are living out in the sticks. We all went to dinner at a local restaurant (where we could watch them make up the food across the counter). I realized we'd never walked in town after dark, and it was interesting to see it at a different time of day. We could see inside houses that were lit up from within. Many places opened up that before I hadn't even known were businesses—little restaurants and bars and a disco. We might have stayed out longer, but it started pouring rain.

Wednesday, after sending off Alice and her friend to La Ceiba on the five AM bus, Chito gave Beth and me a ride to the mountain. We were able to check on the garden, where our few plants, beans, pumpkins, and the zucchini-like *pataste*, are coming along. Of course, so are the weeds. We made a row of poles, using a homemade level which looks like a large "A" with a plumb-line hanging down. This is the spot where we hope to plant some fence-post trees to create a terrace. We also just enjoyed the beautiful day and our little one-room wooden house. We are anxious to get back there, as we now have some tomatoes and other seedlings that are ready to be transplanted.

That Friday, we planned to go to La Ceibita, a community near Tocoa, which has the closest Methodist Church, and attend some Holy Week services. We went downtown about 8:30 AM and waited at Melba's tienda, where she has a nice covered area with chairs, for a bus. However, Melba said that no buses were running that day. We chatted and watched, and weren't ready to believe her. So after a bit, we started walking out of town, hoping for a *jalón*, or ride. (We got one for the last part.) But as we were walking along, we saw many pickup trucks coming into town, piled high with people, coolers, and water toys. Beth had heard that Holy Week was big in Limón, with people coming to party at the beach. At the *Desvío* (bus stop), we sat with Rosa(Chito's wife), and Eva (her mother), hoping we might catch a bus that was going from Iriona to Tocoa. However, Rosa and Eva agreed that there were no buses that day. They thought we might be able to catch a ride at least part way to Tocoa. But virtually all we saw for two hours were pickups, and even bigger trucks filled with people, heading into Limón. Finally around noon, we decided we'd better just head back into town and give up the trip to Tocoa. So, after Rosa kindly gave us each a glass of Pepsi and some chips, we were able to catch a ride back to Limón. We finally understood that the Semana Santa holiday officially takes place Friday to Sunday, and is a true change from the norm.

Instead of being too disappointed, we decided to take life as it comes, and go check out this beach party. We walked down there, and saw hundreds of people and children swimming in the river near where it empties into the Caribbean. (The river parallels the coast for a ways.) Along the beaches there were numerous shelters made of poles and huge palm branches, with more people hanging around them.

Some of the shelters were private, but others served as little restaurants, with gas stoves set up, and pots filled with food. It was lunchtime, so we decided to find something. First, we got a plate with rice and iguana. (This was a new treat.) There was some iguana meat, and three eggs, with a soft but inedible shell. It was in a coconut milk sauce, and quite tasty. I was glad Beth waited till later to inform me that she had learned—also after eating iguana for the first time—that they are endangered. People use their hands to catch the slow ones, which happen to be the females with eggs, thus further reducing their numbers. I enjoyed the meal, but will probably avoid iguana from now on.

We also got a big plate of fish served with rice and beans and half a boiled *guineo* (green banana) and some juice. I was stuffed afterwards. A lot of folks were taking their partying seriously and were fairly drunk so we decided not to stay too long. Later that evening we went into town hoping to find a place that served licuados. We'd seen a sign advertising them recently. We walked by the beach which, to our surprise, had emptied out. Downtown, the central park, which consists of a bunch of cement benches and a little snack shack, was packed with young people, and the disco across the street was blasting music. We were able to find the licuado place, and fully enjoyed them. Saturday was spent similarly, going to the beach for lunch. We went a bit earlier this time, and there were fewer people, but the crowds arrived as we sat there. We just watched them come and swim as we ate our chicken dinner. And again that night we went to town for licuados, this time getting them from the shack in the park.

I had gone shopping on Saturday to buy treat foods that we could make for Easter. In the morning we invented a recipe for scones that turned out more like a torte and tasted quite yummy. We boiled lots of eggs, and made dye by boiling onion skins so we could decorate the eggs. Later we made potato salad and deviled eggs (having splurged on a small jar of mayonnaise), which we ate with stove-top baked beans. For dinner we also had fresh coleslaw. Not everything tasted like home, but it was special. (In fact, coleslaw and baked beans are foods I've never really liked, but it was good to try them and the beans I enjoyed pretty well.) We had also purchased some Snickers bars, in place of the chocolate eggs and rabbits we might have had in the States. The whole week, we'd focused our devotional time on the related stories from the Gospels, and on Easter we sang all the Easter hymns we could find. It was a true celebration.

Beth—The Ups and Downs of Mission Work—May 6, 2006

Up: Esteban came back to town and was ready to work. We were delighted as he did some good work for us in October. Well, the first thing he did was sharpen our machete (showing us how to do it). The second thing was he assembled our hoe.

Down: The first time we used the hoe, the blade came loose.

Up: We went to the mountain with him and transplanted our two tomato plants, cantaloupe, and watermelon. Chito took us out there and taught us how to set up drip irrigation, using a two-liter soda bottle upside-down next to the roots of the plant. We also gathered some two-liter soda bottles on the way.

Up: We also did some erosion control around the fruit trees that had been planted. Esteban planted the pineapples.

Up: We made a contract with Esteban to clean again. The weeds have grown up. They need to be cleaned before we can plant.

Up: Clemente was ready to cut the fence post trees and the yucca starts.

Up: We arranged for Chito to take all three of us, plus starts, up to the mountain on Thursday. We went.

Down: Chito has changed his charges for a ride to the mountain. He more than tripled it.

Down: We got to the mountain, where Clemente and Prairie carried the posts up to the house. The garden had not been cleaned. We weren't terribly surprised, since Esteban had not been around to collect his money.

Up: Chito and Clemente thought that we wanted to plant fence post trees for shade, not for terracing and mulch. (They produce a lot of leaves, good for mulch and fertilizer). This was actually quite wonderful. Clemente had cut forty very long posts. When we got them up to the house, he chopped them in half, giving us a hundred posts to plant.

Up: Clemente was willing to do the cleaning. We easily came to a fair contract. It is less work than last time he cleaned.

Down: Clemente couldn't start cleaning, since he hadn't brought the best type of machete for that work. He also wanted to seek a helper for this work.

Up: Our tomato plants looked great after six days. Some of the soda bottles were still full, some were completely empty. (Go figure.) But the tomatoes looked good. The cantaloupe looked good and two of the four watermelons were still alive and a little bigger than the week before. The yard-long beans are struggling, but have a few blossoms.

Up: We couldn't do all we wanted to do, but like Clemente said, "We did something." We walked back to the road. We can't very well pay for two rides a day when they cost so much. It was a hot day without a breeze. We stopped at the stream to eat our lunch. Clemente showed me how to make a cup from a large leaf. Our walk out was not tough. We were able to hitch a ride back to town once we got to the main road.

Up: Clemente will clean, then we'll all go back again for the all-important terrace planting. We will transplant our okra at the same time (and water the tomatoes). No rain for a month.

Down: The neighbor who can do the water system is still out of town.

Up: Today is May sixth. It is also the sixth day in a row that I have felt perfectly normal, completely healthy. It is great. I was never very sick, but it sure dragged on a long time. Prairie says that I am even walking faster. Well, I hope so. And so it goes.

Beth—National Immunization
Campaign for Central America—May 6, 2006

Last week was the National Immunization Campaign for Central America. The countries collaborate to have it the same week. It officially lasts a week, but since it can't possibly be accomplished in one week, every public health clinic starts a week early.

The immunization program is something that this country does very well. Since the health care system is quite a mess otherwise, this is pretty important to savor. The immunization program is well thought out and is updated as appropriate. The country uses the United Nations health experts (I am assuming the World Health Organization) the way a state in the US would use federal government experts.

The goal is to immunize all children (one hundred-percent) for the usual stuff (including TB). Another goal is to immunize all dogs (one hundred-percent) against rabies. There is no treatment for rabies here. The only thing is prevention. The hundred-percent goal is not considered theoretical by anyone. It is really expected by all.

We went to Limoncito with the team on Monday last. We were eight. I set up doing consultas at the school. (A very good deal—wide shaded porch, nice breeze, nearby bathrooms with running water and soap and my pharmacy, a cardboard box on my table). I sat on one chair, the mother or patient in front of me. I did thirty consultas before one PM. Prairie gave some shots to eleven-year-olds and gave out oral polio vaccine and Vitamin A drops. We were four on our school-based team—including also Warnita and Nildy, from the clinic. Warnita is in charge of the records. Dr. Karen, Elizabeth, the student nurse, and Freddy (a health promoter), went to a post forty minutes away on foot. When they returned, a few went off to a group of two to three houses, a ways off the road, to complete the goal for Limoncito—one hundred percent.

The mayor's car and driver showed up (only forty-five minutes late) to pick us up. The driver has an assistant—so now we were ten. Next we went to Salado, which means salty because the water is a bit brackish there.

Salado is very spread out, so we stopped at most houses. I did one consulta for a sick baby (just a cold). Two kids were not home—our goal was not met that day. It began raining and I was very glad to be among the privileged ones inside the double cab. The young folks outside seemed just fine with the light rain. (Prairie also got to be inside, the only young one to be given the privilege).

They also immunized dogs. That's what Freddy was along for. They sort of walk the dog on his hind legs, one arm controlling the front legs and the other hand holding the muzzle shut. Then the nurse injects the anterior thigh. Quick and efficient. I know nothing about the percentage achieved on dogs.

Warnita knows every child under five in the area. She knows where they live. She keeps all of the records and Dr. Karen keeps referring to her as to what needs to be next. We got back to town about 2:30 PM Then, lunch

Wednesday we were going to go to Plan de Flores, but the transportation fell through and Prairie and I didn't learn of the new plans, so we were left out. I wasn't feeling bad about that. It would have been a hard day. The team spent three days in Plan de Flores—lots of people and very spread out.

Friday we went to La Fortuna. Cooper (head health promoter) has a motorcycle. He and the student nurse left town at five AM, traveled by motorcycle to La Fortuna, and then by horseback (borrowed locally) further up the mountain to get the smaller neighborhoods. This helped a lot as it is usually a mob scene otherwise. Lots of people want consultas on these visits because it is a three-hour walk to catch the bus to Limón!

Dr. Karen helped with immunizations and gave a few adult consultas. I gave forty-four consultas to children and some adults. Our portable pharmacy was getting pretty slim. We had some combination fluoride-vitamin drops. I could give them to the moms as sort of consolation prize when I didn't have what was really needed. We have no asthma medicine, no amoeba medicine, no fever medicine. The mothers accept this very well. It is just not very rare. Fortunately, we had malaria treatment, worm medicine, and antibiotics.

We went to a house for a nice chicken and rice lunch at about one PM. We were all starved and ate well. We had free-range chicken, of course. It is tough. But no one was complaining, you can be sure.

Then back into the truck to return to town. Prairie got to ride in the back this time. (It wasn't the mayor's nice truck, it was Chito's—hired out to Centro de Salud.) The view from the back of the truck is more than wonderful. We could see our house from the other side at three different spots on this twisty mountain road. Prairie wasn't so sure that she would like it. But she did fine.

It is very impressive working with these folks on immunizations. Everyone here is very dedicated to meeting the goal. Everyone helps in whatever way that they can. We work as long as is needed to get stuff done. The staff is paid a small additional daily pay for doing this outreach work—sort of obligatory overtime. They were pretty tired by the end of the week.

Yesterday (Monday, May first) was Labor Day, so the clinic was closed. That means for a week and a day the clinic was closed for consultas—everyone was out doing immunizations. Today was the first day the clinic has been open. We only had about forty patients, so it wasn't too bad. I thought that it might be really swamped. But no. *Gracias a Dios.*

Beth—Daylight Savings Time Began Yesterday—May 9, 2006

Daylight savings time began yesterday. This is a first for Honduras. The government decided to begin observing daylight savings time, but the general population in this rural area is not especially thrilled with the concept. Of course, the school, the public health clinic, and the mayor's office switched to the new time right away. Nildy (volunteer at Centro de Salud) told Prairie that now the elementary school starts at six AM instead of seven and that she goes to junior high at eleven AM instead of noon. It will take a while for everyone to adjust. Since we are in the far eastern end of the time zone, daylight savings time makes the clock agree with the sun better than it did before. Our time zone is now the same as Central Daylight Savings Time in the U.S.

We received mail on Saturday. We hadn't gotten any for almost three weeks. We were really ready; we love getting mail. Included were Easter cards and Easter candy. We enjoyed the candy very much without being the least concerned about the length of time it took to arrive.

Letters from home

A small shipment of medicines from Clinica Metodista arrived yesterday. We were very grateful. We can now treat some of the things we couldn't last week. It has been eight months since the last big shipment of medicines from the government. (We depend on gifts from the United Methodist Church and donations from visiting teams.) We were desperate for IV tubing. Much to my surprise and delight, Eloyda was able to get some for us and it only cost six lempiras (thirty-one cents) each. We never need to run out again. It is a bad spot to be in when we have a sick diabetic and no capacity to administer IV fluids.

Our life is not as interesting as Sor Leonarda's. She runs the shelter for orphans. A boy came to her last weekend, very worried about his little girl cousins. He said that they are naked. In this culture, little boys go naked a lot, but not girls. A girl may take a bath with her brother—he'll be naked and she'll wear panties. Nakedness in girls is sexual abuse. Don't misunderstand, it is not evidence of sexual abuse, it is sexual abuse, itself. A little girl (even still in diapers) is entitled to genital privacy.

Monday morning at 6:30 AM, Sor Leonarda went to the house. Sure enough, outside was a naked little girl. Then she heard a scream inside the house and walked into the bedroom where a boy was taking down his pants with the little girl screaming. (My Spanish isn't sufficient to know if he was taking off his own or hers.) Sor just took them home with her to add to her sheltered children. Of course, she had no legal right to do this. She'll take photos and write a narrative of the incident so that when or if she is accused of misdeeds, she will have a defense.

Sor Leonarda is not especially popular in town. The family values in this community are that what goes on in the family is no one else's business. Sor thinks that abuse of children is everyone's concern. The community would rather look away, would rather not see. This is a lot like in the Fifties and Sixties in the States. Sor Leonarda helps keep me going. She now has thirty-two children. I tease her about all those pregnancies. We have to find humor where we can.

Beth—The Cuttings Come to Visit— May 9–16, 2006

Prairie's parents, April Hall Cutting and Craig Hall Cutting, and her sister, Autumn Cutting, arrived on the late bus on Mother's Day. It is pretty nice to have them here.

In preparation for their arrival, we went shopping in Bonito Oriental, which means "eastern beauty"—masculine case. Our plastic chairs (the ones with arms) had been stolen off the porch one night (in complete silence, I might add). They weren't even ours, but belonged to our landlady. So we really needed to replace them. We didn't have enough chairs for five people to sit down to eat together so we caught the bus to Bonito Oriental to buy chairs and fruits and vegetables. We wanted to share the tropical abundance of things our visitors wouldn't get often.

The bus was crammed. We stood in the aisle for at least forty-five minutes. Every time the bus stopped, it became stifling hot. Some passengers would yell that those wanting to get on wouldn't fit and that we should go on. We didn't, we just stayed there until a few more folks got sardined in. Then, there was a loud clunk! like a big rock flew up and hit the floor of the bus (seemed like just under my feet). Less than a minute later, another clunk! and the bus suddenly listed to the right. Everyone knew that this wasn't good. So we all got off the bus. It was a broken axle.

There are no refunds. The bus folks take no responsibility for the passengers, so we are now on our own. But I've been here before. The very first pickup truck that came along stopped. The driver gave a big smile and said "Fill it up!"—meaning the back of his truck. So we did, about fifteen of us, *Indios, Garifunas,* and us *Gringas.* He took us all to the bus stop in Bonito Oriental and refused any offers of money. I knew better than to offer. I just shook his hand and expressed my gratitude. He said, "At your service, sister," using the form of sister that means religious sister, not family or sister of the church. I guess our uniforms are distinctive. He was so nice to us all and obviously just delighted to have helped out his neighbors of all races (not always what we've observed).

It was very hot, so I called for lots of rest stops. Prairie was patient. Neither of us had spent time in Bonito before. We learned the entire shopping district is seen from the bus route. We walked all over, including a half mile to the licuado store. On the way back to the bus stop, we got lots of fruits and vegetables. We even found the chairs at the last possible place—after checking every place in town that sold chairs.

Then we bought a meal to share. After licuados, we couldn't each manage a whole dinner. Just as we were finishing, along came our bus back to Limón. We hopped on the bus and guys put our chairs in the back. We stood in the aisle—which was even more crowded in terms of where to put one's feet. It was hard to be stable, but before half way home, enough people got off that we were able to sit down. We were very grateful.

One more important stop—the watermelon stand. No one got on or off, but lots of us bought watermelons through the window, including me.

We were sort of using the family's visit to indulge our own hunger for fruits and vegetables. We bought pineapple, mangoes, lemons, watermelon, zapote, avocados, carrots, pataste, sweet potatoes, sweet peppers, even jalapeño peppers. I think I have remembered everything.

Yesterday we went downtown and found some grapefruit, two more pineapples, and another watermelon. (Five people can eat a lot of fruit, you know.) We are enjoying having them here. As I write, Prairie is being the tour guide, showing them the town.

Yesterday was the Feast of San Isidro, an important holiday. Lots of businesses were closed. We saw a few patients at Centro de Salud. As the only doctor this time, this pediatrician took care of a ninety-seven-year-old guy who is developing a hernia. He can't stop work to prevent its progress—no work, no food. He works chopping with the machete. (He looks darn good for seventy-five, not to mention ninety-seven.)

The next day we went to the mountain. More about that later. We were very pleased how we lasted for two days in a row of such physical exercise. We are getting in shape. We are getting in such good shape that pretty soon I won't be able to hold my blue jeans on without a cord. I already look sort of clownish in them. They ride lower on my hips every trip to the mountain.

Time to go back to the house party. By the way, did I mention how cool it is to sing with three-part harmony? The Cuttings are a very musical family. Our prayer times are an incredible musical experience—yes, in Spanish. If the words are too hard, the tune isn't and humming works just fine.

Beth—One Step Ahead Day—May 22, 2006

This morning April and Craig left on the direct bus to La Ceiba. They should get to San Pedro Sula today, then on to Guatemala City on Sunday. It was kind of hard to see them go—obviously, harder for Autumn and Prairie than for me. They knew how to be guests on vacation while knowing full well that we weren't on vacation. They helped us with gardening at the mountain—on a day that was advertised as a hike. We planted the sugar cane and the kale. Also, a tour of the peak, house, garden, and short hike. We took the bus there, then walked. We walked out to the highway and caught a lift to Chito's house and chatted with him about all of our projects. He is quite the communicator. The next day, Mateo was over to talk about the construction of the kitchen and porch.

But I'm getting ahead of myself. Last week we visited the neighbor who we thought could put in the water system. Well, that didn't work out so well. It would have cost a lot of money (about $3,000). The risks were incredible. The spring is on one neighbor's land and the water tank would be on the land of our near neighbor. There is a pretty strong rumor that he uses land not officially his, and is at risk of being indicted for this. We have no idea whether the part in question is the peak where he would like to put the tank. We would be paying all of the expenses while his part would be to supervise the work. The peak where the water tank would be placed is at the same level, as far as we can determine, as our house—not higher—at the same level. And finally, he says that the way to raise water pressure is to use a smaller pipe. Well, I was pretty disappointed, but we had to turn down this wonderful offer. We are back to collecting rainwater as our plan. This should do fine for ten months of the year. What about the other two? One step at a time.

Now that we know that we don't have to plan our space around this long-expected water system, we were ready to work on the dry compost toilet, the kitchen and the porch roof.

Mateo took us out to the mountain this morning. We talked over the plans. He will extend the roof of the house forward fourteen feet from the front door. On one side he will build a free-standing kitchen about eight by six feet. He thinks that this is too small, so he will mark it out on the ground for us to look at, in case we want to change our minds. There will be a three-foot space between it and the house (fire control and egress to the north side of the house). There will be shade on the south side of the kitchen—maybe even a place for a hammock to go. The kitchen will have windows on the three sides that don't have a door. No screens—we will have a window out of which we will pour the waste water.

We talked about the *fogón*, a traditional stove with oven. He recommends that it be made with clay bricks. They make a better oven than cement blocks. We will not have it made right away.

We still need to learn a little more about these stoves and to choose a size and then learn about the chimney setup. Some folks have chimneys, some don't. We want a chimney—less smoke.

We talked about the dry compost toilet. We chose a place for it. When we went back to the house with the drawings, we realized that there were still some details that we were not clear on. We deferred this planning a little. We would be visiting El Pino in a few days, and we knew Carlos (the pastor) had experience with dry compost toilets. He would be able to explain stuff to us and share his experience. We had many reasons to be eager to talk to him.

We planted a few more plants at the mountain today. It was sort of our last chance before we left town. Any little plants left at the house would die. We would see how they did when we returned. The okra and tomatoes are looking good. The other stuff is okay.

A new contract has been written for the kitchen. Also, Mateo will construct our beds. He cut down one of our trees for the lumber and will cut down one more tree which has grown too close to the house. He'll make two single beds and two bunk beds, our first furniture. Step by step.

We are delighted. We are now ready to assemble information about water collection and tank size (for water storage) and tank type. Again, the home-made clay bricks make very good tanks, but they are more expensive than the plastic ones. Always, new things to be learning.

We are enjoying our second copy of *Mil Voces Para Celebrar* (a Spanish Methodist hymnal). It was a gift from the Cuttings and is pretty nice. They gave us a lot of very helpful start-up gifts.I really like one-step-forward days better than those one-step-back ones.

Fighting for Children's Health—May 22–24, 2006

This is a follow-up on the almost 4-year-old girl with congenital heart disease. The mom was told a few years ago that her daughter needed surgery before she turned four. Well, the child's birthday is next month and the girl's mother is getting desperate. She keeps taking her to the foreigner clinic, as everyone who lives here believes that sometimes they finance health care provided elsewhere. But no, unfortunately, it was a misunderstanding that they would pay her way. The misunderstanding was painful for everyone involved.

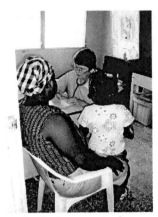

Beth gives a consulta

The mother and I visited Dr. Karen to learn the referral process. It goes this way: we make a referral to the state hospital where a pediatrician consults and can write a referral to the children's hospital in Teguz. As a local Centro de Salud, we cannot write a referral to Teguz. We have a process to go through. At Trujillo, they can do a chest X-ray (which we can't), but neither EKG (on kids) nor echocardiogram.

Then we talked to Sor Leonarda about funds for travel. The mom says that she is doing well enough to provide food for herself and her six kids (and they all are skinny, not just the sick child). So Sor looks into things. It turns out that this is a backdoor family. All six children have the same father, but the father has a wife and lives with her and his two children from the marriage in different municipality, where he has both a good job with the government and a business on the side. As is typical of such backdoor families, the woman is well-schooled to ask for nothing of the man except whatever he gives her (mostly more babies). So, it never even occurred to her to ask the father to pay for transportation and health care. Instead, she asked perfect strangers for help.

Sor Leonarda called up the father and told him his responsibilities (in no uncertain terms). He didn't want to foot the bill. She told him that if he refused to take care of his own daughter, she would turn him in to the authorities. He finally agreed, saying that he knew that she could ruin him if he didn't comply.

Two weeks ago the mom came to our house and showed me the referral written to Teguz for the chest X-ray. We had already had the first consultation at Trujillo—from the same pediatrician who helped us out with another cardiac patient. The chest X-ray demonstrated that the little girl does not have the more serious heart defect that I worried about. The mom looked pretty, though no one would have called her pretty before. She was so happy and so relieved to be getting what her child needed.

Then last week, mom, dad and child went to Teguz for the consulta. Sor Leonarda called the father on his cell phone on the bus, insisting that he pass the phone to mom, too. She wastes no trust on this father. Then she called the social worker at the hospital to take care of a place to stay for mom and child while in Teguz. On Monday, Sor told me that the child had had her consultation and would begin her treatment this week, with a follow-up appointment in September.

Please pray for Sor Leonarda. She lives a very dangerous life.

Last October, I treated an eight year-old boy with pneumonia. He was the most severely dehydrated child I had seen (that survived, that is). After treating him with penicillin and IV fluids, I taught his mom to use oral re-hydration fluid and sent him home with her. Four days later, he was still sick and went to Clinica Carolina (where a visiting team of doctors were working). They did a malaria test, but it was negative. Still confused about his illness, the doctor ordered a complete blood count. As Gloria was counting white blood cells, she saw a malaria parasite. Mystery solved. This helps remind us all about the value of negative malaria tests! They treated him and he recovered.

This week, mom brought him back. He is in first grade, but mom doesn't send him to school because he has one or two generalized seizures a day. These began after his illness in October. He never had them before. Well, I figured that he had neurologic damage (he was certainly entitled to). I consulted with Dr. Karen about EEG versus just starting treatment. She definitely wanted to make a referral. The leading cause of adult onset seizure disorder in most tropical countries is cysticercosis (pork tapeworm). It can invade the brain—very gross. We were in luck. Dr. Karen did a research project on exactly this as her thesis to get her M.D. Yes, we know that an eight-year-old is not an adult, but he is old enough to have this disease—and there are a lot of pigs in town. We have a pig leash law, for whatever that is worth!

The first step is to start treatment. The next step is to send the child to Trujillo, the state hospital, where he will get a referral to go to Teguz for a CAT scan. Of course, the family is in a tight financial situation, so we refer the mother to Sor Leonarda, who may or may not be able to help. But you are starting to get an idea of her track record, aren't you?

Medical follow-up on me. I am in excellent health. Prairie is in excellent health—except for the small patch of skin she lost on her palm yesterday while planting madriado trees at the mountain.

Beth—On Beggars—May 25–30, 2006

Last week on the bus to La Ceiba, a beggar climbed aboard. He was a middle-aged man, neat and tidy, with congenital disuse of his hands (looked like a form of *arthogryposis* to me). He went down the aisle accepting gifts of one or two lempiras, blessing all who gave to him. Then, he sat down next to a friendly young man who helped him organize his money because his hands really do not work. Another neighbor accepted the change, replacing it with a twenty lempira bill. He thanked and blessed them. Then he blessed everyone again. He got off at the next stop, no doubt to get on the next bus going in the opposite direction.

While Prairie's family was here, we wanted them to experience all the interesting eating possibilities, so we planned a dinner out in Limón. Well, the electricity had been off for most of the afternoon, so our first-choice place to eat was not ready to serve. We weren't able to wait for an eight PM dinner, so we chose a different restaurant—big meals, more expensive, more elegant.

We all settled in and ordered our dinners. The meals were served on platters, each with a fish or pieces of fried chicken, lots of tajadas (fried green bananas) and a large platter of coleslaw to share. This meal was much more than I could possibly eat.

Soon a young beggar came in. He was about nine years old and developmentally delayed. He used to live with his family, but seems to be a street kid now. Many developmentally delayed kids end up this way. The families have no clue how to train them. I have been told that the family used to beat him a lot, but then a very kind visiting doctor had a meeting with them, explaining the futility of that. Supposedly his life improved after that. About three years ago, he was still running around naked (like a much younger boy). One day I came upon a man from the neighboring church hitting him with a stick. I said, "What are you teaching him?" It just popped out. The man said, "I'm teaching him to wear pants." I was stunned. Well, now he wears pants.

He has learned slightly more refined begging manners than in the past, too. He calls us Aunt and doesn't paw with his filthy hands as much as a year ago.

So, he came to the table, wanting food, of course. I gave him about a third of my *tajadas* (plantain chips) and tried to get him to go away. He took his napkin full of tajadas and moved down the table between Craig and Autumn. It was clear that he was going to stay until he was fed.

When I had eaten a little less than half of what I had been served, I sent my platter to him. He moved with it to a chair away from the table and started eating. Very soon, the waitress took away the food and platter, took it to the kitchen and moved the food to a disposable tray and sent him outside with it. He went without complaining.

So, in spite of myself, I collaborated with our little brother and the waitress to keep from wasting food (a serious sin in a country in which lots of people don't have enough to eat). And we both had a meal.

Well, we wanted them to have an interesting dining experience. It didn't turn out to be quite what we expected.

Beth—Immigration Laws, Mayan Art, and Good Food—May 31, 2006

First, recognize that this is a privileged communication, you know, strictly confidential. Anything that you are told today may be used against me.

The immigration laws in Honduras are very strict. Interestingly enough, most Hondurans know more about immigration law in the U.S. than they do about their own country. When we tell folks that we have to leave the country every three or four months to keep out of trouble with the law, they are almost always surprised.

When we were in La Ceiba last week, we went to the Immigration Office to learn the latest. We paid our fees for the three months that we have been here (twenty dollars per month per person) and were told that we no longer have to be gone from the country for three days. We just have to leave and come back, even the same day. Furthermore, the entry folks can stamp our papers to allow ninety days free (no every-thirty-day fee).

We were delighted. We spent Saturday traveling here (Copán) by bus. On Sunday, we did our usual day of rest. We enjoyed that a lot. We took some hikes around town, read, rested.

On Monday, we were tourists. We went to the Mayan ruins. It was a slightly overcast day, so we didn't fry in the sun. We even walked the nature trail. The restoration continues and a little more has taken form since my last visit. Then Prairie and Autumn went to the museum. I had seen it once and didn't think it was worth five dollars for the re-run. Well, I guess not. All of the explanatory signs had been taken down in preparation for new ones. But the new ones were not yet up. They saw a lot, but without explanations.

Tuesday morning (yesterday) we went to the new museum in the center of town. It was delightful. Everyone is always telling us what great art the ruins are, but everything is pretty badly weathered and it seems like great history, but not great art. In the museum are some well-preserved sculptures, jewelry and ceramics. They are wonderful. When I see them not mostly destroyed by time and weather, I can see that, indeed, they are excellent art. It was a real treat to go to that museum.

We walked Autumn to the bus which was to take her to Guatemala City. She is flying from there to Portland, Oregon, today. Then Prairie and I moved from the hotel to a hostel. We can cook there. Lots of vegetables are available here that are not available in Limón and restaurant meals are very costly here (and very delicious, I might add).

The order of business of this morning was to go to the border and get our legal obligations met. So we did.

When we arrived at the Honduran border post, the worker said first that we have to be out of the country for three days, second, that we should have a document from the government in Tegucigalpa stating our volunteer work, and third, that she didn't have authority to do us the favor of stamping our passports, permitting us to leave and re-enter—or give us a ninety-day stamp. She would have to wait for her chief to arrive. We said, "Okay, we'll wait." (Like, what else could we do?)

Every time she had a little break in her work, she would

confer with us. Each time she reiterated the same stuff, but said that her boss was a good guy and he would probably approve. He hadn't arrived yet. (When you are the boss, you don't have to arrive at work on time.) She called us by pet names usually reserved for children.

She said that if he didn't show up soon, she would call him on his cell phone when another break in her work came. We trooped across the border to where there is a telephone. She placed the call. We paid for it (thirty-two lempiras). The guy wanted to charge in quetzales. (We were in Guatemala after all.) I pulled out my money from my pocket inside the front of my dress. It all came out—a twenty dollar bill, some hundred-lempiras bills, and a fifty-quetzal bill. He couldn't change the fifty, but was willing to accept lempiras.

She didn't tell us what the boss said, but she had us go back to her office. All of this time, of course, she has had our passports. After all, what good are they to us without her stamp?

We filled out the papers and she called another helper to carry our passports to the Guatemalan office (twenty quetzales each). I handed over the fifty-quetzal bill. There was no change, of course. Finally, she stamped our passports, filled out all of the paper work and informed us that this favor cost twenty dollars. The fee was 120 lempiras for both (six dollars). The rest was for the favor.

So, there we were, feeling so innocent, just paying the bill. But I think that I have just participated in bribing a government official. (Then I started thinking about all that money coming out at once—isn't flashing big bills the subtle way to offer a bribe?) Maybe I have done it in the past without knowing it? My Spanish gets better every trip, after all. This left me with a very strange feeling in my stomach.

We took the next bus back to Copán and won't have to have our passports stamped for ninety days. An unnerving morning, but we have all of our papers in order, so far.

Beth—Trips, Sick Child, Kitchen Construction, Fence lines,
Gardening, and Sewing—June 1–22, 2006

We have had a very interesting week after returning from our trip.

Our visit at El Pino was really very nice (last Thursday–Saturday). We were permitted to stay in the training center. That means that we could be there at El Pino for the evening meetings. We attended a women's meeting on Thursday night and a leadership training session on Friday night. Everyone was very patient with my poor Spanish. Prairie is quite shy, but when she had something to say, she was well understood. It was very nice for us to have this group church interaction. Our group of two has a shortage of variety of ideas, of course.

It was good to get back home. We were really ready for our day of rest on Sunday. We indulged, as we usually do, in a dip in the ocean on Sunday. The water is still fairly cool (for the Caribbean).

We have caught up on the sheet washing after our houseguests and traveling. We carried our own sheets for the trip. When we stay at El Pino, we are given cots to sleep on and we bring the sheets—large sheets—that way a single one serves, half for the bottom sheet, and half for when you might need a top sheet near morning.

On Tuesday, we were going to go to the mountain with Esteban, but a misunderstanding about daylight savings time versus old time ended up canceling that. We repaired Prairie's pants that had given out in the butt. We used some bright lavender sheet-material (very festive against the pale beige) and essentially put in a new bottom.

About noon, Gloria showed up with a very concerned grandmother and mother and a fourteenth-month-old boy with a complicated medical history who is very sick. The story sounded very much like sickle-cell disease with a pain crisis. So we all went down to Centro de Salud for me to give a consulta.

I pulled the chart. This is the same child that last fall I had thought had posterior urethral valve. They did not pursue the specialist that I had recommended. Now I realize that my poor Spanish resulted in me asking leading questions. The mom just agreed with me. The attitude is, "Who am I to contradict the doctor?" So, back to the Spanish studying. We do not have the capacity in town to do a blood test for sickle-cell disease. I made the diagnosis based on history (including some lab tests done elsewhere) and his physical exam. The next evening, the grandmother dropped by to tell me that he was improved. Then we knew why our trip was canceled. We needed to be around for our little sick boy.

On Wednesday, we went out to the mountain. Mateo picked us up and Esteban went along to work with us. Mateo and his son took the zinc roofing material up and put it up on the porch and kitchen area. Then they built one wall of the kitchen. They had already put the skeleton up—yes, framing. I knew the word. I find that my English is getting more eccentric all of the time. I usually have a perfectly useful word at hand, but it will not be the usual word used. You understood "the skeleton of a building," didn't you?

It was fun to watch that come together. We talked over the progress and the plan. Mateo had been concerned that a eight-by-six-foot kitchen would be too small. I reminded him that we are not as rich as his family and we can't afford a great kitchen like Margarita, his wife has.

After he framed it, he took Margarita to the mountain to provide a kitchen consult. She approved of the kitchen, recommending that one wall be left without a window, for storage shelves, etc. This was very generous of Margarita to give us this consult and very wise of Mateo to have sought it. We are delighted.Also, the kitchen and porch are likely to come in under budget. The zinc roofing cost less than expected. Unbelievable. When was the last time any construction came in under budget?

Carlos Ortiz, our friend, the pastor in El Pino, has experience with dry compost toilets. There were some details that we had not been clear on so we got out drawings, pencil and paper and he explained those details. They were pretty important details. When we got back to Limón, we were able to show the drawings to Mateo and explain the details to him. We didn't make a contract to build it yet, but that will be next—after the kitchen, porch and bunk beds. By the way, the lumber for the beds is all cut and stacked inside the house.

This is starting to feel like a real house that is livable—not super-rustic camping.

Prairie is doing internet research to help us decide if we want either a completely traditional fogón, or a souped-up version that makes less smoke and uses less wood. Usually the promoters of souped-up versions of traditional items leave out the disadvantages, so decision-making can be pretty tricky. We want the best of both worlds, of course.

Esteban had cleaned along the fence line. So the first order of business with him was to inspect that. The fence line is a rugged hike. But inspect we must and inspect we did. Many of the old fence posts have rotted out. They are hanging by the wire. The wire looks good. Mateo can provide us with some new fencepost trees to put in. He recommends the live trees for property lines. Makes it harder for a neighbor to get creative about the location of the line.

Then came inspection and work in the garden. Our two most mature tomato plants had died. We knew that being gone for two weeks would put everything at risk of dying of drought. I suppose we are lucky that only those tomatoes died. Sigh. We have one other tomato plant (a full month younger, though) that looks okay.

The kale was eaten by insects. I can recognize it as kale only because I planted it. We have recipes for organic insect repellents. Hopefully, they will be useful. We are in Tocoa today and hope to buy some hot peppers. Our hot pepper plant also got attacked by the insects. It is hard to start organic farming from scratch.

The winged beans that Autumn and I planted were struggling. About one third or fewer came up.

The okra has blossoms and a few small pods. The next time we go to the mountain, we should be able to pick okra. We were scheduled to go today, but Mateo had to cancel. Also there was a lot of rain yesterday and the clay soil would be very slippery. We were satisfied with the cancellation.

Clemente had planted one dwarf *plátano* (plantain) and it has come up. We weeded and put down more mulch. Esteban planted some more of the *madriado* (fence-post tree) for the terrace. Prairie planted a couple more hills of yucca. I planted two hills of *lablab* beans (ground cover, green fertilizer). And that was enough for one day.

Mateo gave us a ride both ways, so we got a lot of work done for our five-and-a-half-hour investment of time. We are stiff again, though I'm not as stiff as last time. I wore Prairie's pants (with the great new patch) and she wore my blue jeans. They sort of fit her, but really hang on me.

On Thursday, we borrowed Gloria's iron to work on our sewing. One of Prairie's dresses had gotten stolen (it was in the barrel). We finished up her new dress. We had started it over a month ago. When April was here, she put the pockets in, helping along the progress a lot. We did the final touches. Looks pretty good. It is a much brighter blue than the rest of our stuff.

On Friday morning, we went back to sewing. We finished the pair of new slacks for me. April had helped with pattern-making on that while she was here too. It took all morning, but we got them done. I won't start wearing them until we wear out one of the other pairs. One pair is enough. We did want to do the sewing while we had electricity and an iron available, though. We altered the pattern so that now we have two sizes of pants, one for each of us. We are very grateful for the sewing experience that April shared with us.

We walked past one of the carpenter shops this week and asked about table-making. We told the carpenter about some little square tables in a certain restaurant that we thought would be perfect. We wanted two. Each table seats four people (a little smaller than a card table) and they could be moved together when needed. He agreed to look them over.

We stopped back yesterday afternoon and he said that he could do them for 300 lempiras (sixteen dollars) each. They will be done on June twenty-first. We made the deal.

It is a very strange life. We spend days and weeks patiently (or not) working on something that hopefully will come to fruition. Then a week like this, when lots of things come together all at once.

We are now reading *John Woolman's Journal* as our shared reading I had forgotten how really wonderful it is. It is nice to have friends like John to encourage us.

Beth—Learning-by-Doing Has Disadvantages
June 22, 2006

We have had a lot of rain and that closes down our internet connection. Actually, the rain doesn't, the clouds do. So, today we are in Tocoa trying to catch up on communications and shopping.

Progress on the house is good. The built-in bunks are finished. The outside kitchen is finished. The garden has mixed news. We finally have some bovine manure.

We are hoping that our garden will do better now that we can feed the plants. We, in fact, have more manure than we need right now. We are not complaining about that.

We are still working on planting the first terrace of madriado trees. We had understood that the cut stakes would survive quite a while and still root. Then we were informed that this is simply not the case. We can see some tiny sprouts on some of the first ones planted, but several others were probably planted that were already dead. Sigh. This learning-by-doing has its disadvantages.

We were able to get some fresh posts. We thought that they were going to be for the fence at the edge of our land, but Prairie cut them shorter (to have more of them) with the machete and planted another fourteen on the terrace. Now we'll just see which ones survive. Last Friday, Prairie and I took the bus and then walked to the mountain. We got there about seven AM. She worked on the madriado while I helped just a little. I put down manure and mulch. I got pretty dirty and smelly, but they let me on the bus on the way home.

We are trying to find some *gandul* seeds (pigeon peas). They provide food for humans and chickens and are good terrace plants. It sounds like they would meet our needs a little better than more terraces of madriado so we look. We got a new email contact today that may be a good lead.

Mateo talked about making the water collection system. It is now the time. After all, we get rain in June and July, then hardly any in August and September. There is no time to waste. He did some research about the cost of materials and planned to stop over on Saturday afternoon to talk details and make a contract. Saturday afternoon came and went. Saturday evening came and went. We are used to this—not with Mateo, but in general. After all, one can't just pick up the phone to change an appointment.

On Sunday afternoon, he showed up, all ready to make a contract. What a temptation! But (just as though I weren't tempted) I told him that we don't do business on Sunday. We didn't talk about materials or cost or time schedule—nothing. I told him that we get up at 5:30 AM and go to work at Centro de Salud at eight AM on Mondays. About 6:45 on Monday morning, he came back to complete the business.

There will be gutters down both sides of the roof with

the roof of the kitchen and porch continuous with the house. They will come together to empty into a raised tank. The tank will be made with traditional bricks and will hold just over 500 gallons of water. It will be at the back of the house—not at the same end as the kitchen. Mateo thinks it would be so big that it would be in the way. Still, he thinks that he can run a PVC pipe from there to the kitchen. We talked about several more details, but it will be in the doing that all will be ironed out.

We now have a track record together and I am confident. It is, however, quite costly, 40,000 lempiras—just over $2,000. Another reason to be in Tocoa is to withdraw money from the bank. Mateo thinks that this project will take about two weeks. I am eager to see the work in progress.

Beth—Of Guitars, Bluejean Seams, Gardens, Rain, and Hummingbirds—June 22, 2006

Well, *both* the local internet connections in town are out of commission. We are very grateful for the emails that we receive. I eagerly read the news, but cannot respond to them. If you sent me an email—thank you. If I get the time to read them I am grateful. But answering seems like a luxury that I don't have.

Our trip to Tocoa today was so I would meet my self-assigned deadline of writing the invitation to potential aspirants and sojourners. June. Just made it.

The other reason is that though we have a guitar we have no guitar teacher, no guitar book. Prairie had found a website today that gave her the basic information so that she can give herself the first lesson—tuning the guitar. A local pastor plays, but he has been out of town, so no local instruction available as yet.

Prairie's guitar

On Tuesday, we had planned on going to the mountain with Mateo, but it rained pretty hard. Mateo didn't show up. We didn't expect him to, but we really had wanted to do some gardening and to take some of our stuff to the mountain.

We started our blue bed-coverlet. We have several scraps of blue fabric from our dresses. Since they are a very simple pattern, the scraps can be pretty big and still not useful for a dress. I have three quilters in my family—Mom, my sister Ann and my sister-in-law Marguerite. We took tidbits of each of their experiences to start our coverlet. We want one layer only; two layers would be too warm. We cut rectangles and sewed them together. Since denim, even lightweight denim, ravels easily, we used bluejean-style seams. I didn't even know that I could do a bluejean seam. But there it is. We got a good start. And a nice project it was for a rainy day. Prairie also did some musical arranging for alto recorder duet. Next step is to learn the duet.

Wednesday was more of the same. We went to the mountain yesterday. We caught the six-something bus and began walking. We stopped along the road to eat our packed breakfast. We chose leisurely prayer time at home and breakfast later. It was about seven by the time we ate. Since we had been up since five, we were really ready to eat. Shortly thereafter we heard a truck come along. Oh, good, maybe we can hitch a ride. Well, we certainly could. It was Mateo! He had driven over to our rental house while we were on the bus. So we all rode to the mountain together.

Mateo had the local water tank, rainfall-collector-constructor-expert in tow. He directed the work; Mateo and German (Mateo's brother-in-law who is Mateo's helper) helped him. They will put the tank on the kitchen end of the house. (The expert convinced Mateo that it was more sensible than the opposite end). They made the wooden forms and put in the rebar for pouring the concrete for the posts and the concrete floor of the tank. The expert answered all of my questions. He makes it all seem very easy. But we are pretty far behind schedule. The rain has interfered a lot, of course. Supposedly, it would have been finished by the end of next week, but it is not terribly likely now.

We did some more gardening, of course. We noticed a few milestones. The entire madriado terrace row is now planted. Prairie planted a lot in the last few weeks. She also planted some posts for our trellis for the winged beans.

We noticed that the peppers have tiny pre-buds. Dutifully, we picked them off. We are told that picking the first ones off makes for a stronger plant and more fruit in the long run. But it sure took a lot of willpower!

Last week I planted some cashew seeds and some *mamón* seeds. Mamónes are in season right now. They often grow wild. They are about an inch long and three-quuarters of an inch wide, with a seed that almost fills the fruit. But they are sweet, with just enough tartness to be enjoyable. They are a nice activity-type snack.

Our okra is not doing much. It is hard for me to be patient. The temperate-climate okra that I planted last fall bore early and heavily. This tropical-climate okra is a little slower, but it is supposedly drought tolerant and yields more in the long run because it lives longer and keeps on bearing. We'll see. The kale is still alive.

Mateo gave us a ride home. That is such a lovely luxury.

Our thoughts turned more and more to packing, transporting stuff to the new house and thinking about when we actually move there ourselves.

Clemente sold us his hole digger and pick. He gave us a good price. They are old and the pick head is a little loose, but it would have cost us twice as much for new ones. He had left them for us to use and I had begun to be nervous about using them so long without returning them. He says that he doesn't use them anymore and he would rather have the cash. That worked well for all of us, 200 lempiras for both (about eleven dollars).

We had made a contract with a local furniture maker for two small tables for the house on the mountain. But the rain has meant that no one is cutting wood, so he has not even started them.

The rain has meant that the zinnias have popped up again in the yard around the house in town, the first new blossoms this week. No hummingbirds yet, but they'll be back.

Beth—Of Fogóns, Water Tanks, Furniture,
and Dry Compost Toilets—July 3–13, 2006

Last Saturday, we walked to the post office to mail some letters and to get our mail. There was some; we liked that.

Then we struck off for Limoncito. It was about ten AM so we didn't expect to find a bus. We hoped to hitch a ride, which is easier to do on the road outside of town. It is hard to do inside town. We hadn't even gotten out of town when along came a bus. Lucky us! It dropped us off right at Margarita's front gate. Her house is right on the highway. The timing was good. She was in her outside kitchen and was ready to talk to us about our fogón. She has a gas stove in her kitchen as well as the fogón. But she always uses the fogón. She doesn't like the way food comes out on the gas stove. When food cooks so fast, it isn't as juicy.

She taught us a lot of the ins and outs of the fogón and said that she would like to build ours for us. We talked about the various kinds of chimneys. She thinks the chimney straight up through the roof works a lot better than a bend just above the stove. Mateo, her husband and our contractor, would help, of course. The chimney would be made of zinc (roofing zinc) soldered to make a long cylinder.

We were ready to make the contract, except for the detail of how much it would cost. Mateo conveniently showed up right then. They conferred while we went to sit under their bougainvillea arbor. When their daughter brought us each an orange soda pop, I understood that the price would be high! I was right 3,500 lempiras. (This is just under $200—a high price.) We made the deal and gave the down payment when Mateo took us home. He wanted another payment on the tank project anyway Then the internet died while I was writing this letter, but, fortunately, I had saved most of it. To continue....

We spent our first overnight at the new house on July fourth. It seemed very strange that it is not a holiday here— just another workday. We worked at Centro de Salud on July third and went to the mountain on July fourth. Margarita, her young woman helper and several children came, too, besides Mateo and German, Margarita's brother and Mateo's usual helper. (Oh, I almost forgot, the tank construction expert was along, too.) It was a pretty lively day. Margarita got right to work on the fogón. She constructed a large box on the dirt floor with clay bricks, using wet clay to hold them together. When it was as high as the bottom of the oven, she filled the center with rocks and dry dirt. Then it was leveled off to make the oven floor.

Fogón stove finished

There is a table to one side (all built in, of course). This is where the wood rests when the stove is in operation. One uses poles, about four-feet long, of wood. The fire is in the fire-box—no grate.

The pieces of wood are pushed into the firebox to keep the fire going. It is a little complicated, but we can learn. The side table is constructed of bricks over the rocks and dirt on the right side of the stove.

The oven is four bricks high. These are fairly standard-size bricks, I think. The top of the oven is a metal plate on which the fire is lit. An oven opening is built in, of course, with a wooden door that slides down from above to close the oven. It is a very leaky oven, but we are assured that we could roast a chicken in it. We have not yet bought a whole chicken, so this assurance is merely academic.

Lighting the fire is a little tricky. One lights grease-wood (a dried pine that is very full of highly flammable pitch) and puts these lit sticks far inside the firebox as tinder. Then one feeds in the wood. Since there is no rack or grate, this is a challenge for the inexperienced user.

The cooking surface is another large metal plate that will easily hold four pots at once. Margarita says that one makes the tortillas right on the stovetop with no pan needed. This is true both for corn and flour tortillas. You just have the fire hotter for corn tortillas.

The stove by now is completed, except for the outside layer of white clay. It just wouldn't be right to leave it red clay. I don't know why. It just isn't done that way. We could make a fire in it, but the clay was still wet, so the stove was not really very useable yet. The chimney draws and Mateo fixed the leak that the stovepipe caused in the roof, so, we are close to being independent in cooking on the mountain.

Back to July fourth. By mid-afternoon, all of the workers had left. We had done quite a bit of gardening when we weren't talking with and observing the construction going on at the house. We were pretty happy to have the quiet. We even built a little campfire type fire. It stayed for a while before the rain put it out. It was the closest thing we had to fireworks.

The night was lovely. The rain cleared up and most of the clouds departed. The moon and stars were bright. (Far from towns and electricity, the natural lights of the sky are quite remarkable.) It was very nice to finally sleep in our new house. We warmed up our food on our kerosene stove. In many ways, it was still more like a camping trip. But it was a start.

Things just aren't going to be in chronological order. We had about a week in which it would have been wonderful to write to you every day, but the internet was down and there was just not the option. Every day there was something that made our day remarkable. Today, it is that the internet functions!

The water tank had made a lot of progress. They were laying brick. Traditional brick is the best for water tanks.

Water tank

The contract was for a tank of 500 gallons. When the tank was at the right height, Mateo said that they could take it a little higher with very little greater expense. It would hold 850 gallons. I said no, we couldn't afford that. Maybe later, we could enlarge it. He assured me that it wouldn't cost much and if we do it later, it would be deconstruction *and* reconstruction and would cost a lot. I asked how much is a little? He didn't have an answer. I asked: "A little in hundreds or a little in thousands?" He still doesn't have an answer. Based entirely on trust I tell him to go ahead. He charged us 6,000 lempiras for it—far too much. He had us over a barrel and he knew it. I was pretty disappointed.

The water collection system takes in water from the south side of the house only. The gutter wraps around the end of the zinc roof, so essentially all of the rain is captured. The pipe that enters the water tank can be moved to the side. This is what one would do when the rain just starts—let the rain rinse the roof clean before putting the water into the tank. It enters a pipe with a screen over it to strain out particulate matter. The whole tank is completely enclosed. The door for cleaning it is a concrete slab trapdoor on the top. One crawls inside to clean out the tank three to four times a year. It is done during the rainy season of course, so that the tank will refill rapidly afterward. There is a PVC pipe with two taps coming out of the bottom. There is a wider pipe from the bottom leading down hill (the one to use for cleaning). There is an overflow pipe at the top—also pointing downhill.

We stayed on the mountain again this Tuesday, just one night. We had a brief rain. Mateo had cleaned the tank and the heavy rain had cleaned the roof, so the rain should have provided good drinking water. And it did rain a little—enough for me to test the system. The water tasted horrible! Sort of chemical, plastic-like. Apparently, this is from the goo that holds the PVC pipes together. Mateo promised to clean the whole thing out the next day. The foul taste will wear off and we should have distilled water eventually. It is said that some people don't find rainwater acceptable as drinking water because it is pure. Most people are used to minerals in their water. Rainwater is completely tasteless, so not everyone likes it. I hope that we will.

The water system is now in, with the kinks (yucky taste) being worked out. Next step is the dry compost toilet. We had talked about it before, so Mateo had it pretty much in mind. We reviewed what the construction would be and where it would go. Then he told us that he would charge us 35,000 lempiras. This was shockingly high. He came down to 30,000 lempiras and understood that I was pretty shocked about the extra 6,000 for the water system. In my opinion, he is still charging us an unfairly high price. Before we made the contract, I got out the bankbook so that Prairie and I could go over our financial status. This cuts very close to the bone. So, we'll be very close to the bone, I guess.

Mateo wanted a down payment of 10,000 lempiras. But, of course, we didn't have 10,000 lempiras. Tomorrow we will go to Tocoa to withdraw money so that we can give him the down payment (and have enough to pay for the stove when it is all done). This will delay things a little bit, but that is how it is.

On Tuesday, we talked about the bookshelf and he started it. We have not found any chairs to suit us. The plastic ones that are very popular here are both pretty flimsy and bad for posture, so they are out. The only other chairs available are hand-made heavy wooden chairs. (Need I mention, they are expensive and take up a lot of room?) So I asked Mateo if he could make us some stools. He made one. As he put it, it is actually a short bench. It is perfect. The first one is just a little high to use as a chair by a table, but is good for the sewing machine and perfect for clarinet or recorder playing. I asked him to make three more, but the other three to be a little shorter. I don't know what he will charge for these.

We went to the carpenter shop yesterday and our tables were done. They are a little smaller than I expected, but they will do. I hadn't given specific inches of measurements, so I have to take what I get. It was threatening rain, so we were carrying umbrellas. Prairie said that if I could carry the umbrellas and the bag and she could carry a table. So, she carried one table home—just over a quarter mile. We'll take the second one home today. This time she put her long sleeved shirt into the bag. She will use it for cushion and try carrying it on her head, I guess.

Prairie—Houses and Monastery—July 14, 2006

Life has been full the last month; things are really moving along fast. I want to give you a couple of scenes from town before we move permanently to the mountain.

In June, a rainy season started, and the world turned green again (actually, it already seemed pretty green to me even though it hadn't rained much in six weeks—but it's gotten even greener). It has been nice to see the soccer field grow some grass, and humorous to watch the players continue their games even when it is pouring rain and huge mud puddles form so that it is more like a slip-n-slide than a proper field. The zinnias in our back yard have grown back, and just came into full bloom in the last week or so. In fact, our yard has gotten so overgrown with grasses and weeds that people who came over would tell us we really need to clean it, that is, either chop the grass with a machete or spray poison on it.

We finally caught up with the landlord, and they have sent some folks to chop the grass and weeds today; we are reluctant to use weedkiller which we think will just seep through the sand into the groundwater. We're afraid, however, that they may chop our zinnias down in the process.

I don't think I've ever mentioned the free-range animals in town. Most people keep chickens, maybe half a dozen adults and always a hen or two with a brood of chicks. The chickens just peck around to find food—in people's garbage piles and yards.

There is no proper solid waste disposal in Limón, so people just dig a hole and throw in the garbage and burn it. Sometimes chickens will come clucking along through our yard as well though we are a bit off any main roads.

We have gotten used to the roosters crowing throughout the night and early in the morning.

Dogs also seem to be free-range. When we first arrived, I couldn't tell if these were alley dogs or people's pets; in fact, I still don't know for sure, because they just wander around the streets looking for scraps to eat, like the chickens do.

The majority of the dogs are pretty pathetic looking—skinny and scruffy with fur worn down in places.

There is a female dog (with droopy breasts from her many litters of puppies) that comes around our house most days and lies in the shade on the porch.

When we have meat, we will give her the bones. We don't know where she goes when she's not here, but we've come to see her as ours in a certain way.

Even more astounding are the free-range horses. Some people keep horses in town; we will see men riding them down the streets or on the beach every so often. The horses are put to graze in grassy areas—such as the area outside the fence of our yard—with or without being tethered to a tree or fence post.

Free-range village dog

Sometimes there will be a single horse, sometimes a mare and her foal, once there was a small herd of about six horses grazing there. People seem to try to get away with as little proper feeding of their animals as possible.

I don't know if I've ever given much description of the various types of houses around town, so I will do that now. The house we live in is made of concrete block with a smooth stucco and painted finish. It has a tile floor, dropped ceiling, and corrugated metal roof. It has screen doors and screened windows made of slats of glass, rather like venetian blinds. People who can afford houses like this will build them; in fact we have watched a modest one and a huge sprawling one go up nearby. Some people have wood-sided houses (actually a type of palm bark) with cement or packed dirt floors. They might have a metal roof or the traditional, pointy, thatched palm-frond roof, which is cooler but also at risk of leaks. The simplest style of house and building construction is made of *caña brava*, a type of cane similar to bamboo. The cane is often just lashed to crossbars and is easily put up in a day. Out in the country, people also make traditional earthen homes with either clay bricks or an earth plaster stuck to a wooden frame.

Building projects for the monastery were pretty much finished by the beginning of this week, so on Wednesday we made a contract for our last major installation—the dry compost toilet. Mateo will build this as well. We are in Tocoa today to get money from the bank in order to give him an *adelanto*, or some money down to buy supplies.

When we've gotten rides with Mateo out to the mountain, we have taken a few more things out there, so that now the basics are there for staying the night. We have spent two nights there in the last two weeks, which was a nice experience. Something like camping out at a cabin, with its rustic bunks, our kerosene stove for cooking, beautiful stars, moon—and annoying mosquitoes.

We anticipate being able to move permanently to the mountain in less than two weeks. We had ordered two small (very small) tables from a carpenter shop in town. They were finished this week, and Mateo is building us a bookshelf and some simple backless chairs. All these trips to Tocoa we've been making (almost every week) have been to collect items to set up our new household—buckets, a washtub, a charcoal iron, a washboard, a teakettle, and all the little things one needs. We have chosen voluntary poverty, and it is always a challenge to figure out what are actual needs, and what are just wants or luxuries. But this construction and set-up phase is about over and I'm looking forward to the new challenges of learning to live at our mountain monastery.

Beth—Refocusing on the Center—July 17, 2006

We've all seen it—when someone gets more focused on getting something done than on what the whole thing is about in the first place? Well, I caught myself in that spot a few weeks ago. I've been there before, but only recognized it in retrospect. Of course, it is very easy to see in someone else. And I've seen a lot of that!

So, what to do? A day of prayer and fasting, of course and if I can get back to centering, I should be able to stay more focused. So, that's what we planned—a day of prayer and fasting. Just leave the gardening, the moving, the furnishing the household, everything.

We are inexperienced in fasting, so it wasn't obvious how we wanted to do it. After a little conversation, we decided to eat breakfast, but not lunch. We chose Thursday, June fifteenth for our retreat. Then we planned our schedule. The prayer and fasting retreat would be from 10:30 AM to 4:30 PM.

Up as usual at 5:30 AM; we had our morning prayers, ate breakfast, pumped water, did laundry, and walked downtown to buy groceries. Buying groceries on a fasting day! Now there's a trip! Then we started with the poetry of John of the Cross, followed by a Quaker un-programmed meeting and a lot of journaling and personal time. We sang hymns and had our usual afternoon prayers and reminded ourselves that fasting is different from skipping a meal (just as being celibate is different from not having a sex life). The differences are not subtle when we're paying attention.

All in all, it was a very worthwhile time. I am reminded that Mother Teresa of Calcutta said, "I am not called to be successful; I am called to be faithful."

Within a few minutes of the close of our retreat, children came to the door selling tamales. We broke our fast with tamales and returned to our active tasks.

Beth—*Gardening is Not a Precise Science*—July 26, 2006

We hope to move to the mountain this week—Friday. But we won't know until it happens.

My expectation had been that we would have vegetables from the garden by the time we moved. It doesn't look like that is going to happen. Our okra is our big disappointment. I planted some last fall and it thrived—but in different soil—in sand. The okra on the mountain just struggles. We get one or two pods a week. I have written all the details to my ECHO [Educational Concerns for Hunger Organization] adviser asking for help. Efrain, the agriculture guy at El Pino, says that maybe the soil is too acid. Well, we bought some lime today. We'll try that.

The one tomato plant had two blossoms on it last week. One pepper plant (I don't know if it is the sweet pepper or jalapeño) had tiny little peppers on it. We planted some more okra, some ordinary string beans and some radishes last week. We had hoped to go to the mountain to check on them today, but that fell through. Our yucca is thriving—that takes about nine months to be ready to eat. The one dwarf plátano looks vigorous and is growing. The sugar cane has taken hold—at least most of it.

Our passion fruit vines look pretty good. Of course, we have no idea how large they should be at this point, but they are green and vigorous looking. They bear in about one year if all goes well.

We have two nice tomato plants ready to transplant in the garden and some more peppers almost ready. The cashew seeds that we planted a few weeks ago are up and looking good. Several fruit trees are in place. But they have a few years before they provide any food. We planted some lablab beans, the spreading kind, useful as ground cover, soil enrichment, and erosion prevention. They have come up and the most advanced of them have started to spread. Half a dozen pineapples look as though they will survive. They haven't actually started to grow yet, though. I think they are not in a good place. We'll try again in a different spot.

I had wished for vegetables by the time we moved. I had hoped for vegetables by the time we moved. I actually had expected that we would *have* vegetables before we moved. And we don't. I am disappointed. Yesterday, at Centro de Salud, I told Warnita about our okra disappointments. She was all sympathy. She is a big vegetable lover, too. It was amazing how comforting that was. In the meantime, we will keep learning about our garden site, trying new things and taking vitamin pills in place of fruits and vegetables. Sigh!

We went to El Pino last week. It was nice to see friends there. They have had a series of visiting teams from the states, so everyone is exhausted. It is always so nice to connect with the visiting folks from the states and with the friends who live in El Pino.

Beth—*Wanted: Library Volunteer—July 27, 2006*
We have a job opening:
Wanted: Library Volunteer

This is a high-commitment volunteer position. No traveling required. Needed is interest in monastic literature, the lives of justice-minded women and men of the past (Dorothy Day, Gandhi, Elizabeth Fry), familiarity with both United Methodist and Quaker thought and history. Ability in Spanish would be useful but not necessary. Our library is missing—even in English—some of the basic books needed for a monastery. At the present time, I can't name the books, authors, publishers that we want. We need a book lover, able to search, browse, critique, and recommend. Finally, we will make some decisions together. There is a book budget. Is it you?

[Note: Several of us helped with this project and it is still ongoing.]

Beth—Moving Day—August 3, 2006

Last Thursday, Prairie and I were convinced that we really wanted to make our move on Friday. We hadn't talked with Mateo for a week. Wednesday, I was under the weather with a gut virus. We had kept on puttering with the packing and planning. We were ready.

About 1:30 PM we left the house. We started walking toward Limoncito. It is easier to hitch a ride on the road than in town. We walked a long way before we got a ride. (It was hot!) But when it came, we actually got to sit in the back seat of the cab (not the usual bed of the pickup) and we were dropped off right at Mateo's house. Mateo, of course, was working. He was working on our dry compost toilet. Margarita was home and we chatted with her. The subject got around to our sewing machine and the fact that it is acting up. It turns out that Will (the water-tank expert) also fixes sewing machines. He just happens to be Margarita's cousin.

Margarita gave us each an orange punch drink (nice and cold, too) while we chatted. She took us to see her chicken coop. She doesn't really have a coop, just laying boxes. Since they live sort of in town, they don't need a coop in which to close up the hens at night.

We spent a few hours talking, until Mateo got home. Someone else had arrived with a chainsaw for him to fix. First he fixed that and then he took us back to Limón, agreeing to pick us up the next morning for our move.

But first, the sewing machine. We went to our house and carried it to the back of his truck. He drove us across town to Will's business, which is in his mother-in-law's house and on the other side of town. Then we went to where Will was working on a new house under construction. He agreed to fix the sewing machine on Saturday. On the way back to the rental house, Mateo asked a few questions about what would be going up the mountain and what would be staying in town, and wanted another payment on the dry compost toilet.

At 5:30 PM, Mateo left and we began our serious packing. We worked until 8:30 and had evening prayers (our last with electric light) and went to bed. We were up at 5:30 the next morning for our last morning prayers on our little porch with the view of the ocean and our last breakfast cooked on electric stove. Is this nostalgia? At about eight AM, Mateo and two helpers showed up to carry stuff to the truck. They arrived about sixty seconds before we were actually ready for them. I even had time to dig up a few of the zinnias that Prairie wanted to take along.

We loaded the truck. One of the guys held the guitar while he perched on the stuff in the back. Prairie and I rode in the cab with the glass for the solar oven on our laps. Mateo drove very carefully and slowly. We were very pleased.

When we arrived at the mountain, the guys unloaded the truck, and carried the two heaviest objects up the mountain. Then they went to work on the dry compost toilet. Prairie and I just went back and forth from parking spot to house. Prairie carried the heavy stuff and I carried the light stuff. We didn't count the trips. But we got moved.

Bad news. We noticed a heavy trail of termites inside the house. We showed Mateo. We had talked about spraying for termites, but he was preoccupied with other stuff and it hadn't happened yet. He promised to return on Monday to do it. He could do it while we were at Centro de Salud. This meant that we would have to move all the stuff into the middle of the room so that he could spray the walls, shutters, doors, built-in bookshelves, built-in bunks. A big job. So be it.

We are now installed in our new house. Slowly, we are settling in. We use the fogón to cook most of the time, but then we use the kerosene stove when we fail with the fogón—or just don't want to invest the time. We are getting a little more slick at the fire-making and controlling. It is actually pretty easy to make the fire. (Keeping it going is the hard part.)

The guys haven't showed up this week to work. They cut wood for the walls last week. I assume that the wood is aging. Supposedly it is wise to let it age for a week before using it.

Beth—A Hard House Call—August 9, 2006

We went to Centro de Salud as usual on Monday. It didn't feel as usual because, of course, we walked from our house to the road, then about half a mile to Rosa's house and tienda. She greeted us cheerfully and gave (not sold) each of us a can of peach nectar. We were so grateful. We never buy peach nectar. It comes in aluminum cans and is an expensive treat. But we enjoyed it.

Soon, along came a car and we got a lift in to town. We heard in the back of the truck that there is a *brigada* in town (a team of health care workers) at Clinica Carolina. One lady was taking her little boy in to have a molar pulled. No one ever says "have a tooth pulled."

So we weren't surprised when there weren't a lot of patients at Centro de Salud. Elizabeth told Warnita (in Garifuna) about a very sick man. She called him brother, but I didn't know if this meant brother in the church or brother in the family. Warnita looked very serious and invited me to accompany her on a house call. Only after we left the house did I learn that the patient was, indeed, Warnita's oldest brother. A man about fifty years old, he looked any age over forty up to ninety or more. He had been a soldier in the war between Honduras and El Salvador twenty-eight years before and had taken a bullet through his spinal cord. There is no veterans' hospital or even any sense of obligation to an injured veteran. He had been cared for by family members for all these years. At first, he used a wheelchair and did pretty well. Now he was dying.

He had been taken to La Ceiba. That hospital sent him to Tegucigalpa, whose hospital sent him back to La Ceiba, whose hospital sent him to Trujillo, whose hospital sent him home.

He had the worst pressure ulcers I have ever seen, with bone open to the air and wearing off, pus—extreme complications. Basically, the hospitals could do nothing. He was sent home to die. He acquired a few more pressure ulcers during this tour of the country's hospitals.

When we saw him, he had the infected ulcers plus a urinary tract infection. He was emaciated, a little dehydrated, and miserable. He could nod in response to Warnita's questions. She cleansed his wounds and bathed him. She even changed the sheets in his bed (you know, the way only nurses can, with the patient still in the bed). Nurses amaze me. Then she started an intravenous line since he was not able to eat or drink. Oh, how he suffered. I was Warnita's assistant. She sort of apologized for that, but we both knew that she was the one with the skills and I was the one to open packages of gauze and hand them to her. He hung in there until afternoon, when Victoria, their sister—who is also a nurse and lives in Francia—a village equidistant between Bonito and Limón—arrived. After his last visit with Victoria, he died. I was ready to hear of his death this morning when Victoria told me. He had been suffering so badly.

It was a very hard house call. I can only imagine how hard it was for Warnita to provide her nursing care for her brother as he died.

Then we saw patients as usual until about noon. The internet was closed and we spent a couple of hours hanging around town, doing our shopping and chatting with people.

We learned how to prevent the entrance of snakes into the house. Last week we found a small (about a foot long) coral snake look-alike inside the house. It slithered away, but it made us think. We do not consider ourselves experts on snakes. We did get an excellent book on snakes of Honduras, written by a Honduran professor, but having a book and knowing something are not the same. The treatment is garlic. Don't laugh— it's not like vampires, you know. Snakes have a very acute sense of smell and they don't like garlic. You chop up four heads of garlic and soak them in water, then sprinkle this water all around the house. The snakes won't come in because they don't want to be around the garlic. We bought garlic. Yesterday, we mixed it up and last night I sprinkled it around. This morning when I shifted my plants and seed bags (which I had moved away from the house to apply the garlic water), I could smell the garlic. This is just part of moving in, I guess. The prioritizing of moving-in projects sometimes gets switched.

Beth—Working Out the Kinks—August 9–23, 2006

We've lived on the mountain for three weeks. Cooking (including making the fire) occupies a lot of our time. We cook on the fogón. The firebox is approached from one side. There is no support for the wood. One must use another piece of wood for that; when it burns up, one must do without. The fire is made about a foot inside the entrance to the firebox. *Ocote* (oak-OH-tey) is used as a fire starter. Imagine slivers of wood that burn very readily—pitch-soaked, but they don't sputter like wood with pitch.

Before you can start your fire, you must have some ocote. You hack shavings off a large branch with the machete, then pieces of small and rotten wood and finally large wood chunks. The best firewood is *nance*. It burns hot and lights rather well if it is seasoned. Mateo and German had cut up a tree for us when the stove was being made. They even split some. But these are small trees and that wood is long gone.

We had hoped Clemente would come out two weeks ago to cut wood and show us how to do it. We got a very small splitting demonstration from German, but no cutting instructions at all. German is about twenty and his demonstration was more about showing off than about teaching. Clemente had cut his foot and wasn't up to getting out to us, so we were on our own. We have been foraging for standing dead trees. Since no one has lived here before, we haven't had to go very far yet. We have also brought back a couple of already fallen trees. This is easier, but of course, the wood yields less heat.

We use the machete to cut suitable lengths—about three feet long. As the fire consumes the wood, we push the wood further in. We have found the whole operation rather challenging.

We have a kerosene one-burner stove that we had planned to use for backup, but one day, when we were buying kerosene, we were accidentally sold water instead. Our gallon container of kerosene is really kerosene layered over water. The wicks of the stove got wet and, of course, the stove wouldn't work. End of backup plan. The wicks are slow to dry out. It rains about every other day right now. Yesterday, I checked and finally, the stove was useable!

Sometimes starting the fire is rather smooth, but not very often yet—though it's getting a little easier. (After all, we practice a lot.) Beans are boiled and then brought to a boil a second and third time each day. (That keeps them good without refrigeration.) We often eat rice with our beans. We have learned to make corn tortillas. Since our garden isn't giving us much yet, there is not a lot of variety in our diet.

Mateo's land and cattle herd are fairly near to us. His son rides up a back way to milk them (by hand, of course) every morning. Cows are milked only once a day here. We carry a two-liter soda bottle over to pick up milk every two or three days. Like the beans, milk must be boiled a twice a day so it stays good. It is a lovely walk over to where the milking is done. So far, Mateo has refused to charge us for the milk.

When we moved here, the dry compost toilet was still under construction. We identified a well-screened area where we used a series of trenches until the toilet was ready. The little clearing was nice and private, but rather steep. We enjoyed it for two and a half weeks!

Mateo had never constructed a dry compost toilet before,

so the tricky part, of course, was the urine diversion. He got that worked out and now we have a functioning dry compost toilet. Just as advertised, it doesn't smell bad. We keep a bucket of water inside to wash hands. Seems to work rather well, so far.

When we first got here, we bathed in the back yard—in the sunshine. My friend, Judy, is a dietician who helps us sort out nutrition questions. Once she said that we'll get plenty of Vitamin D if we don't overuse sunscreen. Well, on bathing days, we got plenty of Vitamin D. But twice while I was bathing, I heard Prairie's friendly greeting (at the other end of the house) to a guest.

Now we put our big laundry tub inside the toilet building. We still bathe by the dipping method, but we have walls and a door to close. I don't miss that sense of personal vulnerability we had while bathing in the open!

On Saturday, Mateo installed shelves in our little kitchen. We had previously pounded in a few nails for hanging implements and pans. Our kitchen is pretty much put together now. The stove still leaks a lot of smoke around the edge of the metal top. We stopped this morning to visit Margarita. She'll come out next Thursday to look at the stove and help figure out how to fix it. The metal plate was not as thick as they had wanted it. They hadn't been able to buy what they wanted and it is now warped—so smoke leaks out. This is not okay. So, we'll all put our heads together over it again.

Mateo also installed another set of shelves inside the house. He cut down the trees, cut them into lumber and constructed the shelves all on the same day. They are not quite dry enough to use yet. So far, most of our storage is cardboard boxes shoved under the bottom bunks. There is plenty of room that way, as long as there are only the two of us—and as long as the cardboard lasts. In the rainy season (November to Jananuary) cardboard has a tendency to disintegrate.

We have one mosquito net so far. Prairie is particularly attractive to mosquitoes—and to other biting insects—so she's using the mosquito net. We bought netting material on our last shopping trip in Tocoa before the move. On Saturday, I took the material out and began the measuring and cutting. Yesterday afternoon I was able to putter with it just a bit, but the mosquitoes have begun biting and this has now moved into a priority job.

We found some great little berries to eat. They are called *pimientas*. They look like very dark purple to black blueberries, but are so sweet and mild that they taste more like blackberries. We have lots of them. A very welcome addition to our diet!

Prairie—Living at the Mountain—August 28, 2006

We made it! We've moved to the mountain. I was expecting it to be a big adjustment, but still I was not prepared for as much stress as there has been. Every day we are learning to do new things, and our routine hasn't quite settled down yet into anything predictable. Luckily, we were able to bring our daily schedule of prayer and devotional time along. This helps. We must remember our focus as a monastery, after all. And it is lovely to sit outside and watch the sunrise in the morning, and enjoy the views of the green hills and the ocean in the distance.

We had planned to move by the end of July, so as the time got close, we started packing things up at the house in town. When we got rides with Mateo to the mountain, we would bring along a few extra household items. The last week in July, we went to Mateo's house in Limoncito to confirm that he would be able to help us move all the rest of our stuff in his pickup. He said it would be no problem to do the move-in that Friday.

So Thursday night and Friday morning were spent getting the last of our things into boxes and bags to be moved. Mateo showed up with two workers just as we were finishing, and they helped get everything packed into the back of his truck.

Beth and I sat in the cab, Thankfully, Mateo drove very carefully all the way up to our place. The guys moved everything down from the back of the truck and then went to building the dry-compost toilet. Beth and I made many trips along the footpath to the house carrying boxes of books, and all our various household items that we had collected over the last several months. We finished about noon.

The last few weeks have been an adventure in learning to live again and settling in at the monastery property. The biggest adjustment has been learning to cook on the fogón. At first we settled for some sad, cold meals of beans and crackers as we learned. One time, when the fire was slow to go, we had a very late dinner of barely-cooked eggs, over-cooked veggies, and soggy spaghetti.

Within the last few days we feel that our fire-starting abilities have greatly improved, and we are just thankful that we do have food to eat.

The first two weeks, Mateo was still working on the dry compost toilet. (We were using a pit in the woods, and bathing in the back yard.) There were close calls a couple times when a male neighbor stopped by to visit as Beth was bathing, so we were grateful when our bathroom was finally finished.

Each Monday, as we have always done, we go into Limón to volunteer at Centro de Salud. Now, though, it is a much bigger deal. From the monastery, it is a one-hour walk up and down hills and across a creek to the main road, where we usually end up walking to Rosa and Chito's tienda at the entrance to the road to Limón and chatting with them a bit before we can catch a bus or a ride into town. It is the same in reverse on the way home, except usually then we are carrying some groceries in the backpack. We try, as much as possible, to do all the errands we might need to for the week. However, the internet isn't working most of the time, and some people we try to visit aren't home.

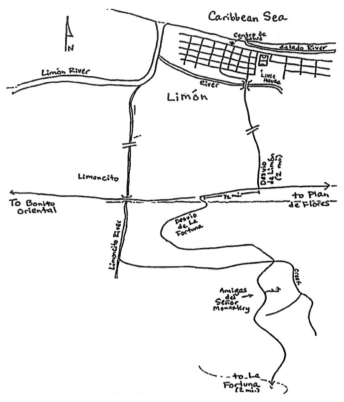

Our neighborhood

Coming into town as visitors instead of as [temporary] residents feels a bit different to me; I can look at Limón with new eyes, and I like it. Somehow I can appreciate its uniqueness better, and visiting with our friends who are around has become a special, more intentional event.

Well, I have more stories I could tell, but I really want to get this update posted before I lose the connection again.

Beth—God Will Take Care of You—August 23–30, 2006

Sunday evening, as we were reading (we take turns reading aloud by flashlight or candlelight) I felt dizzy, light-headed. This was not so uncomfortable except for my history with malaria, which causes dizziness.

Monday morning I woke up feeling pretty good, but still a little dizzy. I wasn't sure if I should try to go to Centro de Salud or not. The other doctor is on vacation and Mondays are the busy day. It is a one hour walk to the highway. Vacillation.

Prairie had chosen "God Will Take Care of You," for one of the hymns for morning worship. We also use *The Upper Room* during worship. The prayer focus for the day was physicians and nurses. Well, if everyone who prays *The Upper Room* is praying for me, I can certainly go to work. Prairie encouraged me (translation, she will carry the backpack more than her fair share of the walk).

So, off we went after breakfast—Prairie with the backpack. Usually I carry it down, toward town and she carries it up, back home. I was fine. We walked to Chito and Rosa's and got a lift into town. My exam room was an oven, no fan, no air moving, lots of sick kids—some pretty complicated (including a twenty-eight-day-old with infection and probably congenital heart disease). I could concentrate only on work, no mental energy left for self-assessment.

The old lady who sometimes sells oranges came to the clinic. Prairie bought us each an orange for now and each an orange for later. That worked well for me.

We did our running around town and caught a lift in the back of a pick up truck right to our road. I was fine. The heat bothered Prairie more than usual, so I carried the backpack almost half the way home. It's pretty nice when a lot of people pray for you.

Beth—Leaping Lizards—August 31, 2006

When we moved from the rental house in Limón we brought a few of the zinnia plants and planted them by a stump in the backyard. We have been enjoying them, as have been several small orange butterflies and an occasional hummingbird. One day we noticed that one of the plants had a broken stem and some of the leaves had been eaten. We weren't sure what had gone on. But several leaves had been eaten off other plants, so we sort of shrugged our shoulders.

Last week, one day after afternoon prayers, we were just sitting in the shade when we noticed a lizard resting on the stump. Well, I knew that lizard folks like to bask in the sun, so I didn't think too much about it. Then, all of a sudden, it was on the ground and one of the butterflies flew off. I wasn't sure exactly what I had seen. It seemed like it launched itself into the air. But, I had seen the same lizard, or one that looked just like it, taking a bite out of a nance fruit a few days earlier. So, it couldn't have been hunting, could it? But it sure looked that way.

We just stayed put and watched. Sure enough, the lizard climbed back up on the stump and positioned itself ready to leap off. It was just above one of the lower zinnias. The butterflies continued to flit, drinking from the flowers. Suddenly, it jumped again. This time it caught the butterfly in its mouth and ate it down. So, I guess it was an omnivorous lizard. What a surprise! We get little biology lessons all the time, here.

Beth—Visitors and Homemade Mosquito Nets
September 4, 2006

Our life has been so interesting I can't give justice to all that has happened.

A week ago Friday, we made our first homemade mosquito net on our recently overhauled treadle sewing machine. The sewing machine worked as it never had before—for which we were very grateful. Now we each sleep under a mosquito net. That's nice.

That same day, Margarita came and tried to make the stove better. The metal top is lightweight and has bent with the heat. She spent a lot of time on it, but the problem seems unfixable to me. She also gave us a lesson on making flour tortillas. Delicious. We found bugs in the flour so we must use it up quickly. We just pick the bugs out.

A week ago Saturday, we had houseguests. A young woman Prairie met while putting her sister on the bus in Copán works near Trujillo. They had corresponded by email and Prairie invited her to visit us. We were still talking about details of her visit when she showed up at the door. She only had that weekend for the opportunity. We were very glad she did came. She brought three friends. (We had told her not to walk from the bus alone.) For lunch, we put more chicken bullion, cabbage, and several eggs into the soup and had it with the leftover flour tortillas. It reminded me of my childhood. My mom always enjoyed having drop-in guests and could put a meal together for any number of people very quickly.

The guests were each very interesting and we could have enjoyed long conversations with them, but it was a whirlwind visit. I walked with the men over to the neighbor's house to see if they could sleep there. No one was home, so the guys took off for town. The women slept in our extra bunks. We didn't have mosquito nets to offer them. When the first net has been pretty well tested, we'll begin on another. Like we say here— *paso a paso* (step by step). It was delightful having them. They are all Roman Catholics, so they understand more about monasticism than the usual Protestant. It was nice for us not to be explaining ourselves so much.

On Wednesday we went to Tocoa. We did a lot of internet stuff, organizing pictures, especially. We also did a little shopping. We went to the Methodist Church in Ceibita (a suburb of Tocoa) for the women's meeting on Wednesday night and stayed overnight at the church. Thursday evening we went back for prayer meeting. The women's meeting was especially nice. Randy, the pastor, wasn't there so we didn't have to have an introduction, we could just participate. There were a total of eleven women and about a half a dozen children. We enjoyed meeting and worshiping with these women very much.

On Friday, we came back to our mountain. But first, we finished our shopping. We bought a second laundry tub and a small kerosene lamp. The larger one was available, but without a chimney. We hopped the bus and got home just past noon. Prairie carried the laundry tub (plastic) like a large hat. Very fashionable. She could only see a few feet in front of her.

It was good to get home. Our lives were much enriched by our contacts.

This week we expect to be a little quieter. There is a visiting medical team in town, with the result that there were few patients at Centro de Salud. That's why I can write to you. We are planning our September retreat for this Thursday. It will be a little different from last month's.

Beth—Financial Report—September 4, 2006

Total construction costs to date: $7,842. There is still an outstanding debt of about eighty dollars. Since the quality of the stove is far from what was expected, we don't know yet whether the last bit will be paid or not. This construction cost includes the house, kitchen, water system and tank, dry compost toilet, stove, built-in bunks and shelves. By local standards, it is a little steep.

Our monthly expenses are a little misleading. For example, when we traveled to Copán, we bought a lot of Honduran stamps and have been using them ever since. In September, again, we will buy a lot of Honduran stamps.

We received donations through Rose City Park UMC of $350 in the last few months. Some other donations went directly into a personal account. We received some gifts of items and I don't have any idea of their dollar value. (Their value to us is far higher than mere money.)

Our tithes have all gone for medicines for the local public health clinic. "Communications" include telephone at more than a dollar each call. The majority of medicines in the clinic are now from you, our donors. Thank you.

It takes forty-five days for a check to clear the bank here. I deposited a check from my U.S. account early in August. That money will be available in time for our obligatory trip to Guatemala toward the end of this month. Now that our construction is mostly done, we expect our monthly costs to be lower.

Prairie—How to Make an Amazing Cream of Vegetable Soup, or, What I did on Tuesday —September 8, 2006

1. After morning prayers at sunrise, get an empty two-liter pop bottle and take a walk to the neighbor's property down the road.
2. Climb under the barbed-wire gate and keep walking down the dirt driveway to the corral.
3. Tell the young man, who is milking cows by hand, that you want some milk and let him fill the bottle.
4. Say thank you, since he didn't charge for it.
5. Walk the fifteen minutes back to the house.
6. After breakfast, change into long pants and sunscreen, grab the machete, and hike down the hill to the garden.
7. Pick whatever vegetables are ripe. Today that means a handful of yard-long beans (a type of green bean, some of which are actually purple, that grow twelve to eighteen inches long), two okra pods, and a winged bean.
8. After tending to the rest of the garden, hike back up to the house.
9. Start up the fogón: shave some ocote off of the greasewood log, find some dry rotting pieces of wood, and some nice cured ones, and build the fire.
10. Pull out the *Tassajara Cook Book* for some tips on how to make a cream soup.
11. Heat some oil in a small pot and add some flour.
12. When the mixture is thickened, add three or four cups

of fresh warm milk.

13. Add a lot of salt, some pepper, and some oregano.

14. In a pan, sauté the chopped green veggies with some onion, then steam them until tender.

15. Add the veggies to the cream broth, let simmer briefly.

16. Enjoy the creamiest soup with another person who thinks it's wonderful, too

17. Enjoy it again for dinner.

I don't think I've ever made a milk-based soup with whole milk before—rich and delicious. And who knew okra could be so nice? We are grateful to be able to get milk at Mateo's property across the way. One of his sons comes by mule every morning to milk their cows (thirty or so, they said).

A Herd of Toros Bravos—September 8–21, 2006

Monday morning brought a new surprise. I woke up with a strong premonition that we should leave as early as possible for Centro de Salud. I didn't know why, just that we should do it. I lit a candle, even, as there was not quite enough light in the house for finding stuff and getting ready. We had our morning prayers (unrushed—we are adamant about that); Prairie made oatmeal on our kerosene stove (hurriedly) and we left.

We had gone about a third of the way towards the highway when we met a man walking in the opposite direction. He said that it was good that he met us. They were about to drive a herd of toros bravos (fierce bulls) along the road. We could continue on though; there was no danger yet.

Around the next curve in the road were the big cattle truck and several men. The bulls had not yet been released. The driver told us where to stand (like we needed to be told) on the opposite end of the truck from where the bulls would come out and that he would be happy to give us a ride to the highway after they unloaded the bulls. With due care, the bulls were released and driven off down the road.

We climbed up into the cab. It was so high that, even though there was a step, I had to tread on the lug nuts for my first step to get up there. We chatted a little, of course, with the driver. I told him that bulls, raised for beef in my country, are usually castrated as that makes them less *bravo*. He said that bulls are not castrated here because they are less valuable that way. I wasn't sure exactly what he meant, so he explained. Castrated bulls go to fat and yield less meat, so they are worth less money. (And people wonder why there is so much heart disease in the States!)

We ended up at Centro de Salud earlier than usual, but there were no urgent patients—just the usual. My premonition had been about our own personal safety! If we had left the house two minutes later, we would have met a herd of half-grown fierce bulls on the road. So, we respect our premonitions.

Yesterday, we left the house later. We decided to do our *Companions in Christ* (study course from Upper Room Books) daily work before leaving the house as the day would be noisy and there wouldn't be a good opportunity at midday or afternoon. We don't use the clock anymore, but the sun was well up when we left the house. We usually take one backpack and have it lightly loaded for Mondays. But we were starting a ten-day trip. We each had a backpack, a pretty full backpack. I needed a rest by the time we got to the creek! I had to readjust the straps to shift the weight pressing on my body. I started thinking that it might be a long walk to the highway. We had gone only about thirty yards past the creek when along came a truck that gave us (and our heavy backpacks) a ride all the way to Rosa's little store.

We chatted with Rosa a bit and soon along came a bus for La Ceiba. We felt very well taken care of yesterday. Someone's clock said that we got on the bus about eight AM.

Prairie—An Unplanned Trip to Belize—September 28, 2006

We made plans to spend a few days visiting the Methodist Church in El Pino and run errands in La Ceiba before heading to Copán and crossing the border into Guatemala like we did back in May. Well, when we were visiting the immigration office in La Ceiba to pay our fees, the woman who works there casually told us that we couldn't go to Guatemala to get our passports stamped this time.

Unbeknownst to us, the laws had changed in August so that the Central American countries of Honduras, Guatemala, Nicaragua and El Salvador have open borders, so we would have to go farther to comply.

We were a bit stunned at this news and the casual way she told it to us. All our plans up in the air! Well, the most obvious choice for us would be to go to Belize because it is relatively close. Plus, the Methodist Church of Northern Honduras and Belize are connected, and that could help us. But neither of us had ever been to Belize before, and we'd only heard rumors about boats that might go there from Puerto Cortes.

So we went to visit Kemberlee, the secretary at Zion Methodist Church, just down the street from the immigration office in La Ceiba. As luck would have it, her sister Stephanee lives in Belize, and their mom and grandma have made the trip numerous times. Whew! Kemberlee kindly called her sister to see if we could stay with her in Punta Gorda, and explained to us about how to take the bus and launch there. Which led to... three countries in one day, two days in a row!

This is how we did it. On Monday, we took a bus (three to four hours) to San Pedro Sula. Beth had been to San Pedro Sula numerous times in the past, but it was the first time for me, so we spent the afternoon touring the center a little bit, including its big beautiful cathedral. We indulged in a treat or two, and also happened upon a wonderful bookstore that Beth had been to a few years ago. Honduran book publishing is, unfortunately, of pretty poor quality, and it is hard to find a bookstore with any books besides required school textbooks. This bookstore, on the other hand, has top quality imported books (in Spanish of course) from Argentina, Spain, Chile, and other countries. We browsed for some time, and purchased four books that we couldn't wait to get home and read (a biography of Mother Teresa, El Zorro by Isabel Allende and more).

Tuesday morning we were up early to catch a six AM bus that would take us to Puerto Barrios, Guatemala. It went first to Puerto Cortes and then followed the coast to the Guatemalan border, where we had our passports stamped to leave Honduras and enter Guatemala. We were surprised at this, because of the open border policy. Hondurans, apparently, only need their government-issued ID card in order to cross. Then, to our surprise, the bus dropped us off at a fork in the road, and we had to catch another form of transportation into Puerto Barrios itself. We thought the bus would take us all the way, and we hadn't changed any *quetzales* to pay a fare. The public bus we got on, graciously didn't charge us. We found our way to the boat dock, checked in at the immigration office there to exit the country (a ten dollar exit fee per person), bought tickets for the launch (eighteen each), and hopped in. It was a lovely ride across the Gulf of Honduras with its blue water, green palm-lined beaches, and the wind in our hair. We arrived in Punta Gorda around noon, and were met at the dock by Stephanee. We got our passports stamped at immigration, and then took a taxi to her house, a bit outside of town.

Stephanee and her husband, Alex, live there with their two young sons Rashad (three years old) and Gregory (one year old). Alex is a teacher and principal at a Methodist school in a small town nearby, and Stephanee is a homemaker. They are of African ancestry and both speak English, Spanish, and the locally-used Creole, (a take-off of English that we North Americans typically associate with Jamaica). We spent the afternoon visiting with them, and in the evening we all took a walk to the beach and a small dock there, where we sipped Belizean beer and listened to Alex tell us the history of Belize as music played in the background from a nearby bar. It was a nice—although brief—visit.

Wednesday morning we were up early as usual and, after having breakfast and saying goodbye, we walked the mile or so into town to get some exercise and a better feel for the place. We had learned on Tuesday that the change in immigration law also meant we didn't have to spend three nights in Belize (which we got out of last time by bribing an official, as you may remember). So, we went through immigration paying Belize's fee of $3.75 for environmental protection, bought our launch tickets, and rode back to Puerto Barrios. We checked in at immigration and got a ninety-day pass just by asking, then caught a mini-bus to the Honduran border. (This time we paid by exchanging lempiras for quetzales with a money-changer at the border). As we were leaving Guatemala and entering Honduras, our passports were stamped. With an entrance fee of three dollars to pay the employee on the Honduran side, we were on our way back. From there, we caught a local (chicken bus) to Puerto Cortes, and from there a mini-bus direct to San Pedro Sula. We waited a short time for the next direct bus to La Ceiba. It got us back to El Pino a little bit after dark.

Now our passports are full of stamps and we are legal again till the end of January. We could only thank God that things went so smoothly with such a sudden change of plans, and we would still get home on schedule.

Beth—Traveling and Voluntary Poverty
September 28, 2006

Day nine of a ten-day trip. It took a full ten days to get ready for this trip, too. Voluntary poverty means that we spend about half of our physical work time doing the daily and weekly chores—washing clothes, cooking and cleaning, gathering and cutting firewood, routine garden and yard chores, bringing home provisions. Things that are special projects must be planned for. One of those for this trip was inspecting and repairing our backpacks as needed. We had one backpack that was in excellent shape and looked like it would last for several years. We had one backpack that wasn't and didn't.

We decided what we could fix and what we couldn't fix. We decided what was essential to mostly assure that it would survive a ten-day trip. We decided which outside pockets should no longer be used as they merely contributed stress to the already stressed parts.

Then we took it apart where it needed to be fixed. We have some strong denim to replace the ripped fabric. It took the gifts of both of us working together to stick with this repair job. We were (by my past standards) fixing a backpack that wasn't worth fixing. But it was what we had—and it was fixable. So, we did it. Prairie has the gift of patience and meticulousness. I have a little more experience sewing, so I was at the machine. I explained what easing is. She said that it sounded impossible, but after hearing that it is an ordinary part of most blouse constructions, she pinned a seam, easing the fabric. I sewed it up. The backpack still survives. (It was not quite that fast, but we got through it.)

When we talked to our friends at El Pino about going to Belize, they were very matter-of-fact about it. We would just do what needed to be done. Then I asked each if they had ever gone there. None of them had. Several of the young adults are very excited about a planned large meeting of youth in Belize in January. The group is doing a lot of fundraising to sponsor the trip. They take it for granted that Prairie and I go to Belize, to Guatemala, wherever. Why? "Because gringos travel. That's what they do." Apparently, this goes along with the unlimited funds apparently available to foreigners who come on mission trips.

Beth—Our Garden—September 28, 2006

This morning (like every Monday morning) we came to town. Imagine our surprise when Centro de Salud was locked up tight. There are two versions of gossip—one is that today is a holiday (the school also seemed to be locked up); the other is that the nurses all have a meeting in Francia. Take your pick. We'll find out next week.

As we were walking around (with an unexpected free day to run errands), we ran into some folks from Plan de Flores with a sick man. Neither the foreigners' clinic nor the Centro de Salud was open. He had had a cough for eight days, but yesterday he had a big-time fever and coughed up blood. No equipment for exam. Diagnosis? Lobar pneumonia is most likely. I wrote a prescription for amoxicillin and sent them to the pharmacy in Bonito Oriental. It is not a government pharmacy, so it was likely to be open. Actually, I think there are two in Bonito. Frustrating, but this family can afford the trip and the medicine, so he will be okay.

About our garden: we had good news and bad news. The bad news was root knot nematodes. We figured that they were responsible for taking out our first planting of tomatoes, and one of the two of the third planting of tomatoes. The second planting died, but I don't know from what. Our remaining, tomato-bearing plant had given us a few meals of fried green tomatoes and we would have a ripe tomato waiting for us for dinner. It was not bearing as vigorously as I would like, so I suspected that it also had root knot nematodes. We had two more plants that were not planted near this one that should begin bearing within a month.

We were then eating jalapeños, as many as we wanted. We really liked them in the beans, of course. And Prairie made cream of jalapeño soup last week. It was a fun change of pace, but won't be a regular item on our menu.

Our okra was bearing. Then we went on a ten-day trip. So

as not to waste the time, we marked three different plants to collect seed. Well, ten days of no harvest told them to shut down and we are now not getting okra. I am told that they are also vulnerable to root knot nematodes.[21] Sigh. We had gotten used to okra. Cream of okra soup could be a routine menu item in my opinion.

We were getting a few yard-long beans. (Actually only half-a-yard long.) We liked them and would like more. We needed to have manure to plant more in that new field for planting, and so all the beans needed to have manure to inoculate them with the synergistic bacteria that allow them to take nitrogen from the air and use it to enrich the soil.

Lack of inoculation meant that our first planting of winged beans fizzled. Our first planting of yard-long beans took a long time, but when they got manure, they started bearing. They had just run out of time. Our second planting of yard-long beans were just beginning to bear. (But one of them decided that it was done after the ten days of no picking.)

Our pumpkins died—some disease, our cantaloupes; also. The watermelon plants had apparently the same disease, but they gave us half a dozen tiny watermelons anyway. The sweet peppers were giving us about three small peppers a week, but they looked a little iffy, so I didn't know how long this would last. (Yes, they too were vulnerable to root knot nematodes).

Our gardening investment for food in 2007 looked very good. The yucca was strong. The sugar cane was growing. The pineapples were looking strong. The passion fruit vines were climbing. The papaya plants were a foot tall. The *moringa* trees (edible leaves) were about two feet tall. Our dwarf plátano plant was growing—but how would I know if it is growing appropriately? I reminded myself of all of these foods that we would have, as we might reap far less than we expected.

We were learning a lot about gardening here. Our mountain

---

21 We learned later—not root knot nematodes, just poor, clay, arid soil.

taught us; our consultants at ECHO taught us; our neighbors taught us.

We noticed with our cooking that I was eating more. I had lost quite a bit of weight with the vigorous physical exercise, but I thought by then I lost enough. I also had learned to like our beans and cornmeal tortillas. We now could make flour tortillas, too, but they are not the quality of the corn ones—yet.

Prairie—Baking, Playing guitar, and Photos
October 18, 2006

With time we are feeling more settled at our mountain home. After about the first month here, we were finally beginning to be comfortable using our fogón. We can now light the fire with relative ease, and have gotten better at finding the best types of wood to use (really rotten stuff that will flame up and heat the stove quickly, and then more solid dry wood for keeping it going). We also finally got up the courage to try using the oven and have had some full and some partial successes. It only heats a little above 200 degrees Farenheit at the most,[22] so it's slower cooking than normal, and since the heat comes from the top (the oven is below the firebox), we've had challenges getting it to cook food all the way through.

Things we've tried: cornbread (came out sweet and moist), chocolate (wacky) cake (only the top half cooked, so we just served the pieces upside down and called it a pudding cake; delicious with milk. (it was Beth's birthday!), dinner rolls made from my mom's yogurt—or soured milk—bread recipe. That last came out nicely and we enjoyed the treat of yeast bread as something like a comfort food. We made baking-powder biscuits, rich and flaky, and happily even the bottoms were crusty. We are learning!

I don't think I've talked about the guitar. Back in May or

---

22 We later learned to put hot coals directly in the oven, which brings it up to standard baking temperatures.

so, we purchased a Guatemalan-made guitar, a bit smaller than standard size. For years I have been interested in learning guitar, but haven't taken the time to find an instrument and practice. Who would believe I'd have the chance to do so in Honduras? But I have. The hymnal we use has a chord chart in the back and guitar chords printed for all the hymns. So, I found some tips on the internet about tuning a guitar and reading chord charts, and took it from there. In July I was able to get a few lessons from the Moravian pastor in Limón who plays guitar. (In return Beth gave him some English lessons.) This helped especially with my Spanish music vocabulary. Then in September I received a guitar book from my mom. From this I hoped to learn a little bit of finger picking. (Strumming can get a bit old, and my thumb gets sore!). Since we've been at the mountain, I've been playing for our prayers and devotions more than half the time. Some songs are just a bit too complicated for me, but overall I feel I've learned a fair amount pretty quickly.

Beth—Hot Spell—October 9–19, 2006

We've had a hot spell. Some days I feel like I am melting. We have cut back on our physically active work, awaiting the rain that will cool things off. We still get a pretty nice breeze much of the time on our mountain. In the middle of the day, though, the breeze is just hot air moving against our skin.

We are in Tocoa today. Yesterday we did errands here. Last night we visited the women's group at the Ceibita Methodist Church. Brief devotions, then crochet lessons. I tried to help a woman who had never done fine work before. She is in her early fifties. She had a hard time seeing the crochet thread. (Yes, it is doily-crocheting with small needles and cotton thread). She doesn't own glasses. It was a challenge.

Today, more errands and then the bus back to the monastery.

We hoped to go to the bank to withdraw some money, but we'll see. There have been several legal holidays. Yesterday, the line at the bank was huge, even in the afternoon, out the door quite a ways. It usually is about an hour wait, even once you are inside the door. Our desire for cash is that we have found a to-die-for Spanish dictionary. It is also very pricey. Often with regards to books, they are either cheap and of poor quality or very expensive and top of the line. This one fits the second category.

The government is experimenting with Monday holidays. It sometimes works and sometimes doesn't. It was Francisco Morazán Day the day we showed up at Centro de Salud and were the only ones. Then this week, we worked all morning, then went to the restaurant for lunch and ran into Dr. Karen. What a surprise! She hadn't been at work. She was mortified to learn that the rest of us had worked and that there were a lot of patients. It is a Columbus Day celebration. I don't know what day the nurses will (or did) take off. Life is funny.

We hoped to find a new kerosene lamp today. Sometime I'll tell you my sad lamp story.

Doña Eva gave us guavas this past Monday. She has a tree with the small pink ones and another with the larger yellow ones. Delicious. Fruit is such a treat.

When we arrived in Tocoa yesterday, we went right to a stand and bought grapefruit juice (grapefruit, fresh squeezed in front of us, sugar, and ice, all mixed in a blender). Delicious and cool. We were happy campers. We are making it a point to eat fruit and drink fruit juice a lot while we are here in the city.

Every day, I thank God for the privilege of living at this monastery. There aren't a lot of big projects or activities to share with you right now. Those have calmed down. The routine of monastery life fits very nicely.

Beth—The Public Health Challenge
October 26–November 15, 2006

We have had a month without sending you a letter. Our lives are busy and interesting and far from the internet.

This Monday, we went to work as usual at Centro de Salud, with the plan of catching the bus to Tocoa to join friends there (from Austin, Texas) who are doing a medical mission trip. They are based at the church that we visit when we come to Tocoa, in the suburb called Ceibita, a suburb.

Centro de Salud had received a donation of quite a lot of short-dated medicines. Dr. Karen wanted them to be shared with the hospitals and public health clinics so they wouldn't get wasted. I said, "Well, we're going to Tocoa today, we can take stuff to the public hospital there." There were four boxes of stuff. Birth control pills, high cholesterol meds and a great high blood pressure medicine—and lots of it.

Then we started seeing patients. I saw eighteen kids and we were ready to leave by a little past eleven. Cooper (not the biggest and strongest employee of the clinic, but the only male) was commissioned to carry the heaviest boxes to get us to the bus. We each had a backpack, of course. Prairie carried two boxes. I carried the umbrellas.

When we got to Melba's place (the best bus-waiting place in town) we learned that the bus to Tocoa had just passed less then a half an hour earlier. So, we rested, snacked a bit, and waited for the two PM bus.

We got to Tocoa a little before four and got off at the taxi stand to take the medicines to the hospital. There were taxi guys and bus guys and the two of us taking care of the backpacks, the cloth bags, the umbrellas, the boxes. It seemed to go smoothly.

When we arrived at the hospital, there were only three boxes in the trunk of the taxi. The missing one was the very valuable one (medically speaking, but probably in money, too). So, we hopped back into the taxi, to the bus station. The bus had already left! But a neighboring driver—who drives the same route—told the *taxista* that the owner-driver had gone to buy gas and then home and gave us directions to his house.

So, we drove around town to the gas stations...no sign of the bus. Then to the house. Ah, here was the bus. The bus guys were happy to see us and immediately brought out the box. I told them what was in it. I wanted them to understand how much they are helping their neighbors who are poor by helping us to stock the public hospital. Bus guys make good money— at least good enough so that they can buy private health care.

Then back to the hospital. I didn't know what the taxi driver would charge us, but he charged us the usual fee for the second drive as though it were a simple one. I think he liked to feel like he was a public health supporter, too. We were very grateful.

We walked into the hospital grounds and saw a woman in a nursing uniform, who directed us to the ER where we found the nursing supervisor and a physician. It was pretty late, by now. The physician wrote us a nice receipt—donation from Centro de Salud, Limón. After all, we don't even know who the foreigners were who gave the stuff to us. He wrote it over the hospital seal and then signed it and sealed it with his own personal (professional) seal.

So, now we were free to join our friends in La Ceibita. The public restroom at the bus station was already closed for the day, but Prairie had a licuado and I had a snack before we boarded the local bus for Ceibita. We waited in that bus just over half an hour.

We arrived in Ceibita just after dark. The folks were sitting at dinner and made room for two more. It was quite a day!

What a delightful group. My friend, David, a retired pediea-trician, didn't come this year. He had had a small heart attack a week or two before. He was fine, but not in traveling mode. (There are certain risks of having retirement-aged friends.)

So many cool things this week, I don't even know where to

start. Tuesday mornings things were usually a little slow, so I suggested to Dick (a retired pharmacist and the team leader) that we go over to the local public health clinic. We took some prenatal vitamins along. I had given Dick my solemn word the clinic would be out and would be appreciative of them.

But when we arrived, they already had visitors—formal-looking folks with a car. Well, the news is that *falciparum*, the very dangerous type of malaria, has been found in a neighborhood near Tocoa and these public health officials are working on this public health emergency. The head physician and the head nurse were there, plus two lower-level workers. They want to get as many malaria tests done as possible in the neighborhood.

It just so happens that this team has a lab technician. One guy came over and showed her how to prepare the slides and how to document them. She did eighty-five of them that day. She is doing more today, but I don't know how many. This was quite a windfall for the public health department. I am so grateful to have this med tech. The current malaria prevention efforts are not very effective. It is a great boost for the public health people to have this large batch of data and so rapidly. Hopefully, this outbreak will be controlled.

One of the workers dropped by later in the day. He had been out in the field cutting weeds in mosquito breeding grounds. He brought more slides and paper forms. We have seen several people with malaria, but it seems to be the *vivax*—the much less dangerous type.

Later, we went back to the public health clinic. Their nurse, Gilma, was charming and hospitable. She walked us through her storeroom, clinic, pharmacy, explaining her work. Dick had not been inside a public health clinic before. We wrote down the medicationss she was missing. She was an auxiliary nurse, and was trained to administer several basic medications. She had about two-thirds of them in stock. This team was interested in helping the patients of the neighborhood. They had already done that by giving enough pre-natals for twenty pre-natal visits.

I told Dick that I was going to take a page from Mother Teresa and asked him to give her medicines before his team was finished. That is, I asked them to give medicines before they knew that they would be left over or not—to risk running out themselves. Well, they did respond. Girma has no working nebulizer. (Her two are both broken.) They took their only nebulizer over to her this morning. If they have a patient with asthma, they'll send the patient to her for the nebulizer treatment.

I don't know if you can comprehend what this means. Foreigners, being willing to risk not having what they need in the interest of the greater good. This is worth noticing. This is worth noticing well. You live, immersed in the self-indulgence and self-importance. It is hard to understand what that looks like from the outside. Well, it isn't pervasive.

The lab tech also did anemia tests on all of the patients while her materials lasted. This was a big eye-opener. Lots of anemia—more than I expected. So, I will be more generous with the iron prescriptions. A good thing to learn. We were learning lots of new things. Our dermatologist took a basal cell carcinoma off my nose this morning with a butter knife.

(You think I'm joking?) I had this spot that worried me, so I asked for him to see it. It's sort of a family thing, basal cell. My Dad had a lot. He numbed it up and scraped away. A butter knife is a lot like a curette—not as sharp as a scalpel, just right for treating a basal cell carcinoma. He says it was about one millimeter. in diameter. Now I'm cured again.

Also, this morning, I asked the orthopedist to teach me how to inject painkiller into a broken bone. This need comes up once in a while, and I haven't known how to do it, so my patients have more pain than they need to have.

I saw a bunch of patients. Busy week. We left the clinic to come into town, partially to write to you.

Prairie is quite the star in the clinic. Her public health clinic training makes her a big help with patient intake. She also translates when needed. Since there are four doctors, she is more of an asset to the team than I am. And that's kind of cool.

We are alive and well and living in Honduras. I'm the one with a little spot-band-aid on the side of my nose.

Beth—Family Planning in Honduras—November 15, 2006

We're still in the Tocoa-Ceibita area. We saw patients yesterday in the morning and came to town to do errands in the afternoon.

In the evening, Pastor Randy requested a class on family planning for the women of the church (and neighborhood, in case anyone wanted to come), so our Peruvian-born RN was the leader of the teaching team. Of course, several of the women in the team decided to attend.

As is usual in Honduran meetings, few people were there on time. We asked their ages, the age at which they gave birth to their first child, the number of children in their families. Then, more women arrived and we started in greater seriousness. The turnout was larger than in the past, ten to twelve women, instead of six to eight. First, names, but I couldn't pick up any new names. They were too hard for me. Then our nurse began her talk (in Spanish, of course).

It was a highly theological talk about the value of the human body (the temple of the Holy Spirit), and the responsibility that we have to care for that body. A fair amount of feminist values. It was pretty interesting, but thirty-five minutes into the talk we still had not discussed any birth control methods. (No one has any confidence in the male partner being a true supporter in this area.) Then the pastor's wife arrived. She told her reproductive history in amusing detail. She is a skilled public speaker with a voice that carries well. She included fun stuff.

The pastor's wife announced, with a lengthy explanation of

the whys and wherefores, that family planning is a sin! After all, God won't give you more than you can handle. We could say that this was unexpected, now couldn't we? At first, I thought that I was misunderstanding the Spanish. Too bizarre. No, I was understanding perfectly well. We are now well over an hour into the class and we haven't gotten off theology. The foreigners who understood the conversation were stunned. The Peruvian nurse was stunned. The Honduran women sat politely and listened.

Finally, the nurse turned to me and said, "Help me." So, I tried. I started by interrupting the pastor's wife, who was all set to lecture on the sins of family planning until midnight. I said that I accepted that her opinion was that birth control was a sin and that I was willing to accept the responsibility for this sin in this class and would like to continue teaching this sin. I was respectful and firm. She was also firm. It was surreal.

She continued to block any teaching. In her opinion, teaching family planning was encouraging premarital sex. A minority of couples in Honduras are legally married. Face it folks, marriage doesn't look so good to anybody in Honduras—the men don't want to be pinned down, and the women figure that the men will sleep around whether they are married or not. So, just what is the point? Marriages don't have any better chance of weathering the storms of life together than commitments not based on legal contracts. But, now I am digressing.

We had some brochures about birth control techniques. Some methods are available in Honduras and some not. We passed them out. We were now very late from the usually scheduled meeting's ending time and the team members who needed to pack up the pharmacy needed to come into the sanctuary to do that. We closed with prayer. I did the out-loud version, thanking God that we have a church where people can safely have disagreements, how we are called to love one another, and prayed for wisdom. We could sure use some wisdom.

After the formal dismissal, I responded to some questions

from a woman who is living with a man to whom she is not married— and that conversation was disrupted too. This was amazing. Too bizarre for truth.

Living alongside poor people doesn't necessarily give you a feel for their lives, I guess. One woman of the church (the pastor's wife) could block the essential issue of birth control. Remember, we are talking about choosing to have only four to six children!

Our poor nurse, who had prepared the lesson, was a bit shaken up. The team leader and I talked to the pastor about this unexpected turn of events. He was also surprised and re-iterated the importance of family planning in this poor neighborhood and he was confident that he could persuade his wife to withdraw objections. This team will be leaving and this class will not happen without someone to lead it.

Patience, patience, patience. It is always about patience.

This was a very stimulating evening and I found it hard to fall asleep. Amazing, just amazing. Truth is far stranger than fiction.

Beth—Back in Tocoa—A Mouse in the House!
November 16, 2006

Both internet businesses in Limón have closed down. That means that you will hear from us when we travel, and only when we travel (unless you send us letters by snail mail—in which case you will get one of those occasionally).

When we were here (Tocoa) last month, we had ordered a seal. In the medical world here, one puts a seal on everything. We have a seal at Centro de Salud and use it for every letter that we send. We decided that Amigas del Señor should have a seal, too.

Finally, we decided on a design and ordered one. Carefully, the sales lady wrote out what it was to say. We ordered it on Wednesday afternoon with assurances that we could pick it up on Friday morning. Well, it was ready, all right. It said: *Amigas de Jesus*. The business was quite willing to re-make the seal and to hold it for two weeks. So, here we are, back in town to pick up our seal and to do a few other errands.

We left with rain clouds threatening. We walked all the way to Chito and Rosa's place. They have a porch, so we can wait protected from the rain; it is a good place to pick up lifts. Finally, we got a lift. By the time we got to Bonito Oriental, I was pretty wet. Prairie got put inside the cab and I was in the back of the truck. It was a milk truck. We only made one stop for milk, though, so it was pretty fast.

About half way to Bonito, the rain began, but not hard. The air stream over the cab actually seemed rather protective. And I was right behind the milk barrel, so didn't get too much breeze.

At Bonito, we got *pastelitos* and were ready to go when a bus for Tocoa showed up. I snoozed just a bit in the bus. I'm drier than I usually am on a hot day—less moisture from rain than I would ordinarily have from perspiration.

Hopefully, I can give you a bit of news while we're here in town.

We have a mouse in the house.
Yes, that's the news.

Beth—Financial Report—September–November, 2006

Tithes this time all went for medicines for the public health center patients. As it turns out, we (meaning the public health center) received donations from visiting teams and the government and actually shared out some medicines with the public health centers in Francia and Las Icoteas (the smaller public health centers in our county). We are well stocked for at least a little while.

Communication in September: We bought enough Honduran stamps to last three to four months. The item for the passport and law stuff included travel to Belize. This is needed every 120 days, so far.

Beth—In Tacoa—December 7, 2006

Yesterday, when we arrived in Tocoa, we tried calling the pastor's wife at Ceibita. We had tried on Monday and last week, but had not managed to connect with her. We weren't very concerned about it since we knew our way there and that we could sleep in the church. We had our own sheets and towels.

We picked up our seal. It is lovely. The ink is a paler blue that I had thought it would be, but I'll adjust. We bought our excellent dictionary. We have been looking forward to it for over a month because we like doing crossword puzzles from the newspaper. (Our current dictionary doesn't have a large enough vocabulary to help much.) Now we can do crossword puzzles with a higher accuracy. We have been delighted to notice how much the crossword puzzles actually do help our Spanish.

We caught the 4:30 PM bus to Ceibita. When we arrived, the church and parsonage grounds were locked up tight. The children in the street said that everyone had left that morning for La Ceiba—yes, the whole family.

The next stop was Suyapa's little shop. Suyapa wasn't there! She was in Tegucigalpa at a big church meeting! A child was sent with us to take us to Irma's house. Suyapa and Irma are the only church people that we know by name.

Irma wasn't home, but at least she was in town. Olman had the key. (Fortunately, we had met Olman the last time we were here—well, we didn't actually meet him, he sang a solo in church.) Back to Suyapa's place where the young woman running the tienda left it in charge of the younger children while she led us to Olman's place.

Olman, of course, was not home. No one was home at his house. We learned there was still one more bus back to Tocoa before bus service ended for the day. The evening women's meeting was apparently not cancelled, so someone has to have a key! As we were standing in the street, thinking over our options, along came Irma on her bicycle.

Irma has the key to the church, but not to the new padlock of the gate of the fence. The muchacha at Suyapa's has it. But since she had never met us before, you could be sure that she wouldn't give it to us.

We get the gate unlocked and the church door unlocked, but there was still one more obstacle. The sleeping room attached to the sanctuary is usually locked with a bent nail twisted to hold it closed. It is easily unlocked from the sleeping side, but not from the sanctuary side. The entrance to the building at that end is from a different yard.

Fortunately for us, the door had been left open. We have sleeping facilities complete with bathroom.

Irma took us over to her house and served us a lovely dinner of scrambled eggs, refried beans, fried bologna, and tajadas. Like many urban Honduran women, Irma cooks her beans and tortillas over a wood fire and the rest on her gas burners. Wood is less expensive than gas, so long-cooking beans get the wood treatment. Everyone agrees that beans cooked over wood fires are better than beans cooked over gas. Irma has no refrigerator, just like us.

Then back to the church for the Wednesday evening women's meeting. Prairie was asked to lead the singing and I was asked to preach. So, that's what we did. It was a short sermon by Honduran standards, I guess.

We fell asleep easily after our busy day. This morning after morning prayers, we caught the six AM bus to Tocoa. We ate baleadas at a little cafe near the bus station and began our town errands.

Prairie—Happy Advent—December 6, 2006

We have just entered the season of Advent, the four Sundays leading to Christmas. Beth and I have decided to observe it by making an Advent wreath and lighting the candles during our evening prayer time (a tradition from my family). We are excited to be learning familiar and new Christmas carols in Spanish. We expect to have a simple celebration on the mountain—perhaps by baking cookies—on Christmas day.

The holiday is a bit less commercialized here in Honduras. We are in Tocoa for a couple days, and stores do have decorations up, and are selling them (yes, plastic Christmas trees, Santa Clauses, and mini lights). A friend told us that normally they decorate the house about a week before Christmas, making sure everything is ready and lit up nicely on the *Nochebuena*, or Christmas Eve, which is the traditional big celebration in Latin America. They celebrate with lots of special foods like tamales and roast chicken.

Living in a tropical country, it is a bit hard to remember that Christmas really is coming up. Leaves are still on the green trees, and people are still going around in t-shirts. But, in mid-November, the rainy season finally hit us, and weather has been cooler, especially at night. (Sometimes I have to put on long sleeves, pants, and socks to sleep comfortably under my lightweight blankets.)

The weather actually reminds me a lot of the Northwest— a lot of overcast, drizzle (like "Oregon mist"), and occasional downpours. Some days the sun is out and it is warm, with a cool breeze creating what I think of as perfect weather, when I can be comfortable (not sweaty or cold) in the clothes I'm wearing. The rain only causes us trouble when there is wind that blows it through the screen windows or under the zinc roof panels, getting the mattresses and floor wet.

Beth—To Town for Groceries—December 7, 2006

We got up a few minutes later than usual. Overcast sky; Prairie has a cold. A cold front came on Sunday and stayed. Sunday and Monday had pounding rain most of the time.

There was too much rain for us to go to town on Monday. That means that we had not bought groceries this week. One can live on beans and corn, but one would rather not. We were wondering how to read the sky. Is today a good day to walk to town?

We had done morning prayers and were just starting to fix breakfast. I was making the fire and Prairie was washing the corn before grinding it to make tortillas when guests arrived. A little old lady (toothless) and her granddaughter stopped on their way from La Fortuna to Limón. They stopped to rest. (After all, they had already walked two hours.) We continued with our breakfast preparations as we all chatted. The grand-mother is probably about my age. We have met two of her sons who seem to be in their thirties.

When the fire was hot enough and the corn had been washed three times and ground twice, we were ready to make tortillas. Grandmother helped Prairie make tortillas (and gave a few tips) while granddaughter and I set up the tables and chairs, set the table and put a few things in the backpack.

We had been out on the porch where it is easy to include the kitchen workers in the conversation, but to eat, we moved into the house. We served what we had—lemon grass tea (with molasses if you like it sweet), beans (heated up from the day before, richer than just-cooked beans), and fresh corn tortillas. While we (the elders) were still dallying over our tea, Prairie began washing the dishes. We had decided to go to town, too, and we would all walk together.

Wendy (the fourteen-year-old granddaughter who lives with her grandmother) asked about our books. "Are they all Bibles?" (Well, almost one whole shelf is.) I explained the different sections of books. Wendy is a student at the La Fortuna Elementary School. Grandma, of course, can't read, but values Wendy's opportunity to get an education. "Do you have a Bible at your house?" No, she doesn't. (If they don't have a Bible, this means that they don't have any books since it would almost always be the first book obtained.) Well, we had two New Testaments (given to us by those same nice foreigners from Georgia who shared their pizza dinner with us last February). So I gave one to Wendy, inscribing it as a gift from us.

We put our stuff together and off we all went. As we were walking down our driveway we heard a car coming from La Fortuna! I hurried up a bit and flagged it down. We got a lift from our driveway all the way to the highway! This lift felt pretty important with Prairie's cold and our uncertainty about weather. Our new friends were planning on staying overnight in Limón; they didn't have to make it back home the same day.

We walked about another mile before we got another lift—this one right into town. We went to Centro de Salud. Yes, they had received the box of medicines from the Tocoa-Ceibita area medical brigada. Yes, they had some questions about them. But some were already on the shelf, being dispensed as needed.

There were few patients, so we didn't feel obligated to stay. Our goal was grocery shopping, mail and email. We bought ourselves each a pint carton of orange juice and walked to the now-defunct internet connection.

Our trip to the post office was rewarded. We both received mail The postmaster (who had his right leg amputated earlier this year) is ready to start learning to walk with crutches. So, I gave him his first lesson. It's not very easy. Each room in the house is at a slightly different level from the others. He is not ready to go from room to room, yet. He promised to practice his lesson faithfully and on Monday, I'll give him another.

We bought kerosene. The lady who sells it also makes big, thick, delicious ginger-and-molasses cookies. I bought five. She opened a bag of four to add a fifth. (Five for two women?) We paid our bill and went on. Melba sold us twenty eggs, a bulb of garlic, a pound of onions, and one carrot. (One was all she had.) Then on to Andrés' for rice, cheese, sugar, laundry soap, half a frozen chicken, baking soda, and flour.

Before we went three steps out of the store, we ran into the old lady who sells oranges. Back into the store, where she could sit down and count out our oranges. I wanted one to eat right then, but Prairie was drinking some peach nectar (colds have their perks). We bought eleven oranges.

Then off to catch a lift, but no one came.

I finished my orange and Prairie her juice. We were full of energy, so we began walking. Less than half a mile later, we got a lift—right to our La Fortuna road. We hopped down from the truck to join a man on foot and two boys on horses. The boys looked nine and eleven. They were actually twelve and fourteen. So we all walked together and chatted some. Their pace was a little faster than our usual pace.

Soon they offered to let me ride. We each had a backpack since we had needed to buy so much. The fourteen-year-old got off his horse and took my backpack. Then he and his dad helped me up. So I rode for a ways (up a very steep part of the road). But Prairie was the one who needed the ride.

Pretty soon I got off and they helped Prairie up. She had ridden a horse once when she was nine. This was a very amiable mare, so all was well. She rode the rest of the way to our driveway.

When I got off the horse, I suddenly remembered that I was supposed to be carrying the eggs! I would have put them down to get the oranges and forgotten them. Those turned out to be very expensive oranges.

When we were riding and walking along, I knew why I had bought five cookies. It was now a little past noon (according to my stomach) so we each ate a cookie as we went along.

Francisco is the dad's name. On Friday, they plan to go to town again, with the horses loaded with yucca, malanga and plátanos to sell. I suggested that they stop on the way into town to sell to us since we do not yet have any of those foods. He agreed.

We arrived home for a slightly late lunch, without having been rained on, with new friends (or at least acquaintances), without exhausting our sick one, with lots of groceries and with hopes of more to arrive within a few days. We were very grateful.

We made a nice chicken soup, with garlic, onion, chicken, one carrot and one small pathetic tomato—these last two cut up very fine. Served, Honduran-style, with rice added in the soup bowl. When you have a cold, chicken soup is the thing to have—even if you have to walk to town to get it. This was the first time since we moved to the mountain that we have bought and cooked meat. Usually our day in Limón is too long for that.

Prairie—Corn—December 6, 2006

We currently have internet access only when we are in a bigger city. (We are in Tocoa right now, running errands and visiting the Methodist church in nearby Ceibita, where we stay). Apparently Andres, who runs one of the stores in Limón, is planning on opening another internet place, but we will have to wait and see; he had said it would open at the beginning of November.

So, on to the news: It feels like we have taken the next big step in our life here: we have bought corn from a local farmer, learned how to cook with it, and now are integrating its use into our lifestyle. That's the one-sentence update. Read on for more.

Buying the Corn: One Monday morning (October thirtieth, to be exact), as Beth and I were fixing breakfast and getting ready to go into Limón, a man came walking up the path to our house leading a mule with packs. He was from La Fortuna on his way into town to sell some of his crops—corn, beans, and plátanos—and thought he'd stop by to see if we wanted to buy some. If nothing else, he'd get to see our place up close. We were interested. We had just been waiting for something like this to happen; we were hoping to purchase food staples from local farmers, and had started hinting this to people we met in the area. So this man, named Polo, sold us a hundred pound sack of corn (whole kernel field corn), a twenty-five pound sack of beans (the standard little red ones), and a bunch of plátanos. We paid him 400 lempiras, or just over twenty dollars. It felt like a real boost for our food security, in that the corn and beans should last for quite a while and we won't have to keep carrying them in from town.

Sorting the Corn: We asked Polo the best way for storing the corn, and he told us that it should be laid out in the sun to dry thoroughly before storing it in the sack in the house. Well, it was a nice idea, but we were leaving town the next day and wouldn't be back till Saturday.

We had an interesting trip to Las Mangas, a small community upriver from La Ceiba, where we stayed with a missionary from the U.S. Besides doing local outreach in religion and agriculture, he also hosts people who are interested in mission work for weeks or months at a time. A big thing we got out of our visit was information on gardening/agriculture, as well as a bunch of seeds and cuttings for various edible greens and other useful things that we have since been planting at our place.) It wasn't until the Friday after we got back that we finally got to sorting the corn.

German has been helping us quite a bit with preparing planting holes for fruit trees, chopping firewood, and other tasks. Just last week, he and his wife Doris put in a clay floor in our kitchen; it had previously just been loose dirt. He had reminded us that we had better sun and sort the corn, or it could mold and turn black. So we spread the corn out on a sheet in the sun, letting it dry out thoroughly, and we sat there picking out molding and discolored kernels. (The discards have since sprouted, giving us an interesting lawn of four-inch-tall corn plants.)

That afternoon, after German had left, we had surprise guests—a couple of Americans my age who are teachers at a place called Finca del Niño, or Farm of the Child, near Trujillo. One of them, Naomi, I'd first met at the end of May in Copón, and she had visited us here with some other friends at the end of August. In was a nice visit, and they were a big help in sorting the rest of the corn.

Cooking the Corn: The day German was here, he taught us how to make pinol, which is ground, toasted corn that is usually cooked with milk to make a hot drink or cereal. We had eaten pinol before, having purchased it as a powder from street vendors in Tocoa. But the flavor is so much better when it is homemade—a wonderful toasted smell, reminiscent of burnt popcorn and fresh-roasted coffee beans. The corn is toasted on the *comal*, or stove-top griddle of the wood stove, until the kernels turn mostly black; they pop a little bit. After letting it cool, it is ground finely and can be stored for later cooking. We have a hand mill that attaches to the counter in the kitchen. It takes a fair amount of work to use. I think my upper arms will gain some muscle.

The next week we again were out of town—this time to Tocoa where we worked with a medical mission team from the States at the Methodist church in Ceibita. What we really wanted to learn was to cook the corn and make tortillas. We'd gotten verbal instructions from some friends, but when we tried it the first time, it didn't seem to come out right. We knew we needed a hands-on lesson to learn the details of how much to put in, how long to cook it, how to grind it. We arranged with German for his wife Doris to come over that Saturday, the day after we'd sorted the corn, but she ended up not being able to. Instead, we made a rain date for the Tuesday after returning from Tocoa.

The day after getting home from Tocoa (Saturday), our

friend Gloria showed up for a brief visit. She was with two others, checking up on her property that borders ours. (She is having someone build her a small cabin there.) Gloria was willing to start some corn cooking for us—dissolving a bunch of *cal*, or lime (like is used to make the lines on ball fields) into the water till it is cloudy, then adding the corn. They said the corn should cook until al dente and you can mark it with your fingernail. We weren't sure how long it would actually take and they left before it was done. So we made our best guess, and after it had cooled we put it through the mill to get a nice fine masa, or dough, and make tortillas. They came out alright.

Then next Tuesday, November 21, German and Doris showed up as promised. Beth worked with German in the yard while Doris gave me a proper lesson on tortilla-making. Apparently, we had cooked the corn the right amount of time on Saturday—about two hours (like beans). By then the hulls mostly fall off. Doris showed me how to wash the corn to get the rest of them off—squeezing it in your hands and rinsing it three times until the water runs clear. She demonstrated how to send the corn through the mill two times: after the first time it is a fairly coarse dough, so you add a little water and push it through again to get the fine dough. Then she gave me another lesson on tortilla making. (The only one I'd had was from someone back in March, when we were living in town and using corn flour and an electric stove.) I got some good tips on how hot the stove-top needs to be (very hot), and how to turn them over so they come out perfectly with browned spots, chewy and not too dry.

The next morning, we had more surprise visitors. (Our life is never boring here.) It was an older woman named María from La Fortuna, who turned out to be the mother of Polo, the man who'd sold us the corn. Her granddaughter was with her, and they were on their way in to Limón. María helped me make more tortillas, giving me another chance to observe an experienced cook, and they joined us for breakfast. After eating, we all walked to Limón together, since Beth and I hadn't gone into town that Monday because it was too rainy. So, in the last couple weeks, our corn tortillas have improved a lot—and being made from freshly ground corn, they have a great flavor.

Impact on our lives: Not only is the addition of corn changing our diet with the addition of more corn tortillas and *pinol*, [flour made from ground, toasted maize kernels] but it is also changing our routine. It looks like we will be spending a lot more time in the kitchen, cooking and grinding the corn and cleaning the mill after use. Right now we are cooking the corn at the same time as we cook beans, every two or three days, and making enough for two days (it seems to last well). Having the corn also makes us more ready to have chickens, because now we have something we could easily feed them and not have to haul it in from town. It also has us considering again the question of getting dogs, which have been recommended to protect us and the chickens, as they can subsist on a mostly vegetarian diet, including tortillas.

And so it goes. The adventures continue, and we will see what happens next. Next week we go to La Ceiba to meet with a lawyer who is going to help Beth apply for permanent residency.

Beth—The Legal Saga—December 15, 2006

We are at the bus station about to return to the monastery today. We came to La Ceiba and El Pino because the attorney that was recommended insisted that I come right away to get started on the residency application. If you are going to consult a professional, best to obey her.

Well, we now know that it was just part of a hard sell. There was no urgency and there is no urgency. It is true that the laws have changed in ways that makes foreign residents feel less welcome (more costs, more frequent things to do). But her prices were out of this world. We decided that her services were not in line with our lifestyle of voluntary poverty. Are you catching on, yet? We would have been dead broke by paying the first installment of her charges. So that question remains open.

Our bus arrived about three PM. She had said that she would meet us. By a little past four, we were at her office. Before five we knew we had received the hard sell. By 5:30, still in her custody, we knew we wouldn't be using her. She put us back in the car, ran a few errands, arriving with us at the bus station too late to catch a bus to El Pino. She delivered us there, herself. It was about seven when we arrived, pouring rain and pitch black.

The ladies (down to age eight) of the church were sewing in the room where we usually sleep. They had three treadle machines and one electric. The project is making skirts, shorts and dresses for the poor children of the neighborhood as Christmas presents. They already have a few dozen done. I asked what the goal was. The goal was to use up all of the fabric. It will last clear until June unless they start making clothing for larger people!

The church was open and Carlos was kneeling at the altar. We went to Doña Ada's place to order our dinner (we were famished) and then joined Carlos for our much delayed afternoon prayers. It is a great privilege to walk in during the middle of praying by a serious pray-er. You can feel it—a physical sensation actually.

Then we ate (and were so grateful to be fed) and returned to the church for the evening prayer meeting. Carlos asked me to help "share the word of God." I didn't know what he meant exactly, but I knew what my answer needed to be. Yes. Well, we told stories together—about listening to God. I told about the fierce bulls.

We fell asleep quickly and easily that night. It had been a long day. The attorney had done us a favor in getting us there, so we became far more alert about what the real reason might be for us to have taken this trip.

We visited the Zion church and asked about the January meeting of the young people. Well, it is part of a district convention. It coincides with a time that we need to go to Belize for passport stuff. We signed up to go in the bus with the youth.

I can hardly wait, a bus full of youth. I'll use earplugs, I suppose. Prairie says it will be interesting. It will. It is also almost a full week of meetings. We ran errands. There is never enough time in the city.

But home today.

Beth—A Trip to the Nursery—December 15, 2006

We came home from Tocoa yesterday. We got up knowing that it would be an interesting day, after all we would be visiting a plant nursery that we had not seen before.

It was a rainy morning. We did morning prayers and our spiritual formation class homework before leaving the church. We caught the seven AM bus to Tocoa after leaving the keys to the church at Suyapa's little store—with her oldest daughter.

We had a big breakfast in a restaurant at the bus terminal. Stewed chicken, refried beans, grated cheese, imitation butter cream, and corn tortillas. We have eaten there before. They don't sell juice, just soda pop, so I went next door to buy some orange juice. Our host soon brought me a soda straw for it—with a smile. He was also right there with more tortillas as soon as we polished off the first batch. We eat a lot in this active life. For example, if we make pancakes, we make the amount I would have used in the States to serve 4 people.

We left our heavy backpacks at the restaurant while we went grocery shopping. The cows are in late pregnancy and so have gone dry. We bought a large can of powdered milk, plus other things we didn't want to carry on our backs in the next few weeks—flour, sugar, rice, and other supplies.

Back to the bus terminal, with a boy carrying our box of

groceries. We go to the appropriate bus to send these items to Chito's place, but the bus guy says he's not sure they'll be going. Everyone had gotten off their bus to ride on the one that is just about to leave. He recommends we send our stuff on that bus. We still have some shopping to do, but we don't want to risk missing the chance to send our luggage ahead. So we take the box and the backpacks to the other bus. And off they go.

Now comes the serious grocery shopping. Rapadura (the light molasses in block form, remember) is hard to get in Limón. The grocery stores won't carry it; only the little tiendas do and they often don't have it. We bought three chunks. Then vegetables: two pounds of sweet potatoes, two pounds of carrots, a pound of beets and another of onions, a head of garlic, a head of cabbage, a little celery, some cilantro, even a cantaloupe. We put all of this in a big sack—the size used to carry a hundred pounds of corn. It was heavy. You can see why we would have preferred doing this before we sent stuff on the bus. But it didn't work that way.

The nursery is only a few miles out of town, so almost any bus goes past it. We caught one headed for Trujillo. The bus guy said that he knew the place and would let us know when to get off. By now we are a little wet. The shopping area is under roofs with overhangs and might be dry, might not be; too many people for umbrellas to be feasible.

We settle into our bus seat and document our expenditures. (Wow! They were high!) Prairie provides a visual screen while I snake my left hand up under my dress to relieve my money belt of another 500 lempiras. All right, now we're ready to just enjoy our ride.

The nursery is a little back from the road, so we hadn't seen it from the bus before. We slog through the mud and step across the temporary creek, up the bank to the house.

A nice lady comes out and asks how she can help us. Our wish list of fruit trees includes nine. I mention a few. She doesn't have any of them. It is more efficient for her to tell us what she does have—nothing on our list. Some of them she has to explain to me.

At least we haven't wasted our time; we've made a new friend. We introduce ourselves all around and shake hands. She really is delightful.

Well, dear friends, this is a small taste of that day, but my time is gone. I will try to finish it another day.

Prairie—Making a Difference Newsletter—Issue 1.[23]
Fair Trade—December 29, 2006

This is an occasional newsletter about how you can help create a more just world, from Amigas del Señor, Methodist Monastery, Limón, Colón, Honduras.

Some people wonder what they can do to make a difference in a world where there is so much injustice— economic, political, racial, and on and on. Americans live in luxury compared to the majority of people in the world, and are said to use forty percent of the world's resources, while being only about one percent of its population.

It's no wonder there are predictions of collapse of the world as we know it—because our way of life is not sustainable.

We feel that our updates about our life in Honduras help give you an idea about how the rest of the world lives, and how we are trying to be conscious of our use of resources. This newsletter is to help give you some more concrete steps that you can implement in your life right now that will make a difference and help create a more sustainable, just world.

Issue No. 1: Fair Trade:

One small step you can take is to learn about fair trade and purchase fairly traded products. To put it briefly, fair trade is when the people who grow or make the products receive a fair price

---

23 We never sent another issue.

for their products (usually by removing the middlemen) ensuring that their families can have a decent income. It also often includes using more sustainable methods in creating products and strives for gender equality. Below are some organizations and companies that we know of that certify, promote, or sell fair trade products. Take a minute to learn about them, and see how you can incorporate fair trade into your life. If you are already aware of fair trade, we thank you for your conscientiousness, and ask you to consider the next step you can take in making fair trade a reality for more people (see AFSC's Trade Matters Project, and Oxfam International).

International Fair Trade Association: www.ifat.org an association of Fair Trade Organizations, who are committed to fair trade products. Read about fair trade, its history, and find hundreds of FTOs around the world.

Trans Fair USA: www.transfairusa.org.
This organization certifies food products as being fairly traded. They have good information about what Fair Trade is and what products can be certified as fair trade (including coffee, tea, and chocolate). You can also search for where to buy fair trade products near you or online.

American Friends Service Committee, Trade Matters Campaign: http://www/afsc.org/tradfe-matters/.
This Quaker program works to make trade fair.

Prairie—Dead Lizards Make Bad Bunkmates
January 1, 2007

On the second Thursday of January, Beth and I had our monthly retreat day. We sat in the shade on the north side of the house doing some spiritual exercises. When we went inside afterward, I noticed that a small lizard—black with blue stripes and large back feet—was inside the house. It scampered about as if looking for an escape, and tried climbing up the screen window above my bed. After watching its antics for a while, we decided to prop open the back door so it could get out. We didn't see it again, so assumed it had finally found its way out and thought no more about it.

That is, until Friday. In the afternoon I noticed a new brown spot on my bed covers but didn't think much of it. Usually, I brush the dust out from between my sheets before getting into bed, but that night, for whatever reason, I didn't. As I was climbing into bed, I noticed a faint unpleasant odor. Then as I settled in, I felt a wet or cold spot near my head. Had some rain come through the window? I wiped the sheet with my hand, and in the darkness felt a long, cold object. I jerked my hand away. What might it be? That's when the clues began to come together in my mind: the little lizard must have died in my bed! Perhaps it had gotten under the covers and suffocated—or maybe I had sat on it unknowingly! I considered whether I should get up and find the flashlight to see if I could see it and know for sure, but we keep silence after evening prayers. Beth was already in bed, perhaps asleep, and I didn't want to disturb her. If I got up, I would want to make grossed-out sounds (they had been running through my mind this whole time) and tell Beth what was going on, since I'd also have to figure out how to get rid of the body. Instead, I decided to just suck it up and try to sleep through the night.

As you might imagine, I didn't sleep very well. The smell of dead body (which I was familiar with from dead mice in my past) was stronger and stronger each time I woke up, and I kept scooting closer and closer to the opposite side of the bed, not wanting my head or hands to get too close to the body. Moreover, I had strange dreams—luckily not about lizards.

When I got up in the morning, I was stiff and tired, and it was too dark to see anything distinct. So I waited until after morning prayers to look at my bed. Sure enough, there was the little lizard, lying dead near the window. Ick. I told Beth, and she made all the grossed-out sounds I'd thought about the night before. I used some newspaper to pick up and get rid of the body, tossing it over the side of the hill for nature to deal with. Then I inspected my sheets: the small brown stain was blood, and it had soaked through all the covers—apparently I'd squished the poor creature when I sat down to read on Thursday. I'd slept with a dead lizard for two nights! So I had to wash all my sheets to get rid of the stains and the bad smell. Beth says sleeping with lizards, dead or alive, is not allowed in this monastery and permission is given to get up and deal with it. Next time I will.

Life lessons learned: If you didn't see the animal leave, assume it is still indoors; and always inspect your bed before getting into it.

Beth—Fruit Trees, Oranges, and Friends,
Advent Continued—January 5, 2007

We were so rudely interrupted by time to board the bus when I was telling you about our trip to the plant nursery on our way home from Tocoa early in December. We had just met the nursery lady and she said that she didn't have what we needed, but we made a friend. To continue:

I was curious. All the books say that trees from the nurseries would give fruit a year or two sooner than trees from seed. How much of that is simply that they are a year older and larger? So we decided to look around. (This in the rain, with umbrellas, mind you.) They are bigger.

The nursery lady had giant guavas. Chito had been talking about these for two months, about how he wanted to get two, one for us and one for him. (We sort of owed him a favor, after all.) Chito had misunderstood the dates of this big shopping spree trip and had expected us to show up at his place last Thursday all loaded down and ready for a ride home. On

Saturday, he enlisted a young police officer to come with him and came to check on us. We were, of course, fine. It was just a silly misunderstanding about dates.

Back to the nursery. We bought two trees that will yield giant sized guavas, one for us and one for Chito. We also bought one Persian lime tree. We live in a county whose name translates to lime and we don't have a lime tree (yet). Thirty lempiras for each tree.[24] I handed her a hundred-lempira bill. She searched for change and found a fifty. So we gave her another forty and she gave us the fifty. Change-making is generally a hassle everywhere. We were pleased that this got resolved so easily. We spoke about various types of oranges. She'll have orange trees in January and that is still a good month for planting oranges. Fine, we'll be back. Then she started bringing out oranges. First she gave us over a dozen of one type, then about two dozen of another type. Wow! We like oranges. (Now I didn't feel so bad about cheaping out and not buying a pineapple.)

We loaded ourselves up with umbrellas, our regular bags, a plastic bag with our new fruit trees, and the big grocery bag (now with some oranges, too). It was raining. We took off, with me leading. I went down the bank, crossed the little stream, maneuvered through the gate, and then turned to look back at Prairie. She was just picking herself up from her fall on the slippery bank. She was bruised and filthy. Yes, she was carrying the big heavy bag.

We made our way to the other side of the road to await the bus and consolidate our loads. Each of us carried an umbrella, a blue bag (which we used like a purse and shared), a bag with the trees, and everything else in the big gunny-sack-sized bag. We waited only a few minutes under our umbrellas, when along came a bus that would take us to Bonito. We got on, counting our blessings.

In Bonito, we staggered (because of the weight of the bag)

24 All the trees eventually perished, even the ones for Chito.

to a shelter to wait for the next bus. Prairie tried to guess how stiff she'd be in the morning. We considered buying some rum. Alcohol is a good muscle relaxant, but enough to relax the muscles also leaves a hangover, usually, that is. And we are a Methodist monastery after all. Using alcohol as a medicine is okay, but having leftovers around the house is not.

There is a long tradition in both the Methodist Church and the Society of Friends that houses of worship be safe places for everyone—this includes those who have been injured by use or abuse of alcohol, by themselves or others. Alcoholism is a serious disease and is to be respected. Our constitution (daily rule, faith and practice) has not yet all been written down, but we know that this tradition fits us. We will not have alcohol available. We decide not to buy any muscle relaxant and hope for the best. Prairie took some ibuprofen. Pain relief, after all, interrupts the pain-spasm cycle very nicely.

Then the bus arrived. We got our stuff loaded. The bus driver is pretty curious about our morning. It was the same bus that we considered using to send our luggage. The driver was satisfied with our rendition of our travels.

We got off at Chito and Rosa's place. There had been a lot of rain. Chito and Clemente listen to the radio weather reports, trying to guess how bad the road would be to our place. Our luggage had arrived and was waiting for us.

Rosa offered us food, which we happily accepted—corn tortillas, rice, and beans with a rich chicken broth, the kind made with real chicken and not bullion cubes. We would get home wet and tired (and Prairie sore), but we didn't have to arrive home hungry, too. We asked what we owed. Nothing.

Eva was still sick, so I pulled out several oranges to give to Clemente. She didn't want to eat, but she could probably drink juice. He delivered them to his house and came back with a plastic bag holding a few hot dog buns and a small pound cake. He said, "The one who gives, receives." (It had more punch in Spanish.)

While we ate, Chito brought the truck around. This was very efficient and made me think that he expected the road to get worse as the afternoon wore on. We loaded up the truck. Chito's new diesel truck had a back seat so we all four rode in the cab. Clemente came along. We sorted luggage by what would be okay to get rained on and what would not.

Part way along the road, we came across Francisco on foot and his two sons on horses. Remember them from when they gave us rides? He hopped in back. Crossing the stream required shifting into 4-wheel drive. This was done by the driver getting out of the truck and adjusting something at each front wheel. A downpour arrived by the time we got to the stream. Chito handed me a "nylon"—a plastic tarp—to hold for rain protection. There was no glass in the window on my side of the truck. I thought of poor Francisco in the back!

When the downpour ended, Chito adjusted the four-wheel drive and started up the hill. A little slithery, but up we went. (Chito, by the way, has a reputation of being one of the safest drivers on this road.)At our driveway, Francisco began the next stage of his walk to La Fortuna. His sons on horseback would catch up to him long before they all reached home. Clemente and Chito helped carry our stuff to the house and took off. We were very grateful to be home.

Afternoon prayers, unpacking, bathing, settling in.

Prairie made a vegetable soup for dinner while I arranged the table, collected fresh greens for the Advent wreath, and put the dirty laundry to soak. Then, while she was still working in the kitchen, I read aloud. We were reading *The Complete Gospels*, in what is sometimes called *The Scholars Version*[25], in English. It's very informative. We finished John's gospel. There was still enough light to read a few pages of the biography of Mother Teresa of Calcutta.

Just another day at Amigas del Señor. (Ha!)

---

25 *The Complete Gospels: Annotated Scholar's Version*, Robert J. Miller, Polebridge Press

Prairie—Happy New Year
January 5, 2007

Happy New Year! And what a year 2006 was for me: spending the majority of it, my twenty-fifth year, in Honduras. I thought I was coming to experience another culture and improve my Spanish (both of which I have done), but I've realized that I actually came to help found a monastery and experience the monastic life. It was not something I had ever imagined doing, and I had some trepidation before coming down here. In the end, it has been a true blessing to have this time devoted to my spiritual growth, focusing on prayer and God's presence in my life.

Back in August, at the same time we moved out to the mountain location, Beth and I began a small-group spiritual formation course called *Companions in Christ*. It has introduced me to many spiritual practices, various ways of reading and studying Scripture, and praying, which I am eager to incorporate into my daily life. I really anticipated the last two sections (which we are now doing) that focus on discerning God's call in my own life and for our faith community—as I continue to try to decide what to do next with my life—what God wants me to do.

One thing that I have decided, is to stay here beyond my original one-year commitment, and wait until May to return to the States. Partly that is to finish our *Companions in Christ* course, partly to continue the establishing of this monastery, and partly to attend my sister Autumn's graduation from St. Olaf College—and hopefully visit some old friends. What I am working on right now is whether I will stay in the U.S. after that or return here for another year at the monastery. There are many factors to consider.

For now, I want you to know that I'll be here until May, so keep writing me snail mail letters. I plan to let you know by April whether I will be here longer, so that you can know whether to keep writing to me here or not.

Thanks for reading, and for all of your support and prayers throughout the year. I hope your 2007 is a year of dreams fulfilled.

Beth—Christmas and New Year—January 5, 2007

We got home from La Ceiba sick with diarrhea and weakness. I barfed but Prairie didn't. We didn't even go to work on Monday, December eighteenth.

On December twentieth, German came over and helped us plant two guava trees and a *mamóncillo* (fruit-bearing tree in the soapberry family) along the road. These fruits bear during different months. When they start bearing, the neighbors who walk three hours to the highway will be able to stop for a little refreshment along the way. So far, the trees look good. German also showed us how to dig yucca. We ate our own yucca on Christmas Day.

Friday, December twenty-third, we went to town. We were very eager for mail. Two of our hoped-for Christmas packages arrived—and a fistful of letters and cards. We saved all of the cards to open on Christmas Day with the packages. We also saved a novel by Isabel Allende to give ourselves on Christmas Day. We are now reading a chapter a day as our Spanish lesson. We also bought as many vegetables as we could. We bought guava and pineapple jelly—the two flavors available. They were wonderful. We weren't able to get any fruit, but we bought a one-and-a-half-pound red snapper.

Saturday was preparation. Prairie baked snickerdoodles. It took a long time in our little low heat oven, but they were scrumptious. I fried the fish. We are only very slowly developing any skill at fish frying. So far, we are blaming the crummy pan. But I really don't know how to fry fish. We had a love feast dinner (fish and flour tortillas), very Biblical, you know.

We enjoyed our Advent wreath a lot.

Our special meal was Sunday noon—Italian vegetable soup. Prairie made decorations in the house, Honduran-style with colorful newspapers (the ads) cut to flap in the breeze. We put them along the bunk beds.

More soup, still delicious, for dinner. Cookies, don't forget the cookies.

Pancakes with jelly (and molasses, if you prefer) for breakfast. Present and card opening, Christmas carol singing, Bible selections in the morning. We took a little walk to admire our new trees, and learned that the batteries in the camera were out of power. No pictures of any of the Christmas stuff.

We had six Christmas cards and decorated around the Advent wreath with them. Fun, though the breeze soon knocked them down.

It was very hot on Christmas Eve and Christmas Day and that seemed very strange. There were beautiful songbirds, though. On Christmas night, a huge, windy rainstorm hit. Prairie sleeps right under a window. She had to get up and move to another bunk. We'll have to do something about weather effects during storms.

New Year's is not something we did much about. But we'll do the Feast of the Three Kings this weekend. I love Christmas.

Beth—Prairie is a Keeper!
January 8–21, 2007

The most important news of the month is that Prairie has decided to remain with Amigas del Señor until the end of June, 2008. This is wonderful—on a personal level for me, as well as for the program. Prairie is not replaceable. Obviously, we will be sent whomever we need. That's why God sent Prairie.

Celebrations are in order, but during the time of discernment, I had insulated myself, in case of the other possible decision, so it will be a delayed celebration. February first seems a good time. That is the one-year anniversary of when we got on the Greyhound bus in Portland to start our monastic life together.

We are being very intentional about preparing for the arrival of whoever is coming next. And we wonder when that will be.

About today. We are in La Ceiba. We just got off the bus, used the bathroom and had lunch.

We got up at dawn as usual today, but had to finish the packing and closing up the house. We decided that the guitar really should go along to the district church meeting in Belize. We each had a backpack—me with the two umbrellas, Prairie with the guitar (wrapped in a dress, inside a big plastic bag, tied with a clothesline). Just as we were leaving the house, we heard a car coming. Well, we didn't want to miss our chance for a lift, so we walked about as fast as we could to the road. (It is usually about a three-minute walk, but a small part is really steep, up towards the road.) We know that sounds are unpredictable, so we didn't wait for a truck, but just kept on towards the highway.

Before we got to the stream, the car showed up. They were on their way to Tocoa. (The route to La Ceiba is through Tocoa.) We were thrilled and climbed into the back of the pickup. There were five or six people, a large sow and eight tiny piglets! As the last arrivals, we got the positions near the rear end of the sow.

When we got to the highway, several people got off as they were headed to Limón in the other direction. That allowed me to sit down. But Prairie was still hanging on to the side rails near the wrong end of the sow.

The little piglets huddled next to the sow until she fell on one. Then they cuddled up to the man in front of me and to Prairie. She said that they were soft and warm.

Long before we arrived in Bonito, Prairie's hat flew off. Just yesterday we were having very serious conversations about our habits and hats, etc. Well, it seems that God is telling us it is time to buy hats in Honduras. No rain today, so that hat was not essential.

We caught up with a bus in Bonito. I looked in my mirror (Prairie's face) and realized that I was covered with dust, not quite enough to mistake my race, but more than enough to look very dirty. We thanked our truck driver and climbed onto the bus for the rest of the ride. The road got a lot better between Bonito and Tocoa. That meant that the trucks drove faster and riding in the back was more dangerous.

It was a very crowded bus, but long before we arrived, it thinned out and we were both able to sit. We pulled out our hankies and did what we could for our faces. In Tocoa, we caught a bus immediately for La Ceiba. And here we are.

We'll go on to El Pino this afternoon.

Beth—Locks and Guitars—January 23, 2007

At the bus station, we went for fruit drinks. Lovely, but as we were leaving the shop, the guitar hit the doorway. A bad sound was made. The hole was easily felt through its light protective covering. *Así es* (life is like that).

When we arrived at El Pino, Efraín was there to greet us. He gave us a little tour of his gardening projects and let us in. He apologized that the door from the outside to the room where we would be sleeping had a padlock on it and he didn't have the key. He let us into another door—the classroom, and we passed through the classroom to our bedroom.

We also got out the guitar, just in case he would know something about guitars and repairs. It sounded pretty good, so we were pretty happy about that. But, no, he didn't know anything. A little later, Carlos, the pastor, came over and we chatted. We shared our guitar problem with him. Well, wonder of wonders, he has had experience in carpentry, including fine repairs like guitars. He has no tools for such work now, so didn't offer to fix it. He told us that the guitar is made of a type of cedar, very good for making nice sounds, but it splits easily. Other guitars in Latin America are sometimes made of mahogany. They don't sound as good, but they are much sturdier. He demonstrated how much nicer it sounds when he puts his hand over the hole—a lot nicer. He explained the type of repair that is best, what type would suffice, etc. He would meet us later to take us to a reliable repair shop. He would even transport the guitar as we didn't really feel good about carrying it on the bus again.

Our plan was to leave early this morning to start our city errands. The English language class met in the classroom while we were showering, eating and settling in for the evening. They were still working when we did evening prayers and went to bed.

This morning when we went to the door of the classroom, it, too, was padlocked shut. With a padlock a size or two larger than the little padlock on our door. Well, there is one other classroom. We went to it. That door had the biggest padlock yet. The main door is a solid U.S.-style door. The outer door, with the padlock, is iron grill-work. So, we were locked in. Okay, we broke the grand silence to laugh. What else could you do, after all?

We did morning prayers and ate our fruit, glad that we had some. (We had picked up some bananas and oranges at the bus station).

We took turns watching at the door for any sign of life outside. Efraín had told us that the retired guy who, as a volunteer, is often around the place had just had kidney stones removed. So, we couldn't expect him to show up. But Carlos had early errands to run in the city.

After a while, Carlos came out of his house and we called to him as he went to his truck. Thank God his truck was working. If he had had to use the bus, he would have gone out another door and we would still be waiting, locked inside! Well, lots of jokes about being prisoners. He had a key to the big padlock and unlocked it. He even gave us the key so that the same thing won't happen tomorrow.

We have spent a lot of time in the last week discussing what the monastic vocation means. So, today, I asked Prairie, "Why do all these things happen to us? Is it just so that we have good stories to tell? Are we called to be God's clowns?" Well, if the shoe fits.

We finished our laundry and hung it out to dry. We had already done some in the bathroom sink. Then to the bus. At the bus stop, a lady came up dressed to the nines. She was wearing dressy slacks and very dressy pumps. No heel strap, and just a strap across the mid-step. She had artificial nails on all ten toes—with the popular fashionable nail shape that women are wearing in the States right now—long nails, too. One could not put those feet into closed-toe shoes. Just when you think you have seen it all, there is something else.

A young lady came up with a man who seemed to be her father (or grandfather). She greeted us in such a friendly way that we were each wondering if we were supposed to recognize her. Maybe, for example, she was part of the El Pino church and we just didn't remember her face.

Well, as the conversation went on, it became clear. She recognized us, or at least Prairie, as *monjas* (nuns). Prairie is wearing her new dress (so it is still a bright blue) and a kerchief that matches. "She looks like a sister," the young lady said.

She is considering her own vocation as a Roman Catholic nun but right now, she is registering for nursing school. We had a very interesting conversation while waiting and in the bus on the way to the city.

So, we arrived in the city, but not early.

Beth—Belize Conference
January 23–30, 2007

We are back from Belize. You may remember that in December, I mentioned that we would be attending the Methodist Church District Conference in Belize? It seems very strange to have a district that includes two nations.

We went by bus. We were fifteen people in a fourteen-passenger bus. Our luggage was on top. Five children aged eight to eleven. They were angels. But it was a twenty-one-hour odyssey to get there. We slept at the old parsonage next to Zion church, having been told that the bus would leave at one AM. We didn't have a clock, so I slept on the sofa near the open front door. That allowed me to hear when someone came to the gate of the compound. Well, they woke me up just fine—at 4:30 AM. We didn't mind at all the extra sleeping time. At first, we didn't catch on that it was so late, but we both noticed how much rest we had obtained from just a few hours of sleep!

Our first real stop was in San Pedro Sula at the Belize consulate. Some of the visas were still not in order and that had to be attended to before breakfast. We now realized that we should have packed a lot more food. Oops.

We stopped to pick up some food at a gas station convenience store. Traveling with wealthy people is very different from traveling on the public bus.

We went through Guatemala. (It doesn't look very far on the map—if the map doesn't show the mountains and the roads.) We went up into Petén, near Tikal, then across to Belmopán in Belize then south to Punta Gorda. The toughest part was just before the Belize border, potholes, clay-like mud, ten kilometers per hour. The ten girls in back had their sliding window open. Splash—white-tan mud over everything.

None of us had changed money at the Guatemala border. How could we have been so stupid? Well, we got hungry. Baby, did we get hungry! But we were all very polite. I knew Prairie well enough to know that she was as hungry as I, but no one said anything. We all shared tiny amounts of foods, sometimes politely accepting, and sometimes politely refusing. No one could have guessed. As soon as we crossed into Belize, we had money to spend and stopped for a meal. It was about seven PM by then. (No, you didn't miss a lunch stop; there was no lunch stop.)We all bought big meals and ate every shred of food.

Back to the bus for several more hours, but now we were only tired and stiff, not hungry. When we arrived in Belize, Stephanee and her husband had a lovely dinner for us. We were quite happy to eat it up, too.

It was a classic church business meeting, but a little more interesting as we were learning how this district and this conference works. It is different from the States. We were visitors, not representatives, and sat in only a little of the meeting. We were still pretty sleep-deprived. (I actually never got over the sleep deprivation.)

We were greeted by our friends, Juan Simpson, Reina, and Wendy.[26] It was nice to already know a few people. We were invited to lunch and were given just enough airtime to present the concept that Protestants might have monastic vocations.

We slept in a dormitory room attached to the side of Stephanee's brother-in-law's house. He was gracious and hospitable, but there was a disadvantage, no bathroom available from bedtime until getting-up time. That was okay—until the diarrhea hit. I won't gross you out with the details. The lawn will grow well.

On Saturday, we attended a local event called Village Life. Sort of a county fair, with interesting traditional foods, dances, cracker-eating contest, etc. We enjoyed it. Maybe it was the coconut tart (or the sweet lemon pie) that caused the diarrhea. Was it worth it? Regret is a waste of time.

Afternoon time was youth performances and now we're back at the Methodist conference. Singing, dancing, posters, poetry, drama. It was pretty fun. Lots of uniforms. In Belize, more public school children attend church schools than government schools. There isn't what you would call separation of church and state. Representatives of the government were given formal welcomes and acknowledgments at the meetings. The church schoolteachers receive seventy percent of their

26 The pastor from La Ceiba and two women from El Pino.

salary from the government and 30% from the church. The teachers wear the same uniform as the kids.

On Sunday, our worship service lasted a few hours. (Sometimes it is good to not wear a watch.) The youth were responsible for the service and there was more music and dance. Very nice. We met in the Roman Catholic hall. It had five rows of three ceiling fans each. That's how big it was. We were very happy to have those ceiling fans going all the time. We arrived late, but still managed to get chairs. Our faces (white) showed us to be visitors. So we were given lovely hospitality. We were very grateful. At the end of the worship service we paraded through town back to the Methodist Church. That was pretty fun. Our little Honduras group was right in front of a marching drum corps with drum majorettes, so we didn't feel obligated to come up with any music.

After lunch we went to the beach briefly. Then we tried for a nap. Prairie slept, but the heat kept me awake. We caught the public bus to the evening (five PM) service. The bus guy didn't even charge us. I don't know why. The bus on Friday had charged us.

It was a lovely service—if you don't count the repetitive greetings of all the important people. No kidding, three different people did welcomes and the total time on welcomes was easily fifteen minutes (says she who wore no watch). As the sermon was about to start, there was a crash and lots of screaming.

So, out to the road I went, with several others. A fifteen-year-old woman had been carrying her nephew across the road—to return him to his mother. They were struck by a motor vehicle (driven, I am told by a drunk government official). The girl was conscious and in a lot of pain from her injuries, but she was medically stable. Had we an EMT kit, she would have been given some nice strong pain medicine right then. But, of course, all we had was one pediatrician with empty hands.

The baby was covered with dust. He must have flown from

her arms. Screaming people all over. Dark. There were a few flashlights. I examined his respiratory and cardiac status in the arms of the first woman who picked him up. Snoring, shallow respirations. With just a little repositioning of his head, his breathing was a lot better. He was transferred to another woman's arms to carry him to the hospital in the front seat of a pick-up truck. At first, I thought that I should go along, but he started whimpering weakly and I realized that I couldn't do anything holding the patient in my arms in the front of a pick-up truck anyway. Good grief!

The bystanders gently rolled the fifteen-year-old onto a sheet of plywood and put her in the back of a pick-up truck. And off they went to the hospital.

About fifteen minutes later, there was quite a downpour but, I am told, the hospital is close and they would have arrived before the downpour. On our way home from church, we heard the helicopter that evacuated them to the big city. We were told that the baby's dad had drowned last August. That family has more than their share of troubles.

We did not expect to get any follow-up. The baby was breathing and should survive, but brain injury is the big risk.

Back at that house, a late dinner of rice and beans. Then to bed; well, not quite. The key to our room was with the folks returning the borrowed table and chairs (for this mob of houseguests). I sat on the front step and wept from exhaustion. I hadn't done that in a long time. Finally we were let in and got to bed.

Monday we got up at four AM for the ride home. The trip was a little shorter this time, only nineteen hours.

We arrived back in La Ceiba to realize that no provision had been made for us to get back into the church to sleep the rest of the night. One of our resourceful companions knew how to force the gate (for cars) enough for us to slip through. Prairie threw our backpacks over the top of the gate. There was a key to get into the church. The choir loft had carpeting, so we slept there. We were very grateful to have shelter for the night.

We were glad to be back in Honduras. The next time that we get a chance to go by non-stop bus from here to Belize, we'll politely decline.

Beth—2006 Financial Report—January 30, 2007

Communication was high in December because we paid in advance for most of our travel expenses for the District meeting in Belize in January.

We arrived in Limón February twenty-first of last year. We estimate that we spent $2,000 in travel before then and that up to $1,000 was spent from our checking account in the States. Our total expenses were, therefore, just under $20,000 for the year. There are lots of little hidden items that don't show up on a financial report—gifts and favors that came without a label of dollar value, that were more valuable than money.

2007 projections include no construction (except maybe a chicken coop, which will be inexpensive). The household set-up category will no longer exist. We have made a commitment that the tithes will be a minimum of twenty percent of our income. We will begin the process of applying to be legal residents—this will be a large expense. Travel to the U.S. will also occur this year.

Beth—Assumptions—February 1, 2007

The conference in Belize was really very informative. So many similarities and so many differences. For example, there is elected a Miss MCCA (Methodist Church of the Caribbean and the Americas) each year. (I guess she even gets a crown.)

We had a stimulating conversation with the president of the district. He asked a lot of questions and filled out the answers with several assumptions. They were pretty reasonable assumptions—but mostly wrong. Maybe you have some of the same assumptions.

The monastic vocation is a call to prayer. That's our main job—to pray. Our vocation also includes the call to voluntary poverty. That means that we live the way other poor people live in order to live in solidarity with them. Poverty does not mean destitution. We have enough to live on. Many things that you may consider essential, we define as luxuries because life and health continue without them.

We do not have electricity. This is because we live in a poor part of the country where there is no household electricity. It is part of our voluntary poverty. It is not because we think electricity is a bad thing though it does help us to live in touch with creation.

We do not have a radio. We make our own music. We don't take time for the triviality of most public broadcasts. We don't miss it. Again, we don't disapprove of radios; they just don't fit our lifestyle.

Cell phone service is available where we live. Many of our richer friends and neighbors have cell phones. We poor people do not.

We cook on wood fires. This is again about voluntary poverty. This is how poor people live in our part of the world. Buying gas would be absurd. We make very good food on our little traditional wood stove. This was a big challenge to learn, but now it feels natural. Chopping our own wood was a great challenge at first, but it is getting easier with practice. Occasionally, we have the luxury of hiring a man to cut wood for us. Our physical strength is increasing, too.

We live, not by the clock, but by the sun. We figure that if we can live more in touch with the creation, we can be more in touch with the Creator. We do not disapprove of clocks or watches. We even own one of each.[27] If I remember, I take the watch to Centro de Salud on Mondays so that I can count pulses and respirations.

27 We have since divested ourselves of clocks.

We do our prayer times outside whenever we can—celebrating creation and the Creator. Occasionally, we call it wrong and have to go back inside because of rain.

Obviously, this is not a description of our whole life. The point, I guess, is to make it clear that we live this way because we are called to monastic life, not because we think that everyone in the world (or in churches) should live this way. It is enough of a challenge to sort out one's own calling without trying to judge the world along the way.

Beth—Guitars, Sandals—February 1, 2007

We are still in El Pino today. We leave for Limón tomorrow.

You heard about our guitar getting broken. We left for Belize with it in the repair shop. We left the fee for the repair job with Carlos and he picked it up for us. It now works beautifully. The patch is smooth, but very visible (like some of our clothing patches, actually). Apparently, there were no adventures in re-obtaining it. Now we will carry it on the bus back home. Very ironic, to take a guitar to the big meeting, only to have it broken before it gets there.

On the day we first dropped the guitar off, one of Prairie's sandals fell apart—irreparably. She carries a special glue when we travel to keep them going, but this time, glue wouldn't do it. We walked around town until we found a place with flip-flops that would fit her. She prefers the kind with a strap over the foot rather than between the toes. We found a pair which were just about a perfect match for the blue dress (when the dress was new, of course). We just put the old sandals in the garbage can and she walked on in the new flip-flops before we went to Belize.

Of course, this is not the best way to break in new footwear. Fortunately, my sandals fit Prairie, too, (if she loosens the Velcro just a bit). We had three pairs of footwear—her flip-flops, my sandals, and my shoes. We just switched around until Prairie's feet adjusted. They seem to have adjusted now.

We had left some items in the old parsonage at Zion in La Ceiba. When we got back, they were locked into the bedroom, but yesterday the pastor was there. He had just returned from Tocoa, so he unlocked the door and we could take our umbrellas and our new white fabric for blouses with us.

We have rested up and have enjoyed meeting up with our friends here in El Pino.

Yesterday afternoon, we had a meeting with the women of the church who will be running the feeding program. It starts next week. On Wednesday, Carlos asked me to consult on the diet. Before our nutritional meeting, the group met to do job descriptions. This is typical Honduras. No need to get the nutritional consult early; no need to write job descriptions early.

We talked about the nutritional needs of children. Together I think we have a pretty reasonable plan of foods to serve. Here in Honduras, vegetables cost about the same as meat. We started with how the head cook would cook at home and then altered stuff a bit. What you would call a good diet is not what these kids will get, but they will get a good diet. No one here has done a feeding program before, so the women are very sober about taking up this big project. Reina, the chief, (her name means Queen) has to buy groceries by check every two weeks. Who ever heard of buying groceries by check? It is just not done—and for two weeks at a time. It will be a big challenge. The feeding program is a joint project with the North Georgia Conference of the United Methodist Church and Emmanuel Methodist Church in El Pino. They will be feeding and teaching about forty children, aged two to six. (Carlos, the pastor, had expressed concern some years ago about unsupervised children during their mothers work time in the pineapple fields. Now, they will get some supervision.) This morning, Eloyda agreed to weigh, measure, and give worm medicine to the kids. We'll come back in two weeks to see how things are going.

I met with Eloyda on the subject of the pharmacy, too.

Our friends from South Dakota, Gloria and Ron Borgman, will be bringing their medical team again to work with her. They do the further-out communities that get even less medical care. We wrote out Eloyda's wish list of medicines and an order sheet for Honduran medicines. A good job. These collaborative efforts are such good stuff. We sent off the emails to smooth the path.

So, we have no exciting tales to tell. We haven't been locked out; we haven't been locked in. We have gotten enough sleep and have eaten well and on schedule.

We are physically back to normal.

We have also put in a few phone calls to an attorney in Tegucigalpa about our residency application. It is complicated, but not nearly as complicated as the first (money-hungry) attorney led us to believe. The cost for both of us will be about half of what the cost was to have been for one. We are grateful.

Beth—In El Pino—February 20, 2007

Well, I told you that this February was hot and dry. Then the cold front arrived. We are not too hot now.

We did manage to cut the big tree that casts shade over the lychee tree. It leans over the fence seeking sunlight. It found the sunshine alright. We decided to cut the tree back so that it wouldn't take out the fence when it fell. We cut into it about five feet off the ground as it leaned over our smaller tree. That worked fairly well as the big tree is soft wood and we could fell it with the machetes. We didn't feel safe using the ax up that high.

Well, we got it down. As it crashed over, it knocked the top off the lychee tree! The instructions in the book are that lychees don't need pruning when they are young, except for judicious shaping. We hope that knocking the top off is considered judicious shaping. Time will tell. We'll let the fallen tree lie before cutting all the branches away from the lychee. Unfortunately, the tree we felled is not good for firewood.

When a cold front comes, it comes with rain. Our water tank is now full to overflowing again. That's nice, but we had a hard time deciding if we would be able to leave the monastery yesterday morning. We planned to go to Limón, work in the public health clinic and leave from there for El Pino. The laundry washed on Saturday was still hanging in the house and was not yet dry. Because it was much less rainy and the cloud cover was much thinner than the day before, we decided to try it.

We were concerned about our luggage, so we used the plastic bags that the mattresses come in like capes over the backpacks. Off we went, with umbrellas, hats, and the backpacks covered with superhero capes. The rain began steadily only for the last twenty minutes of our walk. Since it came without wind we arrived at Rosa's reasonably dry. We were quite a bit later than usual for going to Centro de Salud, but on rainy days we have very few patients. So, we waffled. Then along came a short bus headed toward Tocoa. We had one half second to decide. We decided to go. So we did. The next week when we would talk with our friends at the public health clinic we'd know if we made the right decision.

Beth—Feeding Program—February 20–22, 2007

Here we are at El Pino. We had pastelitos for dinner that Tuesday evening. Delicious.

So, this feeding program. The food is an important part, but the daytime supervision is another very important part. We are coming on the second day of the third week. I mentioned it before.

We came about 8:30 AM when the workers arrived. The head cook went right to the refrigerator to boil the milk. (They buy milk from the local farmers.) Eighteen kids got their morning snack—hot milk and a ripe banana about 9:30. By lunch time there were twenty-two children. The program officially has fifty kids, but the largest number (at one time) has been thirty-two. It seemed pretty busy with this number. I don't want to imagine what it would be like with fifty.

Organized. Before the kids were fed their morning snack, we were busily preparing lunch. I peeled oranges for the juice. Local oranges here have very strong oils in the skin and these oils would burn your face if you tried eating orange wedges. Because of the oils, one peels oranges before squeezing them for juice. There is a cool little gadget for rapid peeling, but we don't have it. I used the continuous strip method of peeling. Most Hondurans peel oranges with the butcher knife pointed away from themselves in a whittling wood posture. They found my method pretty interesting. The oranges were squeezed by hand while I ran another errand.

The two weeks' supply of fruit and vegetables arrived today, a medium watermelon, three small cantaloupes, a giant papaya and a lot of ripe bananas. The pineapples and oranges come from another source. The vegetables were a nice variety, too.

The diet for a possibly malnourished toddler is pretty different from what is publicized as being good for a middle-aged American. For instance, something fried each day is important to get enough oil and enough calories; meat every day for well-absorbed iron, vitamin A and the varieties of B vitamins. The cook says that the kids liked the liver. Thank God—it's got so much good stuff for little ones.

Reina (her name means Queen), who is 19, has charge of the kids most of the day. She is very patient with them. In the morning they all go outside. Prairie decided to be Reina's helper today. That was especially helpful in the afternoon at story-time sias laryngitis.

I was in and out, but it got pretty deafening just before we served lunch, orange juice and what Hondurans call enchiladas (tostadas in Mexico). Then about an hour later we served a very light snack, papaya and cantaloupe. (There was some cantaloupe left over from the previous day's snack.)

They showed me the menus from the last two weeks. I was really impressed. All agreed that the start-up was really hard. The first week, all the kids cried all day. I didn't hear crying today, except when someone got hurt.

Immediately after lunch, the workers cleaned up. The director of the program (also named Reina) swept and mopped the floor. The head cook and assistant cook started making pastelitos. There would be a soccer tournament there that afternoon. It had been delayed by the cold front and rain. They would sell pastelitos to help provide financial support for the feeding program.

(I continued this letter yesterday late in the afternoon, but the internet connection died and that was lost. To continue— I spent most of the day in the clinic. I charted the kids on a World Health Organization growth chart. They are almost all in the normal range, but in the lower half of that normal range. When you glance in the room, knowing that they are two to six years old, you would assume that they are mostly three and four, but remarkably well-behaved for their age—but half are five and six. Few of the five or six-year-olds weigh more than forty pounds.

I did consults on about a dozen of the children. Most had some form of infectious disease. Two had asthma. I thought two were anemic. They serve meat every day in the feeding program, so the low level anemia that is common should be helped a lot. We have no lab capability to check on it though.

When we ate lunch, the head cook offered me beans with the food. Of course, I accepted. I asked why the kids weren't getting beans. Because if she gives them beans, they eat them in preference to the vegetables! There is so much to learn that can only be learned through experience.

I helped Eloyda put the final touches on medicine orders for a team that will arrive in a week. It was a challenge. Prices go up. We cut and slashed expenses until we could meet the budget. I am so grateful for this particular team. They go out to the more remote communities where health care is all but non-existent.

They give the kids fluoride treatments, worm treatments and vitamins.

Last year they gave that routine to 1,300 kids, not counting those who got a real consult with a nurse or doctor.

My kids here get so little, but every time that I thank God for the kids, I thank God for not giving me the adults, too.

Prairie—Twenty-Five Years and Counting
February 22, 2007

Last Thursday, February fifteenth, I turned twenty-five. I thought that to celebrate, I'd make a time line of significant events for each of the 25 years of my life. Probably you will learn some new things about me. Enjoy!

1st year: —Born Prairie Naoma Cutting on Feb. 15, 1982 to April (aged twenty-seven) and Craig (aged twenty-nine) Hall Cutting, at their home, shared with two other couples, on Alder Street in Portland, Oregon.—Baptized at Freemont United Methodist Church.
2nd year: —Moved to Berkeley, California, where my par ents studied at the Pacific School of Religion.
3rd year:—Sister Autumn Rose is born at home.
4th year:—Earliest memories of my life from Glenville, Minnesota where dad was interim pastor for a year.
5th year: —Attended full-day Montessori preschool in Berkeley.
6th year: —Entered half-day kindergarten and learned to ride a bike in Pocatello, Idaho, where dad was Associate Pastor at First United Methodist Church.
7th year: —Walked ten blocks daily to Washington Elemen tary School, where I attended first through third grades.

8th year: —Began two years of piano lessons, Suzuki method.

9th year: —Got a black kitten from our neighbors which we named Midnight. (She died on my twenty-fourth birth day at fifteen-and-a-half-years old.

10th year:—Moved to Epworth United Methodist Church Camp and Retreat Center in the Hudson River Valley of New York, where my mom was camp director.—Started playing clarinet at Rondout Valley Middle School (where I attended fourth-seventh grades).

11th year: —First memory of flying in a plane, to visit Oregon and the Pacific coast in November.

12th year: —Got four permanent teeth removed and then braces put on. (I wore them for thrcc years.)

13th year: —Ears pierced for my twelfth birthday. (I wore earrings [including a second hole obtained at age fifteen] until moving to Honduras.—Cast in the school musical. (I was in a play or musical every year for the next nine, through my freshman year in college.)

14th year: —Difficult adjustment after moving away from a place I loved to Hermiston, Oregon, where eighth grade felt academically like a repeat of seventh.

15th year: —Joined the marching band.(I did parades, half-time shows at football games, and competitions for four years.)

16th year: —Attended two influential summer church camps for the first time: Music, Art, Drama, and Dance at Magruder on the Oregon coast (which I attended for two years), and Youth Leadership Workshop at Suttle Lake (which I attended for four years).

17th year: —Confirmed as a full member of the United Methodist Church on Easter Sunday.

18th year: —Was a voting member at the Oregon-Idaho Annual Conference for the first time, where I became in volved in the gay-rights movement through the Reconciling

Ministries Network.

19th year: —Graduated in the Top Ten of my class from Hermiston High School. —Entered the University of Puget Sound, immediately becoming involved in both the United Methodist student group and the campus gay-straight alliance.

20th year: —Discovered my own bisexuality. (I spent the next couple of years coming to terms with what that meant for me and began to come out to close family and friends.)

21st year: —Began supporting myself for the first time with a summer job, moving to an off-campus house with several other students, and cooking for myself.

22nd year: —Spent my 21st birthday in Milan, Italy, where I studied for a semester. Then returned for a difficult, stressful semester at college.

23rd year: —Graduated from UPS with a B.A. in Music.—spent four weeks in Gualemala during the summer.

24th year: —Was a part of the Lutheran Volunteer Corps, working at Neighborhood House (a center for refugees, immigrants, and lneighborhood youth) and living in the Twin Cities.

25th year: —Moved to Honduras and helped found Amigas del Señor, a Methodist monastery in Limón, Colón.

This year: —I will be taking an eight-week trip to the U.S. from April twenty-seventh to June twenty-second, visiting Oregon and Minnesota. Then I will return to Honduras for another year (through June 2008).

Thanks for being a part of my life!

Beth—Prairie to visit the States—February 22, 2007

Yesterday was Ash Wednesday. So interesting to celebrate it here in Honduras. We never know when we are going to get another cultural exchange experience. The local pastor had to justify an Ash Wednesday service to the congregation. Apparently, Protestantism in Honduras is still very occupied with protesting against Roman Catholicism. It reminds me of stories my Mom tells me about her younger years. Ash Wednesday observance is considered very Catholic here and that is not good, obviously. I asked Carlos about having Prairie sing the invitation to communion. There is one in our hymnal that grabs us both a lot. So, he asked her to do that.

Well, there wasn't communion, but when Prairie got up to sing the invitation part that still remained on the program, the young music leader handed her a guitar (it was even tuned). Carlos told everyone the number in the hymnal and she led the song. Carlos held the microphone by the guitar (after all, they are used to electrified musical instruments). It was so cool. Prairie had such stage presence and, of course, she sings beautifully. I wish you could have been there.

We're putting together Prairie's itinerary in the States. Between her flights in and out of Portland, Oregon she will go to the Twin Cities to attend her sister Autumn's university graduation on May twenty-seventh. It is not clear how long she'll be in Minnesota.

Beth—Monday's Events—March 21, 2007

We have been very glad to have a quiet time, regrouping. On Monday, we needed to draw on all of that stored up physical and spiritual energy.

At about ten o'clock, Monday morning, we were walking down the street in Limón, when we ran into Sor Leonora, who runs the children's shelter. (She carefully avoids the word orphanage.) She now has forty-five kids. As we chatted, along came a teenage girl, carrying a toddler.

Soon she was pulling up her shirt in back, pulling down the neck, pulling up her pants—to demonstrate the marks made from the last beating she received from her mother. They looked a week old. Mom used a piece of firewood. The pieces of wood she uses are usually about three feet long and slender. Apparently, this is pretty regular event.

The girl pleaded with Sor to get her out of the house. Sor explained the long process required (which has not yet begun). She lives with her mother, but her father also lives in town.

We talked a bit. Sor had to leave to pick up her kindergarteners. This girl was scared and wanted out. I invited her to visit us. She leapt at the chance—knowing nothing, of course, about our lifestyle.

She is almost 14 and can't leave home without parental permission. So we decided to find her father, to get his permission (in writing). We walked to his house, then to another house where he probably was, then back to his house (just under a mile in all). He was obviously reluctant to do anything. He knows the situation and has done nothing so far. He suggests that we go to the government office responsible for the rights of minors. He said he would meet us there. No such thing; we would go together. (The word *coward* more than passed through my mind.)

Another half mile. The woman wasn't at her office. This time Dad slipped away. He said he would run an errand and meet us there. Along the way, we bought our groceries and cool drinks. We got to her house and waited. Soon she arrived. We all waited some more. She ran an errand. We ate our packed lunch. We waited some more. The toddler was by now tired and fretful.

Somewhere in here, the girl's cell phone rang and she had to go home to unlock the door to the house. She is the one with the key. Her sister arrived home and was locked out. We went to the house, put the exhausted toddler (who had lain down in the sand and fallen asleep) to bed, then to the house next door where the sister was. I was expecting her to be a younger sister since she wasn't the one with the keys. No such thing! She is an adult, in fact, a rather large adult. The keys are on a long lanyard that our young friend wears about her neck. She handed them over to her sister—who used the keys and lanyard like a whip to hit her. She hadn't even told us about the sister hitting her! This is closer to more normal levels of violence within the family; perhaps this is why it wasn't mentioned. It hurts, but it is not a beating.

We walked back to Dad's house, three-quarters of a mile. He was sitting outside eating his lunch. But at least now he seemed to have a little starch in his backbone. Back to the official's house we went. We all agree that this child needs to be safe. It is clear that only the father had any legal rights here. Since he was unwilling to give written (or even verbal) permission for her to go with us, I suggested that he could be the hero by taking her to his house and standing firm against the mother. (Mother works in Trujillo and is only home on weekends.)

At this suggestion, he switched to the Garifuna language, telling the official something. Then he announced that he had other errands to do and left.

The official was left to explain that this child was given to adoptive parents when she was very young. This explained why her family names didn't match the dad's or mom's. (Those people were likely to have all of the legal papers.) In fact, it was quite likely that he, the dad, had no legal rights at all. They lived in Tegucigalpa at that time.

Well, who were these people? Why did that situation change? Where were they now? They had sent the girl back to her mother for bad behavior. After she had repented, they had accepted her back again the first time—but later, no.

We knew the man. He was now with a different wife. So we went to his house. Our young friend had not been eager to discuss her family name (which is a famous name in these parts), nor was she very pleased about going to this house. It was, thankfully, fairly close. You'll notice that I have given up trying to keep track of the miles walked in this odyssey.

It was an incredibly rich house. The doors were open, but we could get no response to our calling or knocking. We left to get our mail. The postmaster wasn't home, so we went to his assistant's house.

After the mail, we tried again at the ex-adoptive-father's house. Still no answer. By now we were well convinced that nothing was going to change that day (or month). We went to the girl's house, where we had left our backpacks. She pleaded for us to stay the night in Limón. But there would be nothing we could do in the morning either.

It breaks my heart. All day, she held herself together (except to cry once, when the official and the father talked about sending her mother to prison, and the second time when she got hit). But she stuttered more and more as the day wore on.

We walked her over to Sor Leonara's place. We met her in the street again. The child now understood that she must do a legal fight for her safety and Sor is willing to work on her behalf. During the day, we had had a chance to tell the girl a little about our life. She was pretty shocked (no electricity! no near neighbors!), but she was still scared and desperate. She would still be happy to go with us if she could. Sor would take the next steps of investigating with the ex-adoptive father and the Office of Rights of Minors. I managed a short private conversation with her, in which we both understand that this child is unlikely to last even two weeks in our life situation. But we would accept her to keep her safe, pending a safe and more appropriate placement. (Sor has connections with residential programs for street kids that want a better life.)

We were exhausted. We stopped to visit Yesbil's mother. (Yesbil is our young man with rheumatic heart disease and sickle cell; he is doing great.) She gave us each a peeled orange and chatted with us a bit. She bought us some tortillas from a vendor and bade us a friendly good-bye as we left. We stopped for a few more conversations and rest—but no bus came along. Finally, it was 5:30 PM and the sun was setting. We started walking.

We got a lift, right to our road. It was dusk and the air was cool. We walked fast. Our last rest had restored us fairly well. It got darker and darker. We felt our way along the path from the road to the house. Prairie led the way. (Her night vision is a little better than mine.) We made jokes about how absent-minded we were to not have left the yard light on. By the time we got home, it was full night. No moon—but a fabulous star show. We took time to admire the stars before going in to our dinner of peanut butter and tortillas, and oranges. We had bought cheese, but somehow it had gotten lost during the day. We were very grateful to have food.

Tuesday, we rested a lot.

Prairie—Ash Wednesday, Lenten Observances, and a Corn Update—March 21, 2007

Ash Wednesday: We happened to be in El Pino for Ash Wednesday, the first day of Lent. That was exciting. We'd have a chance to observe the special day at the church. Well, what a surprise when we asked Pastor Carlos about the service they'd be having. He explained to us that in Honduras the observance of Ash Wednesday and Lent are seen as Catholic, and most Evangelicals (non-Catholics) see them as wrong. As Beth says, the Protestants here are still protesting the Roman Catholic Church, and ecumenism is almost unheard of. We were pretty impressed by this.

Interestingly, Carlos decided to go ahead and do an Ash Wednesday service. He opened it with a brief history of the tradition of the service and Lent, and told the congregation that they wouldn't go to hell for being there or observing Lent. He was really putting himself out on a limb by doing the service and going against such a strong tradition. Carlos talked about how the ashes used in an Ash Wednesday service usually come from the burnt palm fronds from the previous year's

Palm Sunday service. Therefore, he wouldn't be using ashes that night, "but perhaps this year we'll save the palms to use for next year's service." The service focused on repentance and a re-dedication of our lives to God, and ended with everyone forming a line and going to the front one by one, where Carlos used his thumb to make a cross on our foreheads.

Lenten Observances: At the same time that Beth and I moved out to the mountain at the end of July, we began a small-group spiritual formation course called *Companions in Christ* [See Reading List.]. The twenty-eight-week course included weekly readings and group meetings, as well as daily individual exercises. We had the chance to tell the story of our spiritual journeys, learn about (and practice) various forms of prayer and approaches to reading the bible, discover our spiritual gifts, and consider God's call for our lives both individually and as a group. It was through that course that I was able to discern God's call for me to stay at the monastery an additional year to continue to help in its establishment.

The course was such a profound experience for both of us that we wanted to find a way to continue our spiritual growth in a similar way after we finished. We were hungry for more spiritual practices in our lives, and I was interested in further trying out some of the new methods I'd learned about in the course.

When we looked at the calendar, we found that Lent began the week after our closing retreat in mid-February. (In Spanish, Lent is called *cuaresma* because it encompasses the *cuarenta*, or forty days before Easter—not including Sundays.) In the Catholic church and many Protestant churches like the Methodist one in which Beth and I were raised, Lent is a time for increased spiritual practices, most notably fasting. We thought, "What better time to try out these new things in our schedule?" So we made a list of the various practices we wanted to do, and how to fit them in. They include having a time of contemplative prayer in the afternoons, doing lectio divina (a type of meditative-spiritual reading) several days of the week, an examination of conscience every night, and a two-meal fast each week. At the end of Lent, we plan to review our experience, see how things went, and decide if we want to add any of these things to our regular monastic schedule. So far, it is going very well.

Also during Lent, we decided to focus on spring cleaning for our active work. That means we aren't doing any new planting in the garden until after Easter. Instead, we are weeding and mulching in the garden and around the house, cleaning the overgrowth along the south fence line, doing mending and sewing projects (new shirts, dresses, and pants to replace those wearing out), and sorting through things we no longer need. It feels like we have accomplished a lot in this area.

Corn update: Awhile back, I told about our adventures with cooking corn and making tortillas. Well, in January, we noticed we were having to do a lot more sorting of the corn than previously because of these little black bugs that were chewing holes in the kernels. We started asking friends what we should do about it. The solution was to solear the corn; that is, set it out it the sun for a few hours to kill the bugs and their larvae which grow in the kernels. When we finally had a sunny enough day, we did just that. Plus we tried pouring the corn from one tub to another to let the wind take away the dust, and hopefully some bugs. Unfortunately, we found that the bugs were heavy and not prone to flying away. They would climb up the sides of the tubs, however, so we could squish them by hand. We did a fair amount of sorting that day as well.

Well, the problem continued to get worse. The bugs, called *gorgojos* (weevils), continued to multiply. Not only were we sorting out one third to one half of the dry corn, but also, even after it was cooked, we were having to remove kernels that had the white larvae in them.

Sorting our corn

Finally, one day in February, when I was cooking the corn, I took out three kernels to test if they were done. The first two I squeezed, worms squished out. We decided then that the ratio was too high, and this would be our last batch.

We still had probably twenty pounds of corn left from the original hundred, so we put it in plastic bags to give to our friends as chicken feed. Last week, we gave the last bag to Warnita, one of the nurses at Centro de Salud. She reported to us on Monday that the dust in the corn made her chickens cough, and she had to give them medicine! What an ending to the corn.

Now we are back to buying *maseca* (corn flour) and carrying all our groceries on our backs each week.

We're doing a fair amount of baking as well, like corn bread, tamale pie, and baking-powder biscuits.

We are going to try to get some sourdough started this week.

Beth—Lenten Update—March 21, 2007

We are really having a wonderful Lent. Cleaning up, cleaning out, lots of spiritual practice, almost no travel (just today to Bonito to use internet and get some money out of the bank).

Part of our clean-up stuff includes paperwork: financial management, officially getting associated with the Honduran Methodist Church, struggling onward with the residency applications. These, too, need to be attended to, just like the garden. I am delighted that Prairie has written about our Lenten practices and the corn. Now that we have neither corn nor beans from our farmer friend, we have decided to take two backpacks to town each Monday to carry groceries home. The last few weeks, we have been able to bring home a dozen oranges, too. Very nice.

Since purchases of corn flour and purchased wheat flour cost about the same, our diet has more variety. How about that for a Lenten practice—more interesting food.

We have green beans (cowpeas and yard long beans) from the garden about three times a week (usually only one or two servings each time) and tiny Honduran tomatoes three or four times a week. When these crops started, we had about half a cup a day, but they have peaked. We are very grateful for them. One day, Prairie picked less than a cup, then counted that she had picked more than fifty small tomatoes. We had them as salad that day.

Beth—Finances, January–March, 2007

Yes, our property tax was two dollars for the year. We paid three dollars last year, because we forgot to get it in before the deadline so we missed the early-bird discount. The fact that we have since built on the property does not raise the taxes at all. What a delightful surprise that was!

We are learning how to be poor. We are in Tocoa and just ate our lunch—*baleadas* brought from home (a baleada is a refried bean sandwich made with a flour tortilla), water from home, and little mangoes bought on the street.

Only in the last few months have we started really noticing that if we get a lift, we save money on bus fare. Today we got a lift all the way to Bonito—helps a lot.

Four of the six dresses that we started with are still in use, although one of them, Prairie only wears at home as the next hole may very well make it indecent. We will officially retire it at the end of April. We each have three dresses and one pair of slacks. Keep it simple, you know. The blue fabric fades and a few people have referred to our habits as gray. Well, I guess they are more gray than blue when they are in their last months.

Beth—Easter and Travel—April 11, 2007

We are in Tocoa, today. Prairie is making some of her email arrangements for her trip to the States. We'll visit our friends in Ceibita tonight and sleep in the church there, then back to the monastery tomorrow.

We didn't do any traveling (overnight, that is) during Lent. It was very restful. We also didn't plant in the garden, just cleaned and organized. We cleaned and organized about the house, too. We began the weekly whitening of the stove that should be done, but that we had been doing too infrequently. The stove is made of clay. It cracks. If you smear it with a thin slurry of white clay every week, it stays pretty nice. If you let it go, the cracks get big and it is harder to fix. Now we have the habit of doing it every week.

We did quite a bit of sewing during Lent. We made a pair of pants and a dress for Prairie and a blouse for each of us. We had to make the blouse pattern that Yolanda made for me into one that would fit Prairie. We also modified our dress pattern to make a sleeveless variation. We were pushing ourselves to the limits of our sewing skills. Prairie now even knows how to hand-sew buttonholes.

We also did a two-day Holy Week retreat (Holy Friday and Holy Saturday, as they are called here). Then, on Easter morning, we did our sunrise service at the summit of our mountain. We didn't have a big sunrise show, but we had enjoyed the one the day before.

On Monday, we got a lift into town with a friend of ours who delivers the chip snacks to the stores in town. He always stops when he sees us. This time, we were waiting at Rosa's tienda with several other people. When he stopped to deliver to Rosa, I asked him for a ride. The cab is big and all four of us fit (him, the two of us, and his helper). Well, then another man who was waiting for a ride asked for a lift. But the cab was full. In Honduras, if you give a favor, you label yourself as giving favors and folks just ask for more and more. It is really quite amazing.

So, I was feeling bad about being the one to put him in such a spot. Then the man explained that the bus from Sico (really far away) had just dropped them all off at the entrance to Limón when they had been hoping to be taken into Limón. There was a woman sitting with her luggage—at least four large crates and coolers (two-persons-to-carry coolers). The driver said, "Don't worry." They pulled up near to all of the luggage and then they put the luggage and the folks in the back of the closed truck. Off we all went to Limón (about two miles). I was pretty glad to be riding in the cab, not in the dark closed truck. It was pretty nice to get to be an observer up close and personal to this Good Samaritan. When I said something like that to him, he said that he had just been thinking about his—and then he used a word that means either career or race. This experience helped to put it in perspective. We cheerfully thanked him for the ride and went off to Centro de Salud. I was the only doctor, but still only had to see fifteen patients, but I saw quite a few adults this time.

It is Honduran tradition to bathe in the ocean on Holy Friday or Holy Saturday (or both). I asked our friend (who lives in Tocoa), what the folks do there. They go to the rivers or take the bus all the way to Trujillo or La Ceiba (where there is a beach).

After our work at the clinic, we went to visit a woman who

had walked into town with us two weeks ago. We had told her about Prairie's trip and that I shouldn't be living there alone. She thought that would be a good time for her nineteen-year-old daughter to come to the mountain. We had given her and the daughter a little time to think it over and then visited with them. The daughter is a city girl and is sort of scared of the idea of living without electricity. We'll chat with them again next week.

We have some new temporary neighbors. They are living in the house across the little valley from us. They are living there while they fix up their land for cow pasture—a month or two. There are a dozen of them, from the twenty-five-year-old chief and his wife and their two-year-old son, through a few other couples, including a fourteeen-year-old girl. (Yes, I said, couples) and a year-old baby.) We walked over to visit on Easter afternoon. The ladies have stopped by twice this week to visit. The fourteen and fifteen-year-olds came running and laughing up the path on Monday afternoon. Children, but already living with their male compañeros. The little one, especially, is still such a child. It breaks my heart. This is very common here.

Beth—Sourdough—April 11, 2007

A few weeks ago, I noticed that our bottle of molasses had froth on top. Sure enough, the odor and flavor demonstrated a bit of a bite. It had started to work. We had talked about yeast bread and sourdough, but had not yet tried anything in that direction. We found that we can buy yeast, but in the package size suitable for a bakery, not the size suitable for a small household with no refrigeration.

We got out our instructions for making sourdough. It worked beautifully. We watched it carefully—truly it is alive. We have had sourdough bread, sourdough pancakes and sourdough tortillas.

Since we ran out of corn, we have had to buy corn flour

as well as wheat flour. Much to our amazement, we learned that corn flour, right now, costs more than wheat flour. So we switched our diet from corn, corn and more corn (because it was the cheapest staple we could get) to more wheat flour.

We are enjoying our homemade sourdough products. Just as we took Lent very seriously, we are taking Easter seriously. The church calendar has Easter lasting forty days. We are thinking about treating ourselves to some version of cinnamon rolls during this Easter time. We even ended up with a starched hanky. When we mixed up the sourdough sponge, we put a damp cloth over it. Then when we mixed up the next step, again, we put a damp cloth over the top. Well, the breeze entered our kitchen of course. Normally, we are very grateful for said breeze; after all, we cook with a wood fire. It gets hot in the kitchen. But the breeze grabbed the hanky, and it got dipped into the batter. Sourdough batter is very sticky. When we rinsed it, it was heavily starched. We washed it in the regular laundry and then it was lightly starched. I have folded it and used it at the table as my napkin. Who would ever have guessed that we would choose poverty and be using a starched napkin? Life gets pretty weird sometimes.

Prairie—Lent and Easter—April 24, 2007

In my last update I talked about our Lenten practices, so it seems appropriate to follow up with what we did for Holy Week and Easter.

We really wanted to observe Holy Week and take time to contemplate the story of Jesus' suffering and death—something, in my experience that many Protestants seem to gloss over. We celebrated Palm Sunday with appropriate hymns in our morning worship. Starting that afternoon and through Wednesday we read some of the stories that purportedly took place during that week (Jesus purifying the temple, and the woman anointing him with perfume, for example). We used

Mark's gospel all week for the sake of consistency, with just a couple of additions from John, like the washing of the disciples' feet.

We decided to follow a retreat schedule for Maundy Thursday, Good Friday, and Holy Saturday, which meant that most of our normal work was put aside. We also decided to have no guitar accompaniment during those days to add to the solemnity. I planned a special service for Thursday evening, sort of a reenactment of the last supper, washing of the disciples' feet and then their time at the Mount of Olives and Gethsemane. I felt it was a very spiritual atmosphere, with candles and lamp light, reading the stories to each other, singing hymns, and doing the actions Jesus instructed.

On Friday, the weather was appropriately gloomy with cold and rain. We spent the bulk of the day reading of Jesus' suffering and death in small segments, with times of silent reflection and journaling in between. I found it to be a very good exercise, though my rear end was pretty sore after several hours of sitting.

Beth planned Saturday, which was a bit less intense, and involved imagining ourselves in the disciples' shoes, the day after their teacher and Lord had been crucified. What pain and dejection and disappointment they must have felt!

By Easter Sunday, we were ready to go with the disciples to the tomb and find it empty, and celebrate the resurrection of Christ. We had our morning worship on the summit, like so many sunrise services (although with the clouds, there was no colorful sunrise that day). We had also eaten very simply and fasted during the previous couple of days, so on Sunday we enjoyed some special foods including sautéed potatoes and onions and a meal of refried beans, Spanish rice, and fried tortilla chips.

Since Easter weekend, our guests have included: Polo, the guy who sold us the corn, and who gives near-sermons about God and demons; a group of young couples and children who are living at Lencho's place next door for a time while the men clean up their land; a fifteen-year-old boy from Lauda (a nearby village) who was interested in seeing how we live; Jacinto, a Pentecostal preacher who sometimes stops in on his way to La Fortuna and gives us pep talks about God's goodness and prays for us; and a woman and her daughter from Limón who wanted to see our place and, we had hoped, might be interested in staying with Beth while I'm gone. (It looks unlikely.) It is always interesting to chat with these folks, and we learn so much about how Hondurans live and their cultural and religious outlooks on life.

Now I am about to return to the U.S. for an eight-week visit. I'm quite excited, and will send my itinerary in a separate email. Please keep Beth and the monastery in your prayers during this time.

Beth—A Long Dramatic Day—April 26, 2007

On Monday, we walked towards town, like usual. When we were approaching Rosa's place, we noticed a lot of people and vehicles parked there. We couldn't figure out what was going on. Then as we got closer, I thought I saw a body on the ground. Then it moved!

So, I started walking a little faster. Sure enough, there was an older man lying on the ground. He had a scalping injury— from just above his eyes with the left side worse than the right. Lots of blood. No one had provided any first aid. The folks thought that they could get in trouble with the law if they touched him. And they told me that I should follow their example. I had nothing in my backpack that would be of the least bit of use. He had been lying there for two hours.

I talked to him and he could understand me (even with my thick accent). But when I asked him for his approval to take him to the hospital, he answered, "Mañana." Well, by U.S. legal and medical ethical standards, one must have permission from the patient if he is conscious. He certainly was conscious and was refusing transport! If someone is unconscious, by U.S. law, he is giving permission—which he can withdraw when he becomes capable, if he so wishes. The folks thought that we needed police permission.

The ambulance was there. The driver kept it locked up tight until proper permission was obtained. There was no police officer present at first. I knelt in an attitude of prayer on the road by the injured man and cried a little bit, then prayed, then got up and started doing what I had to do.

The police officer had arrived and was slowly collecting the data for his criminal investigation. Gossip says that the buses were "fighting," which I take to mean, racing. This elder got hit by a bus going far faster than was safe at this T-intersection bus stop. He was apparently run over. He had a pretty bad injury of his left leg, but it was his scalping injury that would take his life if he didn't get help.

I told the cop that he would live with prompt help and would die without it and that we should take him to Bonito to get IV fluids started and then to the hospital. Our Centro de Salud clinic was closed up because of the Immunization Campaign. (It sometimes has IV stuff and sometimes doesn't.) He was surprised to hear that the guy could live and realizing that we would go with him helped. The cop finally gave permission. The ambulance driver called for a rag to cover his wound and Rosa donated a child's clean shirt. We wrapped it around the victim's head turban-style and off we went, Prairie in the front seat with the driver and me in the back with our poor brother. When our patient needed to vomit, I helped him turn to the side so he could vomit on the floor. There was nothing else to do. The ambulance gurney had one strap to go across the patient's waist. By the way, you are probably noticing that now we are transporting this injured, but conscious man against his wishes. But, by now he was actually very cooperative.

The road was rough and shook the man so that one leg or

the other kept falling off the gurney. On the curves, he was at risk of falling entirely off on the side opposite from me. I held his left hand with my left hand—handshake style. It was a memorable image—my pale, freckled, clean hand with his dark-skinned hand, filthy with dust and gravel from the road, bright shiny red blood, dark brown dried blood. We were quite the pair. We just hung on to each other.

At Bonito, the Centro de Salud was open and the nurse and physician were very helpful, but we couldn't keep an IV in the victim's arm. The vein kept blowing —wouldn't take the needle. Off we went with our patient still getting drier and drier. (By the way, we had learned that he also has diabetes—not that we could do anything about that either.)

Prairie had the camera along, but she didn't find our patient very photogenic. His forehead was hanging down over his left eye to his cheek bone. His skull was pretty much bare and there was, as I said, a lot of blood everywhere.

Off we went from Bonito. I had asked Prairie to move into the back to hold up the IV. From there the road was much better, less risk of the patient falling off the gurney. After he vomited, even though he didn't aspirate, it was clear that his mind was starting to wander a bit—effects of blood loss.

The hospital personnel accepted him and took over from there. I was quite grateful for someone else to do this complicated patch job and evaluation for other injuries and finish the treatment.

When we were all still riding along (with lots of his blood all over) I remembered our readings from Julian of Norwich that we had used as part of our Holy Week Retreat and her vision of Christ on the cross with the crown of thorns. She got all graphic about the skin hanging down like wet cloth. Well, that's what was happening with our own Christ figure in the back of the ambulance. And so, I rode to Tocoa holding hands with Jesus, just as graphic as Julian of Norwich. She's quite the gal. If you haven't read her book, it's still in print—500 years after she wrote it. [*Revelations of Divine Love Julian of Norwich*, Penguin Classics, 1999].

After we delivered our friend, I washed the blood off of myself as well as I could and the ambulance driver told us the next stop was the car wash (to clean up the blood, of course). We could do errands if we wished. So we did. We did our telephone calling pertaining to our trip to La Ceiba and we bought groceries and went back to the car wash. We met Miguel, husband of friend Melba, and chatted with him. The Vice-Mayor of Iriona (the home town of our patient) was there at the car wash. The ambulance driver had told him about the whole thing and he had called the family to tell them where the man was. The cop on the site had sent us to Trujillo, but thank God, the physician at Bonito told the driver to take him to Tocoa.

This was more excitement than we had planned on. We decided that even though we had done our shopping, we would go all the way back to Limón just to get our mail. The week before, our postmaster was out of town and the substitute was out and about and we couldn't get our mail. With Prairie leaving town this week, it seemed important to get the mail. There were seventeen pieces. Yeah!

We realized that we had forgotten to get powdered milk, so we stopped at Andres' store. There were no other customers, so we had a nice visit. We finally got to have the chat about the asthma medicine that I would like to have him carry for my kids. It seems like asthma attacks always start in the evening when the clinic is closed. We are not permitted to give mothers medicine to have at home. But I can advise them to have it around. I have waited for a year for just the opportunity to have this conversation without interruption. Cool.

We had also forgotten to get rapadura. We went to the tiendas that sells that and our friend had such a sad face that we had to hear the whole story. Her nineteen-year-old son is in jail and about to be deported from the U.S. Before he went to the States he had gotten in with the drug dealers or smugglers.

She had asked him to leave the house because of that. In Texas though, her cousin took him under his wing and he thrived on the strict control from this older man. The son also sent money—only ten to thirty dollars a month, but that small amount paid the electric, water, and cable bills for his mother. Now she is really worried—will he go back to his bad companions and get himself killed? How will she manage the household finances without those contributions from him? She hasn't seen him in three years, but only has sadness to think about him coming home with a harder time for the whole family. A tough deal.

We were tired. We caught a bus to Rosa's and brought her up to date. (She is sort of the news center, of course, for her location.) She was happy to know that the accident-patient lived—at least until we handed him off. We caught a lift to our road.

We had eaten part of our packed lunch (beans and sourdough tortillas) in the ambulance in town while waiting for the driver to run more errands, but we usually stop for lunch on our walk home. It was a very hot day and we were happy to sit for a bit in the shade, eat a little more, and read some of our mail aloud. We stopped a few more times because it was really very hot.

Back at the monastery, after afternoon prayers, we began dinner preparation. I made the fire in the fogon and started the rice dish while Prairie bathed. The idea was that then she would take over the food preparation and I would bathe. But along came three young men from our neighbors.

They had brought *hijos de plátanos*—young plátano plants to plant for us. Not just to give to us, but to plant for us. Such helpful neighbors! So, we had to decide on the spot where to put the plants. We directed them to the east of the house, what I think of as the back yard. They put down some manure, watered them and now we're set. Cool. They also brought some of the fruit for us to eat. Amazing! Prairie continued dinner preparation as they worked and I watched. We could give the guys drinks of water and a little snack of fried green plátanos before they left the monastery for home. It was darker than I was comfortable with when they left.

Our complete dinner was rice with onions and carrots, beans, and fried green plátanos. Pretty nice. We cleaned up, did our contemplation time, had bedtime prayers and I fell into bed. I slept very well that night. No, I didn't get to bathe. That had to wait until the next morning. But when I took off my dirty dress, at least the blood smell left me, even if the sweat smell stayed.

Well, this was quite the novel. But I wanted you to have the whole picture of the day.

Beth—In El Pino, Prairie in U.S.—April 28, 2007

Last I told you about Monday. Now I'll tell you about the rest of the week.

Tuesday, we did laundry, cut firewood, picked cowpeas and yard-long beans, took some seedlings in planting bags down to be next to the creek while I'm gone, finished packing and did our usual Saturday chores so that the house will be in order whatever day I return.

Wednesday, we left the house on foot. But Prairie had two pieces of luggage—her backpack and a soft-side pull-style suitcase (full of all the stuff that we don't need to have as borrowed stuff anymore). She carried it on her head, Honduran-style. Our path is not really hospitable to pull luggage.

We heard a car coming, and sure enough, we get to the road and get a ride instantly. Wow!

Walked from our road to Rosa's to wait for a bus, arriving much earlier than usual. Bus to Tocoa. Changed buses and on to La Ceiba. We had baleadas for lunch. Prairie had made them before we left the house—using the leftover beans to make refried beans and the folded-over sourdough tortillas. We bought juice in the bus.

We arrived in El Pino to find that a visiting team was present and was, at that very moment, having a communion service. They invited us to join in. What a wonderful blessing! Then I did a house call. We did get to rest, just a little later—after dinner. There was no evening program at the church that night. Often, when there are visiting teams, the church programming is put on hold. The same folks are just too tired from their busy days with the teams.

Thursday we got up early for breakfast at Doña Ada's and on to the bus to San Pedro Sula. Arrived there before eleven AM. We found a hotel that fit our budget, 120 lempiras(six dollars and fifty cents) for two of us. Included for the price: two bars of soap, separate beds, towels, and toilet paper. We shared a bathroom with all the other residents of that floor. The shower had its own door. The toilet had its own door and the two sinks are in the hallway. Our neighbor, shaving at a sink, greeted us cheerfully. Privacy is expensive. We had a fan in our room, too. Never mind all the peeling paint. We washed and hung up our laundry first thing.

We checked out bookstores and found two books that we think will add to our library. Just that much shopping took most of the day. San Pedro Sula is famous for being hot. It earns this reputation, but it cooled down nicely in the late evening. Even though we were right downtown, the streets were pretty quiet by the time we went to bed. We were on the top floor, which included an open, patio-type, rooftop. I especially enjoyed looking down at the traffic. We were right next to a taxi pick-up spot, so there was a lot to see on the street.

On Friday—departure day for Prairie—we walked down to the central square to get an early breakfast. Prairie bought two baleadas to have for traveling food. After all, airlines don't feed travelers anymore. She also took along the leftover mangoes. We got this great deal—end of the day special—a bag of small mangoes for ten lempiras. (I'm guessing about nine were in the bag.) She would have to eat them before landing in the States, but that would be hours from now.

We went to the bus station and bought my ticket. Prairie reminded me that I am entitled to the third age discount (10% off for those 50+). The ticket seller wouldn't sell Prairie's ticket. He said she would have to buy it on the bus and she had to pay full price. I was not willing to send her on one bus and me on another, so we both paid full price. Prairie should have arrived in Portland last night about nine. I haven't heard, yet, of course.

On my solo return trip, the bus broke down on the way to La Ceiba. The bus driver got all the passengers on another bus and even paid the fare. This amazed me. I have never gotten that kind of service from a bus company before. When a bus breaks down, we're usually simply on our own. I joined Janet Corlett[28] and pastors Randy and Pablo for late lunch in La Ceiba and learned a little more about local church politics.

Then back to El Pino where I was put to work right away translating stuff and comparing notes with the visiting team. They have decided to fund two more childcare workers for the feeding program. They thought one woman for fifty kids was the wrong ratio.

At dinner we found that the visiting team served the Hondurans and were apparently going to eat later themselves. This is always a problem for me. After vacillating for a while, I decided to eat with the Hondurans. Usually, when foreigners have one role and Hondurans another, I go with the Hondurans. Salvador (our seventy-something friend who had the big bladder-stone removed in January) was my courtly escort. On my other side was Denis. Denis is a middle-aged man with a huge smile. He is a skilled woodcarver who sells his work and teaches youngsters how to do the same work. His wife is the head cook for the kids' program. He gets around in a wheelchair. Well, I am nothing if not curious. This was a gift of time

---

28 Janet is a Methodist pastor from the Isle of Man; she was on temporary assignment as supervisor to the lay pastors.

for me. I was able to ask him about how it happens that he is in a chair.

He told me. Seven years ago, his sister had died of AIDS. She died in Tegucigalpa about eleven PM one night. He and his mother were headed there for the wake (at least the word he used seems more like wake than funeral to my experience). A big truck hit them. He could hear his mother as she was dying, but he could not move to get to her. He felt something odd in his back and nothing below that. His daughter was two months old at that time. He still gets scared about wakes, he said. His eyes filled just a bit even telling the story. His wife had two babies in the bed for awhile he says—their daughter and him. His story includes the dreams that he has sometimes had of running, riding a bicycle, walking, driving a standard-transmission truck—then waking up to notice that his legs still don't work.

I thanked him for sharing this story with me. Then he thanked me for asking. He said that he thinks most people assume that any spinal cord injury here comes from a bullet in a fight and he likes to set the record straight. He is probably right. I have seen two men with spinal cord injuries—one from a bullet in the war with El Salvador and the other from a bullet in a fight. So, the record is straight.

I wonder how long it would have been before I had heard that story if that visiting team hadn't decided to serve that dinner. So many blessings just fall into my lap. I am very grateful.

Oh, yes, the food was good, too. Well, here I am in El Pino for a few more days, at least.

Beth—Happy Labor Day!—May 1, 2007

The First of May is Labor Day for most of Latin America. The clinic and the children's program here at El Pino are closed as are banks and schools.

There is a visiting team of volunteer builders here at El Pino. They are working as usual. An overcast day yesterday—

perfect for lots of sunburn. And they take it in stride.

Yesterday, I worked with Eloyda. We saw patients in her large exam room. We sat side-by-side, she seeing adults and me seeing children. This allowed us to compare ideas easily. (I also think we give better care this way.) There is no privacy, obviously, but no one would really expect privacy.

I saw an 11-year-old boy. He had an attack of left-sided head pain, belly pain, vomiting and looked ashen. He even seemed to be febrile. I took a careful history and examined him. He has an odd form of migraine. Physicians call it "abdominal epilepsy." He had good grades in fourth grade, but now in fifth grade, because of this illness, he was not doing well at all. I started him on Tegretol, but, of course, we don't carry that medicine in our basic pharmacy. Well, this very charming retired lady, who is part of the visiting work team, gave 200 lempiras (just over ten dollars) to get him started on his medicine. It is pretty handy to have rich friends sometimes.

Besides seeing patients, we packed up a box of medicines and supplies that this clinic can spare for Centro de Salud in Limón. I'll take it to the bus station tomorrow to send it off. I don't like to ship something on the same bus in which I travel.. It would be cheaper to take the medicine box on the bus with me, but it would be less secure. These are very valuable medicines to our patients. It is better to be careful.

We made up a list of the meds we needed. The phone was out of order so Eloyda will call it in tomorrow and I'll make the deposit of money when I know how much it will cost. Our tithes go primarily to pay for orders like this one.

The visiting team also asked for a wish list of things for when their local church sends another team in September. Eloyda and I had no trouble making up that list. Also, they wanted to know how much money to raise to help buy Honduran pharmaceuticals. Eloyda didn't want to name a number, so I did—$1,000. From September to February, no teams come and she is really conscientious about keeping the most important medicines on hand. They didn't bat an eye at this outrageous sum of money.

Lola, the jack-of-all-trades in the clinic, would like to visit the monastery with me. It became clear that all of the single young women in the El Pino church are studying. The few who are not in classes of one kind or another have jobs. But mostly, they have greater interest in men than in a potential life of celibacy. Since it seemed best to have someone come with me, I let the women of the church know that I would accept someone who was not considering herself a monastic candidate (namely a woman who is married or has underage children). Lola is both married and has under-aged children. She also has a job and studies junior high education on the weekends. She has permission to be gone from her job, but we still haven't had a good conversation about life on the mountain. On further reflection, she may decide not to come, after all. Or, I may decide that she shouldn't come.

Saturday, I was ready to sew. The sewing machines were locked in the storage closet so I couldn't. Yesterday afternoon, we got one out. Hopefully, I can at least make some progress on my next dress today. One of mine is on borrowed time. I didn't even bring it along on this trip. All three of my dresses have lasted fifteen months. But that is the one that I had used the most.

Beth—Community of One—May 9, 2007

In the last message you got from me, Lola was planning to visit the mountain with me. Lola has migraines and she had a whopper. She couldn't go, after all. She and I will arrange for her to come another time—hopefully the idea won't get her so excited that she gets another migraine.

I had to decide what to do—go back to the mountain alone—or stay in El Pino. When I was finally ready to make the decision, it wasn't that hard. Life is pretty busy at El Pino and it is pretty hard to live a monastic schedule there. Especially, it is hard to take Sunday as a day of rest. I buy food, after all. And nothing happens around there all day, so it doesn't feel like rest, it feels like penance.

Friday morning I left on my own. I wanted to be at the monastery for Saturday, so I could wash the laundry, cook the beans and, in general, tidy up so that I would be ready for a real day of rest. It was a little odd doing all the chores one at a time. Usually, one person cooks while the other washes laundry. This is a very social time since these tasks are right next to each other. Now, I'm not complaining about the work. After all, one person doesn't make much laundry. I'm just noticing how different it was.

Sunday was delightful. No conflicts of interest at all. Rest, some interesting books to read. Group worship as usual for a Sunday. After a week in El Pino, I kept expecting to be interrupted, but it didn't happen.

Monday off to Limón, earlier than usual. I arrived at Rosa's just as a bus was pulling up. Connie, the student nurse was alone in the clinic, so we got right to work. The two of us saw several patients and then the other folks arrived and pitched in. Monday can be pretty busy, nothing especially interesting this time, just the usual worms, pneumonia, rashes, asthma, diarrhea. The box of medicines (for high blood pressure and prenatal vitamins) and gloves from Eloyda in El Pino had arrived at Andrés' store and one of the nurses picked it up. The storage room for the pharmacy supplies had been recently completely re-organized. I realized today that I ordered some medicines that I needn't have ordered. Sigh. The bill was about twice as large as I had expected, but that's okay. I have a red ink pen. This is the first time that I had to use it in our account book.

No mail arrived this last week, but I had three letters from the week when I had been gone. It would have been pretty hard to have no Prairie and no mail. I bought a few groceries and along came a bus. It was quite the day for buses; I only had to think of one and there it was.

Interesting that none of our friends who had warned about personal safety even lifted an eyebrow with me being alone. Talk is cheap.

I got home much earlier than usual for a Monday. It was a hot walk, so I took my time. I stopped to read letters in the shade. That is something that we do most weeks. A nice break when it is hot.

Tuesday (yesterday), I got out the sewing. When I got out the sewing machine in El Pino to work on my dress, I found that I had made an important error. I would have to remake the facing for the armholes and change the back of the arm-hole. I have to make my own patterns here and I am not very good at it.

When we had made Prairie's sleeveless dress, the armholes didn't match up right. When I fixed it on the pattern for my dress, I goofed. So, yesterday's project was to sort out if it was even salvageable and, if so, how. Well, it was. Two wrongs seem to have made a right. The sleeveless dress is really a little more like a jumper now, with deeper armholes. I finished the second armhole this morning and tried it on. Of course, I don't have a mirror, so I can't say for sure, but I think it is okay. I can finish the rest of it when I get home.

I'm in Tocoa and will spend this evening with the ladies at the church in Ceibita. Tomorrow I go to El Pino to meet María, who has been in the Peace Corps for the last three and a half years. She was introduced to me (by mail) by my friend, Sister Angela, in Mount Angel, Oregon. María will spend a little time with me on the mountain. I think she is used to a faster-paced life. I hope that she finds our slower pace refreshing.

Beth—Irma—May 10, 2007

I spent last night at La Ceibita and thought you might like to know about Irma. Irma is one of the very active church volunteers there. She is twenty-seven years old. Her oldest child is eleven. She has four kids and has been married for the last three years. She showed me a wedding picture—a snapshot. She has been the president of the women's club for the last three years. She keeps saying that someone else should do a turn, but they keep re-electing her. She administers the scholarship program[29] for thirty-five elementary school children. United Methodist Churches in the states send money for uniforms, shoes, notebooks, pencils, vitamins, even de-worming twice a year. She is especially interested in this work because she grew up without a dad and had to work hard selling things after school to work her own way through elementary school. She wants a better life for the children in this community and is very grateful for the scholarships that are sent and are providing for a better life for the children who receive them. She visits the school once a month to check on the academic progress of the kids. If they are not doing well, she visits the parents.

Irma herself only finished sixth grade. She is now the volunteer teacher for the literacy program held in the church. She has ten students. She does first and second grade. There is no volunteer for more advanced grades. One of the ladies in the church group is one of her students. Reading the Bible is a very important spiritual practice here in Honduras. She really was grateful when we all reassured her that listening to the Bible being read is the same as reading. I told her about my Mom, who is ninety and almost blind. She does her reading now by listening. Well, this was nice for her to hear. Nobody likes to feel like a shirker, after all.

Irma is also a volunteer with the public health department. People come to her house and she can collect a drop of blood for a malaria test and give a few simple medicines. Once a month she makes a report of her activities to the local nurse.

Irma is also the designated evangelizing outreach person

---

29 *Becas con Bendiciones.*

for the church. I don't entirely understand that job. She went to a conference to help her with it. We have some really feminist women in this church. They know every Bible story with a woman in it and the importance of that woman's action, decision, or whatever. Very impressive. As a result, the men are pretty much afraid to set foot in the church. (Oops, editorial comment, accuracy highly suspect.)

Irma feeds me refried beans and tortillas when I visit. Last night there was *cuajada*, a type of white cheese, sort of like curds of cottage cheese formed into a mass. I like it and can't get it in Limon. She cooks beans, and other things that take a lot of time, in the backyard on a traditional wood stove. She does her indoor cooking on a two-burner gas stove.

Irma and her husband have bought a television recently. It is a small one, but yet smaller ones are available. She turned it on as soon as she got in. You'll be happy to know that Latin America has its full share of televangelists. I know her well enough now to ask some pretty personal questions as you can see. The television is bought on time—six months. They pay 500 lempiras (about twenty-eight dollars) per month. They don't have a refrigerator. Refrigerators cost more than televisions. That is next on the wish list. Most people in Honduras choose the television before the refrigerator.

The woman who was supposed to lead the evening women's devotions didn't show up so Irma did that, too after about two minutes preparation. Irma also goes about the neighborhood on foot or on her bicycle selling tee-shirts to earn cash for the ministry.

This is an especially busy week for the women's group. They have done several fundraisers so that they can put on a Mother's Day dinner on Sunday evening. They also drew names and will give one another Mother's Day gifts. They were pretty disappointed that I didn't feel that I could stay to help celebrate on Sunday. We are always so happy to see one another that they see me as a bringer of joy. It's really quite lovely. They are all pleased that Prairie will be returning. Prairie has a small fan club of eight-to ten-year-old girls in these little churches.

Prairie—Prairie's Travels around the U.S.—May 22, 2007

I arrived in Oregon on April twenty-seventh after a couple of days' travel in Honduras by bus and then a day on the plane. It was great to have my parents and grandmas waiting to greet me at the airport. I spent the first week and a half at my parents' house, mostly sorting through my belongings. Part of the discernment of my sense of call to stay in Honduras, for at least another year, included the sense that I needed to let go of many of my things in the U.S.. They had felt sort of like a back-up plan, just in case I should return to the U.S. someday and need to set up a household. I realized that if I am following God's call, then if and when I am called back to the U.S., I need to trust that somehow things will work out for whatever it is I end up doing. So I was able to get rid more than five boxes of items—clothes, books, knick-knacks, kitchen supplies, linens. I still kept another five boxes of more sentimental things like journals, photos, and my clarinet and clarinet music.

May ninth through the fourteenth I spent in the Tacoma, Washington region and got to see numerous old friends—fellow graduates, alumni, and staff—at the University of Puget Sound. I hadn't been back since I graduated in 2004. Coming into town, the train rounded a bend and all of a sudden downtown Tacoma appeared with Mount Rainier looming behind it and I had the sense of returning home. That surprised me, because I have never associated home with place in my life, as I've moved around so much. It was a beautiful weekend, with lovely weather and, of course, gorgeous green trees and yards and flowering plants. I also got to spend a couple days in the woods on the Key Peninsula.

Last week I spent a day at Queen of Angels Monastery (Benedictine Sisters, Mt. Angel) in Oregon, visiting a Sister

Beth knows. It was my first experience at a more established monastery, and it was good. On Thursday I hopped aboard the train and two days later arrived in the Twin Cities of Minnesota where I am currently, visiting family and friends. I'll be returning to Oregon on the train with my Mom and sister next week.

Also during my time here, I've been sharing my experiences in Honduras with various churches. I gave a presentation at my mom's church in Sweet Home, Oregon the first week I was back. I then spoke at the church I'd attended in Tacoma, and this week at the church I'd attended in Minneapolis. So these have been another chance to see old friends and tell people about what I've been doing. It's been fun to share songs and stories, and to try to answer all the great questions people ask me.

Beth—Maria's visit—May 29, 2007

Maria was with me for just under a week. Her project in El Salvador required her presence there. She had hoped to be able to do the financial part by telephone or internet, but it was not to be. Her project is really pretty cool. She made an instructional coloring book about earthworms. Here in Central America, many farmers think that earthworms are pests, that they are the little buggers who eat roots. Wrong. The language doesn't help either. There are only two words to use; the most common one is also used for intestinal parasite. The less common one is used to describe worms that are definitely pests for farmers. So, just getting folks to see earthworms as the farmer's friends that they are is a big job.

The coloring book is charming and engaging. It also features the Creator, creating. That's where the problem came in. The obvious source of funding for a Peace Corps Volunteer would be the U.S government. It wasn't approved, so Maria sought donations. What a challenge. Well, anyway, she will get some of the coloring books printed up for the school teachers who are all ready with their earthworm curriculum.

Maria brought gifts. She brought us some earthworms. She set them up in a hanging earthworm farm in the *sanitario* (bathroom). She had it hanging up so that ants, toads, and chickens couldn't get them. She taught me how to feed and water them and we're in business. They should double in number (we have a dozen) in a month. We'll see what happens.

We did another project while she was here. We made two mini-terraces for fruit trees in the garden. We talked a lot, of course.

She also left a lot of her Peace Corps agricultural information. I haven't read all of it. There is a lot. This is a very welcome resource. A lot of our farming questions had gone unanswered. This should help.

Thursday she left, walked to the bus by one of the neighbor teenage boys, and I did my retreat day. A few days later, the young people who are the neighbors also left. I spent a week on the mountain completely *sola*—just me and God.

Beth—Remember the Guy—May 29, 2007

Remember the chips delivery guy who gave us a lift and then also gave a ride to some other people who had a lot of luggage? Remember that he said he had been thinking about his career (or race, as in rat race)? Well, last week he gave me a lift again. He was all smiles and he was alone this time.

He has decided that he wants to be a missionary—town to town, house to house. He wants to do it full time. He took a huge first step. He is now traveling alone. His bodyguard had been a little scrawny guy who didn't carry a gun, so this is not really as dramatic a change as it may sound. He says that now he has three bodyguards, the Father, the Son, and the Holy Spirit. It was a short conversation, of course, but full of information. He is an ecumenical Baptist. He says he robs whatever is good from all of the other churches. His wife is a Jehovah's Witness, but she is not against the idea of her husband being a missionary. Fascinating. I wonder when next we'll run into him and what the next step will be in his journey.

We are told that the old man who was hit by the bus and that we accompanied to the hospital did not survive. We are told that the bus driver is in jail. It will be months before we know whether this is really accurate news or gossip.

A three-year-old girl died last Thursday in Limón. She died of pneumonia. Her family brought her to the clinic when she was moribund. Ignorance can be fatal.

Javier is one of our neighbor boys. He is sixteen years old and partnered with Reina, the fourteen-year-old girl. Javier has been earning a living for four years now. He says that he attended school for five years, but never learned anything and didn't get out of first grade. Then he did construction for three years. He has done the farming stuff for a year and really likes that. We talked a bit and agreed that being able to sign his name would be really good. People have four names here: two family names and two personal names. Well, one of his personal names is Javier. I went into the house for chalk. We used the water tank for a chalkboard and he practiced and practiced his name. I encouraged him to only practice that one name that day. We can add another name another day. A signature here really only requires one of the personal names and one of the family names. I got out our alphabet book and we went through it together. He really does know most of the letters. He liked the alphabet book and he was such an attentive student, it was delightful. He had come over on Thursday afternoon. (I fast instead of having lunch on Thursdays.) I was really aware of how hungry I was. As soon as we got involved in our mini literacy lesson, my hunger was forgotten. A useful experience.

Beth—Saturday Morning—May 30, 2007

I decided to do afternoon prayers early on Saturday. The forest fire was a little too close and a little too interesting. Frankly, I didn't concentrate even with doing prayers early.

The neighbors have been preparing pasture for cows. They cut down the weeds and saplings and then burned them. (This is not the recommended procedure by the scientific folks, but it is the local tradition.)

The fire got away. They usually do (my opinion). Well, this one got away and started going through the forest. I could see that it was a cool fire—that is, it was just taking out the small stuff while the big trees were fine. That was good news.

The fire was south of our house, just across a small valley. The west flank was heading further west, where it would stop by the road. There was a good breeze from the north, which kept it from heading in our direction.

It was the east flank that was interesting. It was going downhill. Fire, as you know, usually goes uphill. I have to respect a bit more a fire that descends the hill (especially in my direction). The breeze from the north was nicely blocked by our mountain, so it was no help. It is an interesting experience, watching the forest fire come towards your home, listening to it crackle. Very compelling, you might say. (I have to pity you poor folks with your televisions!) It took a millisecond of imagination to visualize one fifty-nine-year-old inexperienced firefighter battling a forest fire to save a wooden (pine, no less) house. Not an option. We are at the end of the dry season.

I packed a backpack in case of evacuation. I put in the important papers, the clothing that was in best shape, our most expensive Bible, the hymnal Prairie's folks donated to the monastery and miscellaneous toiletries, etc. (even the keys to the house). I partially closed up the house. Then I changed into a less worn dress, put on my money belt, socks, and boots, then took a front row seat to watch the show. I knew I was ready to leave whenever necessary. It gave me great comfort.

I could see one part from the porch (shaded seat, even). I walked to the west end of our yard to see the other part. What to do next? Pray for rain, of course. So, I did. Then I got out the hymnal (not the packed one, the other one) and sang "Showers of Blessings." It was even more appropriate in Spanish.

Translations are never exact, you know. So, I sang it a few times and a big cloud came along. We had about seven minutes of light sprinkles. Joker! I gotta tell you. I get all the straight lines and the Big Joker gets all the punch lines. So, I had to laugh; it was the funniest thing all week.

We had no more rain, but by dark, the fire had demonstrated that it wasn't threatening me or the house or any part of monastery property. With nightfall, the smoke floated over. It smelled sweet; I have smelled this before when we walked near a burn. I don't know which plant causes it. I went to bed with this smell like incense around me.

Slept well.

Beth—Back to the Mountain—May 30, 2007

I stayed in Ceibita last night. The plan was that one of the women from the church would return to the mountain with me today. The plan was made in a conversation of shouting over cell phones and the quality of sound was terrible. I talked directly with Irma as I thought she was going to come with me.

After all my internet stuff, and after chatting with Suyapa (who lives across the street from the church) I went to visit Irma. Suyapa has five kids at home and her husband had just arrived in the States. He called her for Mother's Day. She was very pleased. We all know how dangerous the trip is for people crossing the border illegally. They hope that he can be there for three years and earn enough to pay off the mortgage. Mortgages are new here and no one is comfortable with them

Irma and I sorted through our telephone conversation from Monday and our options. She thought Suyapa was going to visit on the mountain and it is clear that Suyapa would love to, but she is prevented by her responsibilities. Irma could only come for an overnight. This would not be worth it—all traveling, no real time at the monastery. Well, maybe Marlen.

Yes, Marlen. Marlen is a single woman with one child (kindergartener). Someone was able to care for her. This little girl is one of the great perks in visiting Ceibita. She is short for age (even by Honduran standards) and, as we say, just about as wide as she is tall. She is a living example of someone who doesn't fit the growth charts in any way and is also obviously just the way she is supposed to be. She walks with majesty. Heads of state could take lessons from her. I love to watch her walk.

Marlen, Irma and I had a short conversation about this trip. (This morning I learn that Irma really didn't give Marlen a choice—it's God's work—it's her duty.) Back to the conversation. Some of it was in fast, low-pitched Spanish that I didn't get. Marlen would like to bring a chicken. She used the word that means meat of chicken, not live chicken. I commented that we don't usually eat meat on the mountain. But, do you like chicken?

Yes, I like chicken, but we don't have refrigeration. No problem, we'll carry the chicken live and butcher it there.

Oh.

Sure.

Of course.

Why didn't I think of that?

So, we'll meet at the bus station at eleven AM, and the three of us (Marlen, chicken and I) will take the bus to La Fortuna. The last time I was present at the execution of a chicken, I was about seven. I didn't much like it. Dad lopped off its head and it flopped around, spewing blood from it's severed ascending aorta and splattered blood all over my dress. I ran screaming to the house to change clothes. Hopefully, I can comport myself better this time.

I have bought the vegetables. They are much cheaper here in Tocoa than in Limón—and more available. We can make soup. My backpack was light, so I could handle vegetables. I think I'm going to learn a lot in these next few days.

Beth—In San Pedro Sula—June 22, 2007

I left home on Wednesday for Ceibita. What a surprise to find a mission team there! Delightful people from Maryland. But I wasn't sure if my usual free lodging was going to be available to me. And I knew that my hoped for conversations with the Honduran women would be pretty much out. Irma was busy helping in the parsonage kitchen to feed the visitors. She looked very tired, but just kept on trucking. Irma is like that. The only thing she asked me about Marlen's visit was if Marlin comported herself well. Marlen is older than Irma, but Irma is the mother figure. Marlen's mother died when she was little and her father left. I don't know the order those two things. Marlen went to live with her great uncle, his wife and their five kids. Then the wife died and great uncle raised the six kids as well as he could.

Back to the visiting team. They are interested in doing fluoride treatments. This makes me very happy. Fluoride treatments are the gift that keeps on giving. The dental health issues here are dreadful. There is no sugarless gum or candy. Hard candy and gum are very popular. Chewing on sugar cane is popular. You get the picture. Not just with the children, either. It is common to have a conversation with an adult around the lollipop in his or her mouth.

They invited me for dinner. I was very grateful. I had some diarrhea two weeks ago and it put me off my feed. I lost four pounds—not that I was so sick—but I couldn't face beans and tortillas. I made myself some hot chocolate too soon and now I still don't want to face hot chocolate. So, now I am trying to eat frequently and well. That's easier to do on the road, because I can buy snacks. (And don't have to face beans and tortillas.)

We chatted for quite a while after dinner. When it was well

past my bedtime, I was re-introduced to Delmis, one of the ladies of the church, who would give me a place to stay. We walked over to her house, just a little over a block away. Her mother was there and we had a nice chat about the monastery. They were delighted to have the picture postcard. Their house is a little smaller than our house, but divided into three rooms. The main room is about half of the space. The other two rooms are separated by pressboard that goes up about 7 feet. One is a storage room and one has two twin beds they pretty much fill the room. All three rooms are lit by one bulb that is on the ceiling-less roof in the center.

There are obviously more places to sleep, but in other buildings. Cooking is, of course, done outside as is laundry. They have a flush toilet with a septic tank. It is flushed by carrying water from the *pila* (laundry washing place).

Back to our conversation. Delmis' mom is very worried about her son who had just left for the perilous journey north to the land of milk and honey. I read in the newspaper just yesterday that twenty-five per cent of Honduras' gross national product is money sent home from Hondurans working abroad—no data about the percentage that are legal versus illegal. She asked me to pray for him.

So we four women, Delmis' sister who had shown up, and two little girls (who also just appeared from somewhere) stood in a circle. We sang a hymn and then, since I was leading the prayer, I prayed in a slightly louder voice than anyone else. Group prayer here is everybody doing their personal prayer in a low voice at the same time. It goes on until it is over. It is just fine to say the same thing over and over, even in the exact same words. Marvin is his name and he truly is in danger.

My bed was pointed out to me and I was happy to go to bed. But the rest of the household was up a long time. Delmis' son is a high school student and he did homework for a while. Delmis washed clothes until well into the night. I had been given a maroon sheet as a top sheet, still folded because, of course, one is unlikely to actually need it. I put it over my eyes so that light wouldn't keep me awake and fell asleep to the sounds of Delmis handwashing clothes outside.

I woke up as usual with the sunrise to notice that the other bed was occupied by Delmis and a little girl—maybe two years old. I remembered to clean my teeth (which I had forgotten the night before). I used the bathroom and was back to the parsonage in plenty of time for breakfast. (You notice I'm not missing any meals when I have the chance.) Then I went to Tocoa and hopped the bus to La Ceiba and wrote you a nice letter—which was eaten by cyberspace. I grabbed the *rapidito* to El Pino. I arrived there about four PM and chatted with the women, who are in the midst of a big chicken dinner sale to raise funds. This is to pay back the loan from the women's cooperative that they had taken to send two women to the District Women's Retreat at Roatan just over two months ago.

The day care and feeding program for children was going more smoothly. Two more childcare people had been hired. One of them has a real gift for teaching and managing small children. The mothers' group is feeling very worthwhile to Reina, the program director, but I didn't manage to get all the details. This chicken dinner stuff is taking all the conversation time.

I took a shower, did afternoon prayers, set up my camp bed, went to Doña Ada's for dinner and then to Women's meeting. We met in the church sanctuary and since it was hot, the fans were all running. (When the fans run, I can catch about half of what goes on.) I concentrated on being polite, like a slightly deaf person does. I was asked to lead the closing prayer again. I've been getting used to it.

In the morning I caught the bus to San Pedro Sula. I was able to get a room in the same elegant hotel as last time. I washed my laundry and hung it up. It is strawberry season in Guatemala and I bought a small bag of fresh strawberries (for twenty lempiras, outrageous!). I took them back to the hotel, washed them and shared them with the lady who was washing the sheets of the hotel. She seems to be about my age (which means she is probably ten years younger). She was delighted. I handed her a big, very red one. She broke it into three or four bites. She had never eaten a fresh strawberry before. I told her about how they grow and that when I was growing up we ate a lot of them, all we wanted and that I had never tasted a fresh papaya until I was fifty-two. She accepted a few more berries. It was a very sweet few moments.

Prairie—Back in Honduras After Another Busy Month—June 23, 2007

Well, I've arrived safely in El Pino, Honduras after two flights and a bus ride, with two boxes of books and other good things I'm excited to share with Beth. I'm glad to be back and look forward to settling back into the routine of monastic life when we return there on Wednesday.

My full U.S. schedule continued after my last update of May twenty-second. I had a lovely time in Minnesota with the beginning of summer weather—hot and humid. I got to visit family including aunts, uncles, cousins, and more distant relatives in Minneapolis and my dad's hometown near Rochester. My parents and grandmas came up for my sister's graduation from St. Olaf College on May twenty-seventh. Lots of good visiting.

Autumn, mom, and I traveled together on Amtrak back to Oregon where we jumped right into packing mode. My parents were hard at work trying to find an affordable apartment for the next several months before their new home is built. They still didn't have one by the time I left the next Wednesday for a visit to Salem, Portland, and Hermiston. I visited many more family and friends, and spoke to several more groups on that trip.

By the time I got back to Albany on June eleventh, my

parents had secured a two-bedroom duplex in Corvallis. That week was Annual Conference, the yearly meeting of the United Methodist Church in Oregon and Idaho. The rest of my family attended, and I went up there to Salem for several worship services and to staff a table for Amigas del Señor. In the middle of all that, we did serious moving as well—Thursday evening and all day Saturday—with the help of many friends and their trucks and trailers. By the end of Monday, after days of packing, moving, cleaning, Conference, and not enough sleep, I was wiped. Happily, Tuesday was my Sabbath. We went as a family to the Oregon coast and had a lovely relaxing time.

This Wednesday, I went back to Portland for two last presentations, and the final details of packing and other business. Overall it was a wonderful, if a bit tiring, visit to the U.S. I enjoyed so much getting to see old friends and meet new people, and sharing my story with so many. I appreciate all of your hospitality, love, good wishes, and prayers. Do continue to keep in touch, and keep seeking what is true for you in life.

Beth—Aliens: Illegal and Legal—June 26, 2007

Prairie's flight was a few hours late, but all went well. She had received a gift of Nutella and it was confiscated at a security check. She obviously looked like a shifty character who would blow up the plane with her little jar of Nutella. Is there paranoia around or what?

We planned the timing of her journey to avoid an expensive trip to Belize in order to stay legal in the eyes of the Honduran government. You will be happy to know that she is legal. We have started the process of applying to be legal residents (the Honduran equivalent of having the famous green card). It is an incredibly complicated process and every official source gives different information, often in error. But we have forged ahead. We now have our birth certificates properly signed and sealed as required. When Prairie was in the States she got herself fingerprinted to have the criminal background search done. The latest information we have is that I can't get finger-printed here, would have to go to the States to do that. But maybe, just maybe, we could have that done at the American embassy here in Honduras. So that is the next thing to pursue. We only decided in February, so it's not like things are moving slowly. We even have our own attorney in Tegucigalpa. So far, we consult him by telephone. He comes highly recommended.

We are still in La Ceiba and El Pino. Yesterday, I worked alongside Eloyda and Prairie with the children's program. The children's program is getting smoother all of the time. It is delightful to watch. Several foreign work teams come down every year. Now there are toys; there are tables and chairs for the kids in the classrooms and, frankly, I don't know what else. We sleep in one of the classrooms. So, each weekday morning, we pack up, fold up and store our cots and each evening, move back in. It works very well.

I ordered some medicines to ship to the public health clinic in Ceibita. Last week the medical team from Maryland showed me a list of medicines that they needed, that they no longer had. The majority were kids' meds. So what could I do? Randy, the pastor who works in La Ceiba and Ceibita, will take the meds with him next time he goes.

Well, back to the immigration stuff. We are told that if I don't have my passport stamped and if I don't leave the country every three months, I will be earning a bigger fine. Said fine will be much smaller than the cost of the every-three-month-stamp and much less costly than trips to Belize. Trips to Belize are costly, both in money and time.

So, I have decided to wait. When we know that we are (or I am) about to leave the country, I'll go in, pay the price, be legal again and be able to travel. Why am I telling you all these de-tails? Because the blunt version is: I am now an illegal alien in Honduras. I never imagined such a thing would happen to me. But that's what I'm doing. I used my passport at the bank this morning and the teller didn't check whether it was up-to-date or not. I think that this is a small risk and the rule is bizarre and unfair enough for me to feel fine non-violently resisting it.

Well, that's all the news that's fit to print.

Beth—A Patient—July 18, 2007

I keep thinking about my eight-year-old first grader who lives in Plan de Flores. (Plan de Flores is about twenty minutes by bus east of Limón.) His mother brought him in sick and with yellow eyes. Apathetic, tired and sick, he sat on a chair while Mom and I talked. He cooperated listlessly in his physical exam. Mom was very interested in learning about hepatitis, including that hand-washing is big to help prevent spread of the disease in the household. The treatment is high protein and high sugar diet, rest, and time. This family is poor, not destitute. They eat meat once a week usually (just like us). They have a few chickens so mom can be sure her sick kid gets an egg every day. They can also get cheese. They have oranges and coconuts and can readily have the chunk molasses, so will have sweets. Of course, I don't know who will be going without— that is, whose share the patient will be eating. Mom asked a lot of good questions. One question: "Does the egg need to be prepared in any special way?"

They live near the school. When she does let the child go back to school, I asked that she would fetch him home after two hours the first few days until she is sure that he is strong enough for the whole school day. She actually seemed thrilled with this instruction. I am guessing it is rare for the mother to feel that she has more authority than the teacher—but that is only a guess.

After our work at Centro de Salud and our usual Monday errands, we began walking home and quickly caught a lift. The same truck that gave us a ride picked up this family about a mile out of town. They had let one bus pass them. They got off at the intersection where their route split from ours (and our driver's). Mom, dad, little boy and baby in arms took off walking. Was this sick eight-year-old going to walk all the way home? I don't know. But I keep thinking about him.

Beth—Paso a Paso—July 18, 2007

We have a bell

We Have a bell! Actually, we have two bells. We are very happy. The outside bell used to be a wind chime that someone passed on to us. It now is a bell. We removed the clapper and now it is on a stick and we ring the bell by striking it.

Since it is a triangular-shaped wind chime, we actually have three tones to choose from. This is just one of the many wonderful and useful gifts that Prairie brought back from the States. Mostly, the gifts were wonderful books, some for our use, some to share with public schools and some to ponder over at length about how to best use them.

We will send an email to anyone who wishes it with a list of recommended Spanish-language books for donating to a local school or library for persons coming to Honduras. This list is far from inclusive; it is only the ones we have personally reviewed and can recommend. It does not include those we have reviewed and do not recommend. We find that often

Spanish-language books in the States are culturally unhelpful although the words may be a great story or message. Often the pictures are an advertisement for big-time personal wealth. We are happy to review any books you may want evaluated (any age). Just send us the book. We will not return the book. (Reviewers never do, you know.)

After I wrote to you, I managed to get fingerprinted at the police department in La Ceiba. They didn't even charge me. There was a visiting team in El Pino and a person was willing to take the application back to the States to mail. *Paso a paso.* Step by step. It looks as though we actually will be getting our legal residency done.

Javier, the sixteen-year-old neighbor who wanted to learn to sign his name, has dyslexia. Not a big surprise. The first clue was that he had spent five years in first grade, then left school and there was no horror story (unlike Clemente who quit first grade sixty years ago because the teacher beat the kids).

Javier practiced and practiced his first name and then got two letters mixed around. So, I got out the number book. He couldn't do two and five. (They are too much alike if you have dyslexia.) So, I explained how his eyes work. Then we got to work on his surname: Aquino. He passed it and passed writing them both together. We are both very pleased that now he can sign his own name.

The really great news was that we found lots of legumes growing wild in our yard. In fact, our favorite creeping ground cover just happens to be a legume. We now know how to groom our yard in a way that will help make it productive. Our knowledge and experience keep growing, even if our vegetables don't.

We are in Bonito today. We ran out of money and came to make a withdrawal from the bank. While here, we get to communicate with you. We also bought some fruits and vegetables. They are such a treat and so hard to get. We will be feasting for a few days. We even scored a papaya! The lady said it should be ripe in three days. That's good. We can have pineapple tomorrow, mango on Thursday, and papaya on Friday. I am in hog heaven.

Beth—Gardening Update: Pineapple!—August 8, 2007

The big news in our garden is pineapple. As you know, we have not had a lot of gardening success. But our first pineapple plant has begun to blossom. We planted eleven pineapple plants fifteen months ago. They can take up to two years to provide fruit. The pineapple is a compound fruit. Each of those little eyes is where a blossom has fallen off and represents a fruit that has fused with the others. We were delighted to see that the first one had begun. It looked a bit like someone had spray-painted red inside the pineapple plant. It looked like a miniature red pineapple. In the two weeks that we have watched it, the blossoms have come out—little blue lavender petals. The ring of blossoms had moved up from the bottom to the equator of the globe. And the whole thing is bigger, a little bit. It's fabulous. We have three books that tell about pineapples, but none tell us the time expected between the beginning of blossoming until the fruit is ready to pick. We'll just have to watch and see.

Our friend, Polo, gave us twenty pineapple starts, which we planted last week. They are good plants for a hillside. Some folks say they can even be used for terrace barriers. We are planting them in such a way to make that possible. We also planted some forage peanut plants with them. Forage peanut is a low creeper that doesn't produce any edible peanuts, but puts nitrogen into the soil and is good ground cover. In theory, at least, with a lot of forage peanut plants we would have little weeding and little fertilizing to do. Well, we checked yesterday and the forage peanuts that I planted last week with the new pineapple starts look great. We had a nice gentle rain—just right for recently transplanted little guys.

We can also see the beginning of a slip coming out under the growing pineapple bud. This can be removed later and planted. Pineapples are the rabbits of the plant kingdom. Our friend, Warnita, also gave us seven pineapple starts last week when we visited her. When we have about a hundred plants, we'll start being more discriminating about the quality of planting material. Right now, we plant anything we can get our hands on.

It was time to clean our water tank. Actually, it was about a month late, by most recommendations. But the rain has been pretty unreliable in this usually rainy time of the year. Well, Saturday began with rain and overcast. We decided that was the day. We did our laundry and began draining the tank. We filled our laundry tubs and buckets. Prairie climbed up to the top of the tank, lopped off a couple of branches of the tree that overhangs the roof, cleaned up the entry spout and the manhole cover. Then down into the tank she went.

She found three little frogs. She had to crouch down to fit inside, but said that it was really pretty easy. My job was bringing her a scrub brush and a rag. I was not much help at all. Long before noon, the tank was empty and cleaned. Then, with great cooperation, more rain fell, so the tank could begin to refill.

Cleaning the water tank

Tuesday is a big laundry day. No washing on Sunday, of course, and on Mondays, we are not only gone, but we sweat a lot walking home with backpacks of groceries. We didn't think there was enough water in the tank for doing laundry and still have any left over. so we went down to the stream to do laundry (stopping on the way to admire and photograph our pineapple).

We spread a plastic bag on a large rock. Prairie used it like a scrub board while I washed the smaller items by hand. Of course, we stood right in the water, a very cool activity. It went very fast with two people and no water-carrying. Then back we went up the hill to hang the laundry on the line.

We used one of the tough sacks to carry the wet things. The water leaked out as we walked, making it a little lighter with each step. It was all very slick.

Prairie—Readjusting to Monastic Life—August 9, 2007

Readjusting. It took me some weeks to readjust to monastic life after returning from my trip to the U.S. At first I was impressed at how well I slipped right back into using Spanish; my comprehension didn't seem to have diminished at all. Getting back into the monastic routine took more time. The schedule itself wasn't a problem; I was quite glad to be back to our regular routine of prayer and work, and our tranquil location in nature, with the mountains and the breeze. But it took my mind some time to come back from the stimulating, distracting world, and to center again more fully on God. It also didn't help that I came down with a cold almost immediately upon returning (which I then shared with Beth), so that physically I was weak for some time. However, after about four weeks, I was feeling healthy and grounded again.

A visit from Larry: During the first week in July our friend Larry Smoak came to visit from Las Mangas, where he is a missionary. He had told us he was planning to come sometime that month, but we were pleasantly surprised when he found us on the street in Limon that Monday. He spent a couple of days at our place, giving Gloria's cabin a test run as our guest house (with success, I believe). We took advantage of his many years of agricultural experience in Honduras and asked for his advice and ideas for our gardening. He suggested a couple of reasons things haven't grown really well on our hillside garden, too much shade and acidic soil. Happily, that same week we took a step on the first one when we hired our neighbors to come over with their chainsaw and cut down a number of the shade-producing trees. (They also cut down a big dry nance tree which would supply us with firewood for many weeks.) Larry sent us a soil-test kit so we could verify the nutrient deficiencies in our garden. One up-side is that pineapples like slightly acidic soil.

Two friends have given us about twenty-four pineapple starts, which we are planting. Plus, one of the pineapples planted last year is finally blooming. In a couple of months we might have some fruit to eat!

We are getting our papers together to apply for residency, and are planning a trip in September to do another Belize border crossing to stamp our passports. Plus, we're eagerly anticipating the visit of a couple of my cousins and their six-year-old daughter in October. Hope all is well with you!

Beth—Follow-up on Marlen's Visit—June 20, 2007

When I left you last, I was expecting to go home with a chicken. Apparently, Irma persuaded Marlen that bringing a chicken was a bad idea. A chicken is a very expensive item—in fact, a whole chicken is worth more than Marlen earns in a day. (It is worth more than many Hondurans earn in a day.)

Marlen is an Avon lady! And I was wrong about having only one child. She has four.

We hopped on the bus and it was packed. We couldn't even sit together, but, at least, we both got to sit. Marlen was not prepared to ride in a bus full of Garifunas. The Garifuna are of African ancestry[30] and often speak in their own dialect. They also laugh and joke a lot more than the Indios. (Marlen is an Indio.) I was a little surprised, since her local pastor is also of African ancestry—but culturally is anything but a Garifuna.

Marlen was impressed at the long walk to the house, but made herself right at home. She made the fire and starting cooking dinner before I could even think of it. I was very grateful, too. Why? Because we arrived home to learn that the termites had made a fat trail to the top bookshelf and were busily munching our books!

Marlen fixed dinner while I cleaned up the books. Yes, we have termite-proofed the house—worth a lot, that stuff? Ha! Only one book was seriously damaged and it is far from a favorite, although I do look stuff up in it once in a while.

The neighbor boys dropped by. We hadn't yet done afternoon prayers, so I called Marlen from the kitchen and I invited the boys to participate. The older ones were very nervous and giggly about it. We just ignored that and continued our usual schedule. (I use the royal "we" since Marlen doesn't know the usual schedule.) The two younger boys easily engaged in the story, one of the healing stories, then "But don't tell anyone." I like it.)

It seems that often when we arrive home tired, late in the afternoon, company drops by. That's the way it goes.

Marlen and I had a lovely dinner. We had sort of a fuel wood emergency—that is, I thought we did. In Ceibita, Marlen (and Irma) cook using the ribs of African oil palm fronds. Here, Marlen used our nance bark. It worked very well. One has to feed the fire more often and more ashes are produced, but it made heat. This was just the first of the many practical how-to-live-simply-in-Honduras lessons that I received.

Marlen recognized volunteer guava trees growing by our kitchen (from a guava snack last September). She also could at

30 Garifuna, descendants of Carib, Arawak and West African ancestors.

least sort out the different volunteer citrus trees. She was eager to take two of the little lime trees. We also dug out one of the aloe vera plants for her to take home. She was really impressed with all of the pine trees and pulled up about a dozen tiny pine trees to take with her to plant.

On Thursday morning we went down to the stream to bathe and to wash the laundry. I have bathed in streams before, but she showed me how to do the laundry in the stream. She made it look easy.

On Friday, we walked down to the road to dig some white clay for her to take home. She is very impressed with our white clay stove. We even found a little of the red clay. She wants to make a little candleholder like we have made that we used at our evening prayer time.

I found her hacking at the *ocote* (greasewood, used to start fires) with the machete. I asked, "What are you doing?" Answer, "I'm cutting some to take home." Well, I had no idea that the log had so much good ocote in it. It looked to me like only about half of it was good and the other half would be waste. I didn't know until the next week when Javier came over and chopped it up for me that I had a huge amount to store up.

On Saturday, I walked Marlen to the bus. We managed to get all of her clothing and her souvenirs in her backpack and a large plastic bag. That clay was wet and heavy. The bus didn't come until about eleven AM. We waited at Rosa's place. Marlen is not an experienced traveler, so I was not willing to leave until I saw her actually get on the bus.

It was an education. Just when I thought that I had started to know how to do stuff, along comes Marlen and breezes easily through all my rough spots, solving problems for me that I hadn't even known that I had.

Life is funny.

The last Friday in July, which happened to be the one-year anniversary of our moving out to the mountain, we decided to walk the two hours up the road to the community of La Fortuna. We had been there in the past, doing immunizations with the Centro de Salud team, but went in a vehicle and were busy the whole time. This time, we decided to make it a pure adventure with no schedule, just going with the idea to get to know the community a little better. We stopped at the first house we saw by the road after about an hour's walk. There, we sat under a cacao tree and chatted with the housewife about the crops, animals, and fruit trees they raise. They have cows, and are rich enough in milk that they feed it to the puppies, several of which were playing at our feet, all roly-poly, and looking healthier than any I've seen in this country.

Then we kept walking till we reached the first house of the cluster that makes up the village proper. There a woman invited us into her spacious kitchen, with walls made of cane and a palm thatch roof. Her husband joined us for a conversation about the things they raise. The woman served us several snacks, including fresh hot milk from their cows, corn tortillas with avocado—from a tree in their yard—limeade (freshly-made with limes right off the tree), soup, and grilled partly-ripe *chatas* (a type of banana). How generous and delicious!

The third home we visited was much more humble than the first two. The eighty-one-year-old *partera* (midwife), who Beth knew from the past, had a single pot of beans boiling on the fogón inside her mud house. Even so, her daughter-in-law made us limeade, and her son gave us several avocados to take home; they live next door. We talked about the ten-year-old granddaughter she cares for and about trusting in God. The partera was suffering from an eye infection and so the next Monday, Beth sent her some medicine from Centro de Salud by way of another woman from La Fortuna who was walking the same road home.

All in all, it was a very interesting day, though we were quite tired by the time we got home after the long hot walk up and down the hills. I like the feeling that we are getting a little bolder in our interactions.

Beth—Friends—August 10, 2007

So much has happened in the weeks since we visited Bonito to write to you—although many of these things you will never hear about. On our anniversary of moving the monastery to the mountain, we decided to visit La Fortuna. It is a two-hour walk, and we were always going to do it someday. Well, living here a year really reminded us that the someday had arrived. We had a lovely day of exploring. The views along this mountain road are lovely. There is one pretty high peak just before we descend to La Fortuna. We got a lot of exercise that day. I will tell you about one of our visits to houses.

We visited my old friend, Doña Amelia, the midwife. She is eighty-one years old. The young women are not interested in being midwives; they want modern life styles. So she has no apprentice. She tells us that right now she only has one pregnant woman in La Fortuna, and that the woman knows a lot about chidbirth.

This is a very good thing, because Doña Amelia is not able to work right now. She has a bad eye infection. It had been going on for a month or two, but in the last three weeks, it was so bad that she has lost most of her vision. She told me that she could see that I had a face, but that she recognized me by my voice. She lives in a modest house with an earthen floor. She had put a plastic tarp and a small pillow on the floor. She had been resting there (it is cooler) during this hot early afternoon. Her co-mother-in-law, a charming, toothless, skinny old lady, had led us to her house. I had not heard the expression before, but, of course, when it was explained, it was obvious. Doña

Amelia's son had married the daughter of this lady, hence, they were co-mothers-in-law. Spanish can be so sensible.

Doña Amelia's daughter-in-law made lemonade for us. Doña Amelia turned hers down. She has no appetite with her illness and she had just had a corn drink (like a very thin mush). We talked for a while, although we didn't want to tire her out. I examined her eyes and looked at the medicines that she had. This is really a bad infection and I couldn't tell if there is another problem besides the infection. Why, you wonder, would a health care provider not seek care with such a serious problem? I didn't ask. My guesses include poverty and age—it is a three-hour walk, remember.

We talked about her family. She has a ten-year-old granddaughter who lives with her. The mother, who lives there, isn't mentally stable. Apparently, she usually does well but has anger attacks. It is clear that Doña Amelia is concerned about what will happen with this granddaughter when she is gone.

She had a lot of questions about causes of illnesses. She wanted to know if her arthritis was from poverty or age, and also about the eye problem. Of course, she couldn't examine her own eyes, so wasn't entirely sure that it was an infection. Old people go blind, you know, so she wasn't sure. I had seen her take care of a little girl with a displaced wrist fracture, so it took me aback a bit to realize how little of the basic principles of health and disease she understands. This is a different country, you know. It was so nice talking with her about the monastery. She is one of the very few who *get* it.

They sent three fresh eggs and five avocados home with us. We ate fresh scrambled eggs for our dinner that night. We were pretty hungry after our big active day. We enjoyed the avocados for three straight days.

That was a Friday. On Monday, I asked in the waiting room if there was anyone from La Fortuna. A lady identified herself as from La Fortuna and graciously agreed to take medicine to Doña Amelia. A week later, we caught a lift (in the back of a pickup) and one of the other passengers was another of Doña Amelia's sons. He didn't seem to know her status very well, but thought she was doing better. Hopefully, we will learn more this coming Monday.

Our friend, Gloria Lacayo (lab tech and past hostess for me) was in a motor vehicle crash when a visiting health team was in town a few weeks ago. They were leaving for a more remote community to give medical care. Most of the team was in a bus, but she was one of four people in a pick-up truck. Another bus went by, raising a cloud of dust, so the team's driver didn't see the other car coming. It was a bad crash, all five people were injured, a few seriously. Gloria's right leg was broken. She had been in the front seat, holding her microscope on her lap. The microscope falling got the blame for her fractures—both tibia and fibula. They took all of the injured people to Tocoa for health care. The most seriously injured went on to La Ceiba, where they were treated.

Gloria's fractures required pinning. She also had glass cuts on her forehead from the windshield. We visited her at home six days after the accident and she was in good spirits. Her neighbor, Rita, was taking care of her again (as she had done after the gallbladder surgery). The visiting team took care of all of the medical bills—and, I am sure, more. She had heard that all of the visitors were well enough to return home to Pennsylvania, where they live. Their visit was cut short and the outreach clinics just didn't happen. All received state of the art health care. It is available here in the cities and for those who can pay. Gloria has been told that she can't walk on this leg for five months. Recuperation times are very long here. It seems a bit bizarre until you look at how much more physical just ordinary daily life is for most people. She gets lots of visitors, and we loaned her our new copy of *Ignatius of Loyola* in Spanish.

We spent yesterday at Ceibita and Tocoa. We visited Gilma, the nurse at the public health center. She is a lively lady and was happy to see us. Yes, she had received the five gallons of medicines we sent in June—just what she needed. Yes, she would very much like to send a message to the medical team that would be visiting in November. They had left her a glucometer (to check blood sugar). She has found it extremely useful and needs more test strips. It is so useful that she had even checked out the cost of buying those strips out of her tiny cash box. (No good— entirely too expensive.) We also sent a list of the other things they may be able to help her with. She is delighted that the team is hoping to provide treatments to the children.

We were delighted to be able to meet with the women of the church Wednesday evening and at last night's prayer meeting, open to all, it was still mostly women. I preached. I'm getting used to this last-minute sermon preparation and preaching Everybody gets a chance to preach. So far, they haven't asked Prairie to preach, but her time will come. Her quiet personality has protected her so far.

Today, we head back to the mountain. We always pack so much into our trips, we get pretty tired. It will be good to get home.

Beth—Gardening, Composting, Reflecting
September 12, 2007

We did a lot of gardening. When we do a gardening day, it is usually two or three hours of vigorous work in the garden followed by the aerobic climb back to the house. We could do more in a day, but with the heat and the experience of overuse injuries, we are very moderate.

Since our neighbors used their chain saw to cut two large trees, we have not had to use any of those vigorous mornings searching for, cutting down, trimming and dragging home the kind of standing dead trees. we use for firewood. We will not have to haul wood in September at all. Sweet. We can keep up easily with splitting and cutting the long limbs to useable lengths. This gives us more mornings for the garden.

Larry Smoak had loaned us a soil test kit. The news was bad. It wasn't all bad; some was worse. Very acid soil, except where the urine from the dry compost toilet has buffered it, and low nitrogen. Fortunately, pineapple likes acid soil. We think we'll plant more pineapple. We have forty plants in the ground now.

We started a compost pile in the garden. It took five of our gardening mornings to do it. We put *sacos* (sacks) on top. They will sort of keep it dry with the rain. Then we planted legumes, and then some more legumes. We cut and mulch them and then mulch some more. We have given up the idea of planting okra this summer. Sigh. That will wait. Our native legumes are thriving. Now that we know that they are not weeds, we give them preferential treatment.

One day we decided to experiment with working in the shade of the afternoon instead of in the morning. It went fine. Then I started aching. I couldn't figure it out. Why should I be so achy? We didn't actually do more. Then I remembered. I take two Naproxen tablets every morning when we are going to be active. I have a bad shoulder and a little arthritis in one foot, but when I take the Naproxen, I do fine. Well, it wore off, of course, in twelve hours.

This was a sobering lesson for me. The difference in my body was dramatic. When I take medication, I can keep up (pretty much) with Prairie. And we think of ourselves as living in voluntary poverty? Poor people here don't take Naproxen— not even once in a while. They can get acetaminophen at the public health clinic, where they are told to take one tablet (half the dose recommended in the States) and are given only ten tablets. Now I realize that I am living pretty substantially above the average poor person in Limón. Even middle class people take pain medicines much more rarely than I do. Today, all I did was walk an hour to the bus carrying my packed backpack. I was careful to take my Naproxen first[31] (which I take with a

---

31 I no longer take any pain medication routinely. The osteoarthritis doesn't bother me

Tums to protect my delicate tummy).

This is my confession today. I live in pseudo-poverty.

Our baby pineapple is growing. Our dwarf plátano has a baby. (That's what they call the tiny plants that come up along side the mother plant.) We're very pleased. Prairie says it is still too little for the picture to be worth sharing. She doesn't get into babies the way I do. It (the dwarf plátano) also has a bud. We are very excited about this. The plant is about five feet tall—more convenient than the usually much taller plátano plants. We hope the fruit is not dwarf in size!

We have shared cuttings of our chaya (spinach tree) with three friends. Eva and Clemente's family were all shocked (but very polite) to hear that we fertilize it with urine! Perhaps not shocked that we do it, perhaps only shocked about the way I talked about it. I don't think urine is talked about. In the country, most families have neither bathroom nor outhouse. No one talks about human waste disposal.

Eva and Clemente

When I have been here much longer, perhaps someone will tell me more. In the meantime, I shock my friends and eat greens fertilized with our own urine.

The wild Blueberry-type fruit is in season and we have been

enjoying blueberry pancakes. Once we even picked so many we made a stove-top cobbler. Yum. We get a few cowpeas three times a week to add to the rice.

Of course, the major work of a monastery is to pray. The work of the monastery went well during this month of not traveling. People go to a monastery because they realize that they are among those who too easily get distracted from God by all the hustle, bustle, and interesting things going on. Somehow praying with toucans in the background doesn't distract me the way all the old worldly activities did.

I killed a few tarantulas and a mouse in the last month. These were not my finest moments.

Beth—Hurricane Dean Creeps onto Shore
September 13, 2007

Oops, I forgot to talk about the hurricanes. Hurricane Dean caused a yellow alert here. We were working at Centro de Salud and I asked Dr.. Karen if it would be a good day for her to do our check-ups (that we need for our residency application). She very calmly replied that she would be very happy to, except that she needed to attend the meeting the mayor had called regarding the hurricane warning.

We split up to get our errands done more rapidly, made sure that we bought plenty of provisions and took off. It was stormy, though only a yellow alert. Not much happened after that, weather-wise.

A few weeks later, also on a Monday, we learned of Hurricane Felix, a class five hurricane, with a red alert to start several hours later. I now take you to my journal entry of Tuesday, September fourth, the day Felix was due:

'We are in red alert over Hurricane Felix. Everyone who lives near the ocean or a river is told to flee to safety. None of the public buildings in Limón qualifies as a safe place in times of hurricanes, so each person or family is on their own to find a place of safety. We offered hospitality to Juana Nidia, whose house is entirely too close to the ocean. She said that she needs to stay in town in case there would be injured needing care. I reminded her that she must survive in order to care for the injured. Supposedly the hurricane was to have arrived in the wee hours of the morning. We had one big thunderstorm and now we had another. We washed the laundry and hung it inside to dry. It would take a long time. We had to cook up the beans. They take so long that we could bake something in the oven on the days we cook beans. Today—sourdough pizza. There is extra dough, so we will also have fried bread—with cinnamon sugar. We are taking turns tending to the cooking. Earlier in the morning, we had enough light so that I could sew a bit. But not anymore; the storm is heavier. When we got home from Limón yesterday, Prairie did storm preparation while I cooked dinner (after baths and prayers, of course). Our *sanitario* now looks like a greenhouse—aloe vera, *gandul*, basil, small orange trees, small guava tree, two tiny *leucaena* trees (a leguminous tree that I have been wanting for a long time, seeds a gift from Larry). We bought kerosene for the lamp yesterday (just a coincidence), so we are well prepared. Well, we were well prepared for a very calm day. Nothing happened.

We had left instructions with Juana Nidia to send a messenger (they have a motorcycle) to let us know if we would be needed to care for injured. Needless to say, we did not receive a summons. I had some concern about Sor Leonora and her fifty-two kids. The shelter for orphans is very close to the ocean. Later she told me that they all went to the office—a house only a few feet higher, but several rods further from the ocean. They would have fit in like sardines. But all went well.

Limón was founded when the ocean was further away. There used to be a quarter-mile-wide stretch of beach between the first street and the ocean. But over the last forty or fifty years that stretch of beach has been eaten by the ocean and now the town is right on the beach.

Prairie—Nature's Bark Bigger Than its Bite (Hurricanes)
September 13, 2007

Hurricane Alerts[32]: When we went to town on Monday, August twentieth, Dr. Karen was on her way to a meeting at the municipal hall regarding a yellow hurricane alert. There was one in the Caribbean that could bring big rainstorms to Limón, and she was on the emergency preparedness team. Beth and I got a bit excited at the idea. I'd never experienced a hurricane, and she wanted to make sure we got all our groceries purchased, and then get home in time to be ready and sit it out. (She had experienced a bad hurricane and storm season here in the fall of 2005). We split up to do our errands and got soaked in the rain that was already coming down. The next day and the rest of the week it was sunny and clear; we hear the hurricane hit Jamaica.

Last Monday, September third, when we arrived at Centro de Salud in Limón, it was Juana Nidia, the head nurse, who was on her way to a similar meeting. This time, Limón and the whole Department (State)of Cólon were under a red alert for a category five hurricane. The word was it was headed straight for the North Coast and Limón. We saw signs put up around town: "No school today because of Hurricane Felix. Save yourselves! Evacuate areas near the sea and the river!" There was something humorous about the sign, as it was a lovely sunny day, but Limón has been hit hard by hurricanes in the past, and especially the resulting flooding. We invited Juana Nidia to come out to our place for refuge if she needed to, as her house is close to the beach.

Beth and I did all our regular grocery shopping, and noticed there were a lot more people than normal buying kerosene—

---

32 Advisory messages are issued by the National Hurricane Center, giving details as to where the storm is located, its intensity, its direction and its speed of movement. Precautionary measures are given for ships and coastal residents near the storm center. Advisories are broadcast over most radio and television stations.

in case the electricity went out. Then we headed home and took all the precautions we could think of: we moved all our seedlings and loose items from the porch into the bathroom for some protection from wind and rain, and brought lots of firewood and ocote into the kitchen. Before bed, we closed all our window shutters; the storm was to arrive in the wee hours of the morning.

Well, there was some loud thunder and a little rain during the night, but we could still do our morning prayers outside on Tuesday. After breakfast there was more rolling thunder and rain. We did our regular washing and hung laundry up inside, knowing it might take two to three days to dry. In the middle of the morning the wind came up with a pounding rain; we had to shut the south window shutters, and even so rain came in underneath them, and leaked from the roof and under the back door, creating big puddles on the floor. It didn't last terribly long and was only as bad as some of our winter, rainy-season storms last year. The rest of the day was gray, but no rain to speak of.

By Wednesday morning our clothes were dry. There were patches of blue in the sky, and the temperature was unusually comfortable. By Thursday it was sunny and super hot again. On Friday a visitor stopped by and we heard that Felix ended up hitting the Nicaraguan coast, flooding some big rivers there, affecting parts of Nicaragua as well as the La Mosquitia region of eastern Honduras. We were thankful that we happened to be in town both of the days the hurricanes were announced, and that we didn't get hit; we pray for those who did.

Tarantulas: A smaller disturbance has been all the tarantula sightings we've had recently. One day, following afternoon prayers a few weeks ago, I saw a big hairy tarantula—some five inches in diameter—near the stool where Beth had been sitting. It startled me, but didn't bother me too much as it was outdoors, but then I went inside to put things away and there was an even bigger tarantula on the floor in the house!

I jumped up onto the bed and called to Beth, who put on her rubber workboots and grabbed the broom. She came over and stomped on it, smearing guts all over the floor. Then, since she was now dressed for the occasion, she went outside and killed the one out there.

A week later, there was one in the bathroom, which I killed with my boots. This last week I saw one on the outside wall of the house. As Beth went to put on her boots, the tarantula started crawling across the doorjamb. I told Beth, and she just closed the door right on it. A couple days later, I walked into the house and there was another tarantula crawling on the bunk where Beth sleeps. She smashed it with the back of the shovel this time. Tuesday we saw one in the garden, but didn't kill it.

Maybe it's tarantula season. The last time we'd seen any was about a year ago. We are very ready to learn more about them. We don't even know how dangerous they actually are. Our dictionary said they're poisonous but not lethal. And I must admit, it's fascinating to watch them move—slowly creeping along, an undulating pattern to their many legs....

A Wildfire: The same day we had the red alert for Hurricane Felix, just as we walked home along the Desvio de La Fortuna, there was a fire on one side of the road. It wasn't the first time we've seen such a thing, but the flames were bigger and higher than in the past, and the smoke was blowing across the road where we had to walk. So, we wet our hankies and put them over our mouths and noses like bandits, then ran quickly through the smoke. Beth noticed how much heat it radiated. Luckily the fire wasn't extensive, and the rest of the walk was fine. We've learned that most of these fires are not natural, but set by landowners and farmers to clear the land of brush.

Cultivated Nature in Limón: About a month ago we took an extra trip into Limón one Friday to visit Warnita, the auxiliary nurse at Centro de Salud. Though she was on vacation, she was available to show us some of the cultivation she and her husband do. Like many of the Garifunas in Limón, they have a plot east of town where they grow yucca (cassava), a starchy root vegetable. There are a couple of varieties: sweet, for eating freshly boiled, and bitter, for making *cassave*, a cracker-like food and staple of the Garifuna diet. It is known as a good famine food (available and storable in times of extreme poverty or famine) as fresh yucca only stays good for a couple of days out of the ground.

On our walk back from her plot, we stopped right near the beach at the house of her relative. The woman invited us to sit on a bench under two palm trees. Then she took a long stick with a rebar hook on the end of it, and knocked down three big green coconuts. Warnita used a machete to slice off part of the fibrous outer layer, cutting a hole into the center seed (the brown nut that is sold in stores in the U.S.). We each took a coconut and drank the water out of it—sweet with a bitter edge. Then she split the coconuts in half for us, cut a piece of the outer shell to use as a spoon, and showed us how scrape the white, fatty flesh out of the seed and eat it. What a special treat; a real taste of Caribbean living!

Beth—El Pino, More About Tarantulas
September 19, 2007

Well, we went to Belize to have our passports stamped, hopefully for the last time. I am now legal again. It was very expensive. We spent more in one day than we usually spend in a month. It was also pretty tiring.

One of our stops was the butterfly museum where we received one of our tarantula lessons. The proprietor is a Mennonite from Iowa who has lived here for forty-three years. We were hoping to buy a book on insects, but he doesn't sell books, just posters and pictures of butterflies. He has a live tarantula—not hairy like ours, so it looked pretty different. So it was a show-and-tell lesson. We have received several lessons on tarantulas. Thank God, they all say the same thing. Tarantulas are not dangerous. Their bite, when provoked, hurts like a bee sting, but doesn't do any big damage. We have been killing them unnecessarily. And so we learn.

5 inch tarantula in garden

Monday, in El Pino, the clinic wasn't open and the children's program was closed for inventory so we went to La Ceiba. We got lots of errands done in one day, but I arrived back at El Pino really tired and was up in the night with diarrhea and a little vomiting. This seems to be my body's way of rebelling when I have asked too much of it.

Yesterday, Prairie worked with the children's programs. They liked both her Spanish version of "Where is Thumbkin?" and another song about a rooster. She put in a full day. I rested and reviewed books that the children's program had received. Reina, the director, and I shared our thoughts on the books. Far more than half are very appropriate, an amazingly high percentage. Several have more than one copy and she will share them with the Sunday school and the public kindergarten.

Pastor Carlos has been reassigned to La Ceiba, but has not yet moved. He has been here for five years and is much beloved. He is a person of prayer and love, rare in any profession. The new pastor has arrived, Antonio. He was tapped from Costa Rica, in part because of his experience in administration. The children's program has six employees; the clinic three. There are other projects, but since they aren't focusing on children, nutrition, health and education, I don't get very involved in them. Carlos and his family will move in the middle of October since the moving money hasn't yet materialized. Meanwhile, Antonio is commuting from La Ceiba.

Antonio is a city guy. He started with office hours. Office hours? Who in rural Honduras has heard of office hours? He will have a lot of adjustments to make. He even used notes when he gave his first sermon!

Last evening was the meeting for teaching.[33] With two pastors sort of involved, it is more like no pastor involved. Reina got short notice that she was teaching.

It was the most amazing meeting. There were twelve adults present. She used Acts, chapter twelve, the story about Peter's chains falling off before he walked out of prison. Then, of course, the story came up of Paul and Silas in prison who stayed put when their chains fell off. You can hardly think about one without the other after all. And the questions arose of staying versus leaving.

It was in this meeting that people began talking openly about their fears and insecurities about the change in pastors. No fear was too outlandish to air and all opinions were respected. Some of the fears are also quite realistic. Lots of tears, a tender prayer for Carlos and Wendy as they move on. The healing has begun.

What a privilege to be able to be present for such a meeting. We are accepted and included as though we attend every week. Such openness is truly a gift. There are many spiritual giants in this church. Of course, they don't know that. As soon as you decide you are a spiritual giant, you shrink.

33 Think about Sunday School class.

Now we are in Tocoa on our way back to the monastery. We took a direct (and more comfortable) bus this far. I am still not entirely normal and appreciated the comfortable seat for a little snooze. Prairie read the newspaper.

Beth—It's An Interesting Life—October 11, 2007

On Oct. first, I gave a consulta to an older lady from Plan de Flores whom I remembered well. I had treated her a few years ago for niacin and riboflavin deficiency. She also has dementia. It was quite a problem that day because I was seeing patients outside, in the shade of the school building. She kept coming back asking for glasses. I had no door to close (and no glasses to give, of course). Well, I am happy to say that she had no signs or symptoms of either niacin or riboflavin deficiency this time. In my life, I have treated only three people for that. Two of them were elderly women who live in this county. You have to be pretty low before clinical signs show up (especially as dramatic as hers were). It is a poverty thing. You know how skim milk looks sort of blue—that's the riboflavin. When cream is present it covers it up.

Unfortunately, the dementia is still a powerful factor in her life and having a door to close didn't help. Several other consults were interrupted. We had adult multivitamins, so I could add them to her other medications. She is a sweet lady, who just can't remember stuff very well.

Later, when we were at Andrés' store buying groceries, a lady tried to pay for part of her purchases with her watch. She and Andres talked about it until they could come to an agreement about how much the watch was worth. Soon, she finished her transaction and asked Prairie for money to buy sugar. Prairie turned to me; I said, "Go ahead, her mother is sick." So we put her sugar on our bill. It comes in a two pound bag—eighty cents (15.14 lempiras).

It is an interesting life. We are poor enough to sew patches on our socks, but we live in a country where most people don't own socks. We wear socks almost half of the time.

October third was Day of the Soldier here in Honduras. Mostly, however, institutions are going to Monday holidays. So Centro de Salud was sort-of closed, but Warnita, Prairie and I worked anyway. Most patients thought we were closed so we had very little work. This allowed us to walk all over town to do our other errands.

We had decided to participate in the Pray and Fast for Peace Day on October eighth, sponsored by several organizations in the United States—organizations that, like us, understand that you can't end violence with violence. I wonder why that is so hard to comprehend!

It was suggested to do a dawn-to-dusk fast and we did. We got up early and ate breakfast before dawn prayers. (A nice hearty breakfast, I might add.) Mondays are a big calorie-burning day, so we were aware of the sacrifice of fasting that day. We drink plenty of water on fast days.

We did our running around and hitched a ride earlier than usual. Then we walked home, stopping along the road for un-programmed worship. Whenever we have a fast day, we replace the meal skipped with a spiritual practice. Makes sense—feed your spirit instead of your body.

We arrived home earlier than usual and had time for rest after baths and afternoon prayers. We did special prayer services for all three of our usual prayer times. It was very helpful to us.

We ate our dinner after sunset. I suppose I don't need to say it, but we ate with much gratitude.

Beth—An Encyclopedia for the Library—October 11, 2007

One never knows how quickly or slowly something will happen here. Let me give you an example.

As you may know, I have a strong sense of support for public education and the public library system. Here in a country with a bankrupt government, they need a lot of help. We have stayed in contact with the public library in Limón and notice that it doesn't have much. The major clientele are the junior high students looking for answers for their homework.

The librarian had no encyclopedia and only a one-volume dictionary (that we had given her a few years ago). We valued the idea of providing such reference material, but didn't know where we could obtain it or at what price.

In November of last year, we came across the Océano[34] store in Tocoa. They sold reference books and had several types that might be suitable for our public library. One set sold for about $780 (14761.67 lempiras) and the other for about $720 (13626.16 lempiras). The saleslady talked non-stop, offering us a free two-volume Honduras encyclopedia if we bought both. She obviously misunderstood our financial situation. She let us look at the books, but wouldn't give us any peace while we did so, so we just left—in the middle of one of her sentences, no doubt. She had offered to come visit us. We didn't give her instructions for getting to our place.

Well, we thought about it. You know we do Quaker process for decision-making. Quaker-time and Honduran-time are congruent (slow and deliberate). In August, we decided that we should try to make this happen. I sent an email to friends who have a big heart and more money than is good for them and asked them to send a check. They did.

In September, we received this news. Good news. Of course, since we don't get to the internet often, turnaround time is slow. We stopped at the store on our return from Belize, La Ceiba, etc. The saleslady wasn't there. We left a message for her that we were interested and had a donor, but we didn't know yet which set was the suitable one. We would like to have her bring them to a meeting at Limón in which the teachers could review them and make a recommendation. We got her name and telephone number.

34 A publishing company.

The next Monday, our day was so busy that we didn't get to the library during its morning open hours. No problem, we would try again next week.

We did connect to the library, but the young woman wasn't who we thought she would be. The librarian is on vacation for October and will return in November. Okay, no rush.

About a week later, the saleslady showed up at the monastery (with her Man Friday, of course). She had decided which one we should have. She is a teacher and she knows. Then we had another high- pressure sales talk.

I thanked her for her expertise and her opinion, and told her that I really needed the opinion of the local teachers, who, of course, are expert about what is needed in this community. I gave her the librarian's name and telephone number. The prices have gone up in the year since we began this investigation.

That brings us to this week. On Monday, we visited the principal of the junior high to ask him to set up such a meeting. He listened politely and told us that he has visited the store and has reviewed the materials. He told us which one he recommended. It was the one the saleslady had recommended. This is a little surprising since it was the less expensive one. This teacher is one whom I know and I respect his opinion very much. He was the mayor for a while and I liked what I saw then, too.

This choice was a little disappointing in one way. The other set would have been the one we would have selected for seventh, eighth, and ninth graders back in the States. These kids just don't have the academic background to benefit from an ordinary encyclopedia. This theme-ordered didactic encyclopedia would be of greater use. Someday, maybe someday they would be ready for the other one.

So, we now accept the decision of—which one?

We are still not in a hurry. There is a great dearth of trust in Honduras and great concern that items of value will walk away. The principal recommended that we be sure to entrust the volumes to a specific person. The set comes with CDs too. We thought we could give them to Mamuga, a Garifuna organization that has an office, with computers, near the library. It is open to all members of the public—Garifuna or not. The principal said that the school's computers aren't working. If and when we give them the CDs, they are to be sure to hand them off to a very responsible person. He happens to have a computer here at the junior high and he happens to have a library here at the junior high, but the students do not have access to that computer and the general public does not have access to the library. So we thought we had better stick with our first plan and talk with the Mamuga people. The Mamuga office was closed (Day of the Soldier holiday, transposed to a Monday, you know). We were pleased with our progress on this project and plan to visit Mamuga next week.

Tuesday, who should show up at the monastery? You got it—the sales lady and her Man Friday. She had called the librarian. The librarian has moved to the states and there is a new librarian. She got the telephone number of the new librarian and set up a meeting. The new librarian, a kindergarten teacher, an elementary school teacher and a junior high teacher were present. Needless to say, they produced a document advocating for the encyclopedia that the saleslady recommended! One must never laugh when negotiating such an important purchase, but there was a temptation.

The saleslady was prepared to take us to Bonito to the bank to withdraw the money to pay for the encyclopedia set. After all, no one walks around with that kind of money. I mentioned that the bank in Bonito had burned last month. Was it open already? Yes, the Man Friday said, he saw people outside the bank this morning as they drove through. Well, okay. I put on my shoes, got my passport and bankbook and off we went. We left our lunch (of leftovers) sitting on the table inside the house. (Here in Honduras, you do all socializing outside. Inviting someone inside is a very big step of intimacy.)

Well, the bank in Bonito is next to a credit union. The driver had seen people waiting at that door, not the bank. There is a new building being prepared to house the bank, but it, of course, is not yet ready. So, on to Tocoa. Since the day before was a bank holiday, the bank was packed. I am now of the third age, so our saleslady got me in the front door (in front of people who looked older than me). Then inside the crammed bank, she got me to the front of the line of third-age people. This is all very irregular. Later she told me that all of the tellers are her old students. She was very proud of how fast and efficient this all was.

While I was in the bank, Prairie bought a few ripe bananas, lychees, and a green papaya to enjoy with her cousins when they arrive on a visit (today).

We stopped at the saleslady's house and they picked up meals and ate them in the car as we continued our trek. Prairie commented that it is good that we know how to not eat now. (And how nice that we could make little comments in English that don't have to be edited.) We stopped so Prairie and I could buy twenty-five pounds of corn which I wanted to take home while we had transport. (We paid three lempiras a pound—up fifty percent from last year, but still half the cost of buying corn flour.) This was a nice favor to us and it also helped the saleslady to understand in a concrete way a little more about our financial situation.

Next stop was the public library in Limón. It was now getting on in the afternoon, even with speedy Man Friday at the wheel. The library was closed. We stopped at the mayor's office for information. We could leave the box there if we wanted. (I didn't want to.)

They took us back home and helped us carry the stuff to our house. We finished the transaction. She counted her money and I counted the volumes. All okay. It cost $781. Pretty cool. So now we have the volumes here at the monastery. We will take them to the library one or two at a time when we understand better just who the librarian is and if she really is on vacation. And what about Mamuga and their computers?

It was late for lunch and for afternoon prayers. We did prayers and then ate our lunch. Immediately, we made a nice hearty dinner and ate it, too, by lamplight.

Our saleslady got the mayor's office telephone number. Lucky them. We don't have a telephone. Lucky us. We know how to contact her if we ever fall into a bundle of money. She really does have some great stuff, still untapped.

This one lady will do more for getting reference books to students than any number of outsiders could possibly do with whatever higher motivation than profit and making her quota of sales in a month.

Beth—The Cousins Visit—October 31, 2007

This is a combination of celebration and confession. The visit of Prairie's cousins was a lovely success. They are very good sports and just dealt with whatever challenges came up. They didn't manage to see a toucan or a coral snake, but they did get to see two tarantulas—one full-grown and one half-grown.

One of the cousins has a lot of dietary limitations. At least it would seem that way in the States. But we bought all the stuff she could eat and we all feasted on our restricted diet. It was pretty nice.

We even had a special meal in Limón. A friend of ours was delighted to make a special meal for us and really got into the details of the diet. We had grilled and smoked fish, *cassave*, rice, tajadas, a cabbage salad, and a lovely tomato sauce (that the rest of us could and did eat). We stuffed ourselves. We kept it for a surprise, since we couldn't be sure that she would be able to do the exact menu we had discussed. Oh, the drink was *guanabana refresco*. I suspect that your local restaurant wouldn't be able to duplicate it. Actually, none of our local restaurants could either. It was the home-cooking touch. Fabulous. We took the leftovers home and ate them for dinner. We didn't need to make anything to add to them.

They got to see our monastery, our road, the town of Limón, and met some of our friends. Even the six-year-old walked all the way (over a mile and a half) to Rosa's place on Monday morning. Singing "We are Walking in the Light of God," and marching. It takes a lot of verses to walk a mile and a half when you are six years old. But, she had Prairie to keep her interested. One of the adults went in with me so that I could do the regular work. Prairie took the day off from clinic work to be her cousins' tour guide.

We transplanted the baby plátano plant. We made tortillas from corn—including boiling and grinding the corn. We did a lot of life-skills-in the country activities.

Now comes the confession part. We really don't know how to have guests yet. We bought a lot more vegetables than we could eat in the time they were here. We bought a green papaya with no clue how long it would take to ripen. It ripened about a week after they left! So we feasted on papaya—just the two of us! It was a big papaya. One has to be a little careful with feasting on papaya; it is a mild laxative. Well, none of the vegetables or fruit went to waste, but we were eating them for a week after the cousins left.

We are on the road again. We are in El Pino today and will go to Tegucigalpa tomorrow. We have all of our papers in order, we think. We'll deliver them to our attorney, who will get us legal residency—we hope.

Beth—Getting Our Papers in Order—November 2, 2007

We are in Tegucigalpa. We spent Wednesday in the bus from La Ceiba to Teguz. The views from the bus the last few hours were really great. Teguz is in the mountains. The roads don't seem to faze the drivers, but I come from flat Wisconsin. I found it exciting.

Yesterday was pretty stimulating. Our attorney wouldn't give us an appointment. We were to call him before coming. Tuesday we called and the secretary said the lawyer was out of town and we should call early Thursday morning to talk to him. The secretary wouldn't even consider making an appointment. Well, this is the big city. In smaller towns, every corner just about has a business offering to sell you the use of their telephone. Not here. Teguz is in the twenty-first century where everyone has a phone. How would we call on Thursday morning?

We got up early and nothing was open but the cathedral, so we went there and enjoyed a lovely mass with even some beautiful Simon and Garfunkel music. One never knows what one is going to get. When mass was over we went to the attorney's office (without calling ahead). We had managed to buy an *Escuela Para Todos, 2008* (a Central America almanac) at a street vendor.

The secretary had called Enil, the attorney. He would be in shortly. So we did the riddles from the almanac. The secretary joined in. (I know, I'm a bad influence. She was supposedly working.) When Enil arrived we dived in. What a process! He made sure that both of us understood everything. We were very grateful for this. Often when we have complex conversations in Spanish we come away having understood different things. The hard part was that neither of us is a Spanish expert and each is as likely as the other to have it straight or not. He looked over our documents—all in order—but we were still missing one additional document from the church.

When we finally understood most of the process, the attorney began explaining the expenses. First, there was money to go to the police department. No, they don't actually do a criminal background check, they just get a certain amount of money. Second, there was an expense for a stamp (looks like a postage stamp). It doesn't do anything except make the papers look official. Third, there were forms that must be purchased from the Congress of Attorneys—at a high cost, of course. So the attorney organization got their cut. It went on and on. Quite fascinating.

After a few hours of this, we were ready to go to the bank to get money. He took us to a bank at the food court of a local shopping center. Enil invited us to lunch, but it was Thursday and we were fasting. Yes, I know, Jesus never turned down a meal invitation that we know of—but he did say something about how it would be different when he wasn't here in the flesh. The lawyer ate his lunch while we did the banking.

The bank was a small branch and wouldn't give us as much money as we wanted. They had an upper limit of how much they'd give out. So, we were off to another branch to get the rest. Okay, it is so nice to be in the third age—and go right to the special line for elders and pregnant women. This didn't take long. By now, I was carrying a thick wad of money worth over $2,000.

Then back to the office to pay the fees. This is the first time that the attorney had the office door closed for our visit. All of the rest of the time, the door is open. Whenever anyone walks into the outer office, he asks the secretary to inform him. He answers the telephone every time it rings. A woman came with an urgent problem and he had us move into the outer office and saw her with the door closed. He later told us she had a personal problem (like we couldn't tell).

More than half of the $2,000 went to government fees. We'll get receipts for all of them, of course. We paid half of his fee now and would pay half when we got the residency papers. It all became even more complicated when Enil tried out his English to help make sure that we understood. (Better to just stick with Spanish.)

Then we needed to get pictures taken, so the attorney walked us over to the photographer's place. It is graduation time, so that was interesting, too. Just us, and dozens of adolescents getting their graduation pictures. Apparently, they don't really do ceremonies with caps and gowns, only pictures with caps and gowns. The kids passed them on to the next in line when done. There were about five sets that got passed around. We had to take our glasses off for our pictures. It is too bad that we had to hand in those snapshots; we had pretty interesting expressions on our faces. Surprise, curiosity, what else?

We waited for the photos to be developed and then we took them back to the office. More forms to sign. Among other things, we signed a statement that we are not communists and that we are not going to try to overthrow the democratic government of Honduras. (Reminded me of 1950s U.S.A.)

Finally, we have finished with everything. Today we will stop by to be sure that the church letter will be forthcoming. We got an email today that implies all will be well. I am so grateful. The attorney walked us to a bookstore before returning to work. We spent some time looking things over and bought a few small books.

Yesterday was All Saints' Day (and also an anniversary that I didn't understand) at the cathedral. There was a mass in honor of women in the afternoon. It was already late for our afternoon prayers, so we went to mass again. It seemed a nice luxury to have someone else do all of the leading. We could just follow along and not have to strain our brains. We are pretty ecumenical, you know.

By then, it was dusk. We went to a Chinese restaurant for dinner. Chinese restaurants are a splurge—also, one of the few places in which one is served vegetables. We ordered two dinners to share. We finished the food for breakfast in our room this morning. We were happy to have no more responsibilities for the day.

Beth—Books and Rain —November 6, 2007

We are now in the Tocoa-Ceibita area. We spent last Friday in Teguz finishing up legal details, moving to a hotel close to the bus station, and book shopping. There are a lot of bookstores in Tegucigalpa and too many interesting books to choose from. It is a bit disturbing that most of them either come from the U.S. or Spain. Why is this disturbing? One reason is that folks in Honduras who like to read are providing financial aid to the richer countries. Another is that the thought processes of thinking Hondurans are being influenced more from outsiders than from their own country folk. We bought a few books and will review them at leisure when we get home.[35]

Saturday, we caught the bus at seven AM to get to Tocoa by four PM. As we were coming down the mountains, we could hear brakes squealing. Then we could smell the brakes—more exciting than I cared for. At the lunch break, a fresh bus arrived and we all changed over, but by then, we were out of the mountains and the biggest risk was past.

Rain. Cold front after cold front. When we got off the bus in Ceibita, another lady got off, too. Her husband was waiting for her with his pickup truck. She told us to just climb in. We rode with the kids in the back until we were actually into the neighborhood and then walked the rest of the way. We had managed to fit our book purchases into our backpacks. The streets were flowing with water. I took off my shoes and socks and put on flip-flops. Prairie already was wearing flip-flops. We walked to the church and the parsonage.

Our friends in Ceibita are all well. It was good to see them. Soon, the visiting medical team from Texas showed up. Many are repeaters from last year. So nice to see them, too. More rain. Not as many patients as expected showed up because of the rain.

Yellow alert. The public health clinic and public schools were closed. We decided to go to Tocoa to do errands Monday afternoon. But the water was going over the bridge. We might not get back to Ceibita the same day. So we canceled. There is

---

35 Later we gave most of these books to to Larry and Allison Smoak. (Lerry is now married to Allison.)

still some rain today, but less.

Yesterday (Monday), Prairie worked as a translator and intake person. The church sanctuary is a big echo chamber and one shouts. She lost her voice. Today, she participated with the teams going out to interview neighbors. She listened and took notes. (When her voice gets better, I'll get to hear about all she learned.) I saw patients. We were pretty busy. There is a dentist, so a lot of teeth are being pulled. The neurologist is helping the dentist, while the family doctor and I saw the medical patients, but he came to help me when I had a complicated patient.

These are delightful people and hard workers. It is hard to leave. But we are really pretty tired and need to get home. I suppose you can tell that I'm tired.

This afternoon, the river is lower and there isn't active rain, although the sky is pretty gray.

Beth—Robbery and Reconciliation—December 12, 2007

This is our December trip to the internet café. We have been pretty busy lately. Merry Christmas and Happy New Year!

Now to the news: When we arrived home from our trip to Tegucigalpa and Ceibita, we found the monastery was robbed on November seventh. Prairie is writing something about that, so I won't repeat it. It was not a lot of fun.

We stayed at Gloria's house in town for about a week while we assessed the situation. The morning after the robbery we went back to the monastery to put a new padlock on the door and to clean up a little. We hired a car for that. Since we had the car, we packed up the encyclopedias and the new medicines to take into town the same day.

We are now in the long break from school. The school year starts in the middle of February, so that's when the encyclopedias will get the most use. The librarian had received only the first volume of the encyclopedia so far. She was just delighted to get the complete set. She was so happy to hear that my mother is a retired teacher and librarian that she hung on every word of her librarian's tips. They were—that reference books NEVER leave the library, no matter how trustworthy the library client is and this means even the mayor. (I suspect that the librarian job is a political appointment.)

The public access computers are still not functioning. Some time next year we expect them to be available again.[36] In the meantime, the CDs and DVDs that go with the encyclopedia are being kept at our place. The thieves were not interested in educational material.

The medical team that came to Ceibita had given us some useful medicines for Centro de Salud (especially high blood pressure medicines). It was good to get those things delivered.

So, we reported the robbery and gradually realized that we are the ones who are supposed to investigate it. Well, gossip is a wonderful thing. We have, in fact, identified all three young men. We have sent them and their parents written and verbal invitations to a meeting of reconciliation on Friday, Dec. fourteenth, at ten in the morning, our time. Please pray at that hour for our little peacemaking efforts. The meeting will be in the open air (no traps) in the street next to the mechanic's shop in Limón. The mechanic is enthused about the idea. Mateo and his boys will be there. That is pretty cool. I didn't invite them, but I had them deliver some of the invitations. They are apparently our volunteer bodyguards. Juana Nidia and Warnita are our real bodyguards and we did invite them. They will hold the whole operation in prayer. Right now, I could go for a really boring week, butI don't see one happening soon.

It looks to me as though these young men have three options: change their lives a lot (which are going down the toilet pretty fast), spend some years in prison, or keep on with their

---

36 After several months, we realized that Mamuga was not going to repair its computer system. We gave the material to the junior high. They hope to open a computer lab soon for the students.

current behavior until a neighbor kills them.

Not pretty, not pretty at all.[37]

So, that's the short version. The longer version is that we are very conscious that our first responsibility is to pray. Even with the extra trips to Limón and La Fortuna to investigate, set up meetings, etc., we have kept our spiritual practices firmly in place. We have had to be pretty darn flexible in terms of times (and even sometimes days of the week), but you have never seen us more committed to spiritual practice.

There is no one trained in conflict resolution here. Most of our friends just support the throw-them-in-jail path. Jails here are very dangerous places. They are not places that you want your neighbor to have to enter. And we are called to love our neighbor. Well, we will do what we can. Good grief!

Prairie—The Details of the Robbery—Dec 12, 2007

Much of the stress of the last month has been due to the fact that we were robbed. The afternoon of Wednesday, November seventh we returned from our trip to Tegucigalpa and La Ceibita to find the doors and windows of the house wide open. Beth and I had discussed in the past the possibility that we might get robbed someday, and so we guessed that someone had taken the opportunity during our absence. They'd busted the latch on the door and gone through all our stuff, undoubtedly searching for cash. Fortunately, we had all our money and documents in our money belts. Chito had given us a ride to the monastery that day, so we went back to the road to see if we could catch him and tell him what had happened, but there was no sign of him. We figured we were on our own, and returned to the house.

Then came the surprise: the robbers were still around! There

37 In August of 2008, their father and younger brother were murdered—apparently in retaliation for another crime committed by these two brothers. They have since moved away. We have no news about their cousin, the third man involved in our robbery.

were three young men (including one with a revolver) all within a few years of twenty, by my estimate. One of them took me by the hands into the house while Beth tried to stay outside with the gunman—though they soon came in as well. At first, Beth and I tried friendly tactics, introducing ourselves to them and chatting. The guy with me asked me if I was scared and I said no. Then I asked him if he believed in God, and he said he didn't. I couldn't think of anything else to say, so I just started praying silently. Then Beth said it was time for our afternoon prayers, and so we started singing hymns. As we sang, two of the guys started tugging at my clothes and removed my glasses, saying they wanted to "make love" to me. The other one went around closing the window shutters and doors, but Beth followed him and opened them back up.

At one point, I tried to escape out the back door, but they pulled me back in. The back of my legs scraped on a bench, and later developed bruises. One of the guys pulled at the ties on my dress and it ripped. When the gunman heard that sound, he indicated for them to stop. Beth and I ran out of songs we could remember, and now I was starting to get scared and imagine the worst, as they were using more force to get me towards a bed. The gunman had put his arm around Beth's neck to stop her from moving around and put the pistol to her head. She ignored it, however, and said she was sure he wasn't interested in using it.

Just at that moment there was a cry from outside—it was Chito!—and the three robbers and would-be rapists fled. He had returned because earlier, when two young boys had helped carry some boxes to our house, they saw it open. When they went to find Chito, he'd gone to see if Lencho, our sometime neighbor, was in. God works wonders. I had truly thought we were alone on the mountain, but God heard our prayers and we were saved. I have a new understanding of God as my savior.

So, we grabbed our still-packed backpacks and left with

Chito. He gave us a ride into town, and we stayed with our friend Gloria for a week as we recovered. In the end, the robbers only took our two machetes and a few small tools, as well as my money belt with about $130 in it. At first we thought they'd gotten my passport as well, but happily, it turned out to be in with Beth's things. They had also taken the guitar (probably our possession of greatest monetary value besides books), a bed sheet and a mosquito net. But, the next day when we returned to put a new lock on the door, one of the people who came along found all the items stashed in the brush near the path. I was happy to have the guitar back, undamaged, except for a little rust on the strings.

Chito had called the police when he returned for us; there are two officers stationed in Limón. They got a ride out to our place (as they don't have a vehicle), but weren't inclined to search for the robbers as it was getting dark. One of the policemen fired a few shots into the air as a warning.

The justice system here in Honduras is quite a contrast to the U.S. It took us a week before we learned how to make a report to the police. We were told that the way to get the men arrested is to find out their names and report them to the Justice of the Peace. We were rather shocked that the burden seemed to be on the victim to investigate. But, as Chito had seen the robbers run off, he recognized them: two brothers whose parents live in La Fortuna, and their cousin from Limón. Living in a small community, people know each other, and we learned a lot by word of mouth. After about four weeks, we had learned all their names.

In that time, Beth and I have discussed a lot about what we should do, and have been given lots of advice. What we really want to do is follow God's lead and make peace. Jesus taught us to turn the other cheek, love our enemies, and forgive. And so we have spent a lot of time in prayer and discernment. I think about these young men whose lives are going down a bad path, and also about the safety of others in the community. We seem to have the power to get the robbers arrested and likely jailed for a long time. Moreover, people have heard the rumors about them, and around here, sometimes they will take justice into their own hands. I don't wish death on these young men; I have hope in God's grace and the possibility of them turning their lives around.

On Monday, Beth and I sent each of the young men and their parents an invitation to meet us in the open air in Limón this Friday. We don't know if any of them will show up, or what exactly will result, but we trust in God's love and ability to perform miracles. Please keep us, the young men and their families, and the whole community here in your prayers. That is the greatest help and support you can give.

We harvested our first plátanos. And they were very nice. We ate most of them while they were still green and gave some to Chito—who had given us the baby plant—and have saved three to try ripe (if they don't rot before ripening). We are very pleased.

Beth and plantano with babies.

The same plant has four babies. We cut down, and then cut up for mulch, the mother plant. The largest baby is already looking very much like an adolescent. We moved one of the babies and it is about knee high. Still at the original site are two other very little plants. Little by little, step by step.

Our sewing has gotten complicated. The sewing machine got messed up, but good, and we couldn't do anything about it. The last sewing machine repairman was pretty costly, so we wanted to find a new one. We asked for informed advice. Each Monday, we would look for this guy. Each Monday, he wasn't home. Well, we each have four blouses. One of Prairie's has been patched a lot of times and each time that it is washed, we wonder if it will be its last. Finally, we decided that we had to move forward on the blouse making—by hand. And so we did.

When we went to town this week, he was home. He came out yesterday morning and fixed the machine, teaching us a lot at the same time. He recommended that we buy five bobbin holders (so we have spares). Well, today in Bonito, we were able to buy one (five? good grief). So, now we are ready to finish the blouse with the sewing machine. It should be much easier, but we had made some progress. It just takes a long time..

Before the repairman had left, there was another male voice in the porch. It was Rigo, the guy who built Gloria's little cabin. His daughters were with him to visit. Well, we had already washed and hung up the clothing and had had most of our sewing machine lesson, so we entertained visitors.

It was a busy day.

A week ago, the young friend who helped me plant the two coconut trees showed up with another friend. They gave us a couple of cacao fruits and planted a couple of the seeds. The first seed has sprouted! Stay tuned. We even made some pinol with ground cacao seeds in it. It doesn't quite taste like chocolate, but has all that cocoa butter in it—a good drink.

On our fateful robbery day, we had bought an orange seedling—grafted—in Tocoa. We got it planted in November too, planting some pigeon peas around it to provide ongoing soil treatment. Looks pretty good. The guy who sold us the tree said that we should be eating oranges from it in two years. I told him that if we don't, I'll be there to eat his. He agreed. He would give us a sack (bushel) of oranges if ours doesn't bear that quickly. So, we are very optimistic.

Today, we bought thirty oranges in Bonito. The vendor was delighted. She sent her son (or grandson) to pick them. She charged us fifteen lempiras (seventy cents) for thirty oranges. We will be feasting on oranges.

Well, time to go. There's a bus to catch.

Beth—Update—December 28, 2007

No one showed up to our meeting. We weren't terribly surprised. We learned just this morning that the gun was a loaned gun. Also, everybody—but everybody—in La Fortuna knows what happened and who did it. Our friend, Mateo (who built the monastery buildings), has told the gun owner what happened and has advised him not to loan his gun without lots of care. This is helpful to know. I have not been comfortable with that young man having a gun. Everyone reassures us that these guys will not be bothering us again.

This morning, we sent a verbal message through Mateo to the father of the boys that we want our remaining stuff back and that we want to forgive, but we are struggling with that. So, time will tell.

Justice in Honduras, like in the United States, is focused on punishment, not on restoration of damage done or reconciliation. Here, as U.S. citizens, we supposedly have greater protection from the law. This protection takes the form of actually arresting and prosecuting offenders against us. The same crime against Honduran women would not attract much interest in the local justice of the peace or the police officers.

So, time will tell.

Merry Christmas! We had a quiet, peaceful day and lots of special food. We are now in Tocoa, visiting our friends in Ceibita. We may even go on to El Pino to visit more friends. We're sort of vacationing. By that I mean that we have no functional goal in visiting. We still keep our monastic schedule, of course.

Beth—A Trip Home—December 29, 2007

We have made the reservations! Autumn will be here with Prairie, so it looks like I will actually come to visit.

I'll leave here on Tuesday, February fifth, arriving at my mother's house in Wisconsin in the wee hours of the morning of Wednesday, February sixth. I will be in the Wisconsin-Minnesota area for about two weeks before going to Portland by train. The exact dates have not been set. I'll be in the Portland area 3–4 weeks, leaving Portland on Tuesday, March 18 (a night flight) to arrive back in Honduras on Wednesday, March 19.

Autumn will come about two weeks before I leave. That gives her a chance to learn the ropes with both Prairie and me here to help. I am very grateful she will be coming. Autumn will be flying home the same day that I arrive here. That gives us just one trip to the airport in San Pedro Sula. Sometimes, we can be efficient.

We are in El Pino today. Our time in Ceibita was very nice. We are learning that New Year's Eve is more of a holiday, even a church holiday, than Christmas Eve, which is more of a holiday than Christmas Day. We are planning on going back to Limón on Monday. But if there might not be buses, this could get interesting. We have said that we would work in the clinic on Wednesday, January second. We'll let you know.

Beth—Arriving, Coming Home—January 27, 2008

We met Autumn at the San Pedro Sula airport yesterday about noon. We three took the bus back to El Pino, arriving in time for a dinner at Doña Ada's little restaurant and the evening program at the church. Autumn had traveled all night and had slept hardly at all, but when called on to participate in the class, she was able to do it with grace.

Today, we are running errands in the city. Whenever we go to the city, we need to take money out of the bank. We are being more careful not to have more cash than a month's worth of expenses at home. Being robbed does change some habits, I guess.

It has been a very cool rainy season and is just beginning to warm up. This makes it very strange for garden work. Some days are cool and comfortable and some days we swelter. We have to re-adjust to the hot days again.

The plan on Monday had been to see patients in Limón, order medicines, hop the eleven AM bus and arrive in El Pino about 4:30 PM. Well, we started out fine. We were up slightly earlier than usual, walked to the highway, and chatted with our friend Doña Eva and her daughter-in-law, Ana. Ana is concerned about her six-year-old. They live two miles from the kindergarten and she doesn't see how she can send her to school. Things are more complicated by the fact that Ana is illiterate so she can't teach her at home. Doña Eva can read, as can her son, the father of this child. So, we will give them one of our alphabet books to get the mother and child started. I think I'd better pick up some reading glasses for Doña Eva, too, when I'm in the states. She is in her mid sixties.

We caught a ride the rest of the way to work with our friend Justo Paz. (I love it—his name means just peace.) He farms rice and gave me some more information about that. The rice is almost ready to be harvested. He rents a combine.

I saw patients. The medicine order didn't go so well. Warnita and I had made a list of about a dozen medicines that we needed. The pharmaceutical company only had three of them. Sigh. Maybe next week. Next week I will bring the telephone numbers of two other companies. Meanwhile my kids have no cough syrup and no anti-allergy medicines. The adults have a small amount.

We left Centro de Salud about eleven and picked up our mail (always a treat, because there is almost always something). There was a light rain falling; we waited a bit for the bus and realized that the eleven AM bus just wasn't coming. We each ate one of our homemade baleadas [tortilla and bean sandwich] and started walking. By then the rain had stopped and it was just overcast. Soon, along came a truck with folks in back. We hopped in and were dropped off just over an hour later in Corocito—more than half way to Tocoa. It was overcast the whole way. We were very grateful. We caught another bus to Tocoa, then another to La Ceiba. At the La Ceiba bus station, we quickly bought provisions for a picnic dinner and breakfast and caught the bus to El Pino. We arrived there just before 5 PM.

It is always such a treat to be at El Pino. We really feel like part of that congregation. Arnulfo, who is in charge of the buildings, is on vacation. So Reina and the supervisor of construction helped us find the folding cots, the necessary keys and got us situated in the guesthouse. We put up three cots, all ready for Autumn's arrival.

Last month, I told you about the congregation and the new pastor all reeling in pain over the cultural differences. Well, many still are, but the supervisor of the new pastor had called a few meetings with a few key people and the healing has begun. When cultural differences are so huge that it seems like you have just been assigned a heretic to be your pastor, there is a lot of concern.

We were privileged again to hear about the personal work that one of the congregational leaders is doing to help in her own healing and in the healing of the congregation. The Holy Spirit is at work again in that church. It looked pretty grim there for a while.

Beth—The Long Trip Home—February 6, 2008

We did the quick (week and a half) orientation to monastic life for Autumn. She is a very apt pupil and there is the temptation to brag. Well, suffice it to say, I felt confident about leaving Prairie and Autumn. Prairie had been gradually taking over more and more of what had been my responsibilities before I left.

Monday morning (February fourth), we took our backpacks and walked to the highway. Since my backpack was quite a bit heavier than the others, they traded off with me some. We caught a lift all the way to Tocoa almost right away.

First order of business: public bathroom. Second order of business, call the attorney. We have been in the process of getting Honduran residency. Once that process gets to a certain point, one doesn't have to do the expensive passport stamping thing. Well, we are not at that point.

It was obvious that we couldn't do our usual Monday work in the clinic and still get to La Ceiba in time to go to the immigration office, so we had given our excuses the week before.

We called the attorney. He had nothing for us, but asked us to call him again in the afternoon. We caught the bus to La Ceiba and got there in time for a late lunch. We went downtown to Zion Methodist Church, where we could leave our backpacks while running around town. Jerry, the custodian, was there, but he never has much news, and none of our other friends were around.

We went to the immigration office. It would cost $120 to pay the fine and have a clean record for leaving the country the next day but I could pay at the airport—if they notice that the passport is not in compliance, the official said. We waited a long time while she called her expert consultant in Tegucigalpa. Then she stapled the official notice of what I owed into my passport. Our attorney was out when we called him again.

We went to the bank and withdrew money for living expenses for the monastery and for paying the fine in the airport the next day. We tried calling Eloyda, the nurse at El Pino, to start our medicine order process. But couldn't connect with her either. So, we caught the city bus to the bus terminal. By now it was after three PM and it was time to be arriving in El Pino.

We bought oranges on the street for snacking. We bought coconut bread products, bananas, and a cantaloupe, both for our breakfast the next morning and as for traveling food for me. When we got to the bus terminal, we bought some cheese and then went to catch the bus. When the little bus from El Pino pulled up, Eloyda climbed out! We were delighted. She made a date with Prairie for the next morning to go over the medicine list. This is the first time that Prairie has had to handle a medicine order. It would have been nice if I could have been part of it, but she will do well. There is always at least one medicine not available and we just have to deal with it.

Even with our conversation with Eloyda, we were able to climb into the little bus and get to El Pino by about four PM. Tired. We bought drinking water.

We did our afternoon prayers. Since some of the brothers of the church were hanging out near where we usually do our prayers and one especially likes to join us, we invited them. Autumn has had the responsibility of planning and of being the emcee for the afternoon prayers, but, with guests, we all shared. One copy of a song doesn't go very far with six people (and isn't much help for the illiterate ones, anyway). It went well. We are getting over our self-consciousness of monastic prayers in public and semi-public.

We set up our beds, took showers and went to dinner. We had decided to eat at Doña Ada's place, the idea being that my next travel day would be long and tiring. A solid meal to start out would be good. We had a lovely dinner. We stopped to see one friend, Reina, who is in charge of the children's program. The kids were to attend their first classes for the year on Tuesday (yesterday). She and her team are ready. It was a long day. I fell asleep during one of the Psalms in bedtime prayers. The Psalm ending woke me up, fortunately.

Yesterday morning, we were up at just before five (only a little earlier than usual). Morning prayers and a light breakfast before the Cutting sisters walked me to the bus. When it pulled up, I was on my way and the young women were on their own. They planned on working some with the children's program, doing the medicine order, washing their laundry, and catching up on internet responsibilities.

The bus ride put me in touch with a couple of carsick travelers. I graciously gave up my window seat. The wind was too much for me anyway. The carsick one could have that spot Then another carsick one. Well, I moved twice. Am I bragging about my niceness? No, I am sharing my gratitude about arriving at the airport with no vomit on my clothing. Neither of the sick ones got messed up either. We were all very satisfied.

Taxi to the airport. When I was checking in, the guy checking me in looked with some disapproval at my passport. I told him that I was going to take care of that next. Well, the disapproval wasn't about me, it was about the official note saying that I had to pay the fine. He said that religious don't have to pay that. Well, I suggested, perhaps that is something between the Roman Catholic Church and the government, since most religious are Roman Catholics. He said, no, it's about the role. Okay.

What do I know? He called over a guy with a cop-looking uniform and showed my passport to him. He looked it over and agreed with the airline worker. Then he just ripped all of the offending pieces of paper out of the passport. Just like that. Well, I could have done that the day before, but it would have been illegal for me to do it—but I had thought of it.

So now we have a new discernment question. When we hitch a ride, we keep track of that. The money that we would have spent on the bus, we put into our tithe account to donate. When I return, we can decide if that is what we should do with the fine that we didn't have to pay. There are always discernment questions. If our financial management isn't a spiritual practice, then we fall into the dreaded duality mess. You know, it goes something like this: money is bad, all physical things are bad, only spiritual stuff counts. It leads to things like wars and other kinds of dangers—like self-righteousness for starters. So, our financial management is an ongoing discernment question. We get one settled and another pops up to take its place.

I had arrived early to the airport to be sure that I had time to do whatever was required. I spent the time writing in my journal and reading the newspaper in the departing passengers' area.

San Pedro Sula to Houston. Hours of layover. Tempting bookstores. I didn't buy anything, but I noticed how tempting they were. I arrived in Minneapolis about ten PM with another hour-and-half wait for the shuttle. It felt pretty cold to me. I had put on my slacks under my dress in Houston. Now I got out my traveling sheet and used it for a shawl and a pair of socks for mittens. That worked very well. People are so polite; no one said a thing about this strange get-up. Marguerite, my sister-in-law, met me at the shuttle drop and brought me to Mom's house. Mom looks great. Her ninety years sit lightly on her, it seems to me.

So, I am back in one of my homes, the one in which I grew up. I am tired, but, thanks to layers of clothing and an electric blanket, I am fine with the cold.

Money, Notebooks, and Pencils—February 22, 2008

Everyone has challenges with their budget. So why should I bother to tell you about ours? Because we had too much money. How could such a thing happen? A long story, of course.

From about last July, we were aware of having money that we had decided should be donated, but nothing came through. Let me elaborate: Our priority of giving donations is the purchase of bulk medicines for the public health center. It didn't need anything from last February until this January. Prairie reports today that the medicine order that she made the day I left Honduras went smoothly; it cost just over $500 and the medicines have been delivered and are being dispensed as needed.

The local Roman Catholic priest had been buying groceries for the poorest people, without regard for denomination or belief or lack of belief. He is skinny and gets around by bus and bicycle. (This means he is not corrupt.) He got transferred and not replaced so this is no longer an option for alms

Sor Leonarda had gotten a good set-up for her fifty orphans. She now has a fund for medical care; she has salaries for her workers; she proudly told us that she has food security for the first time ever and that will extend for some months at least, but she didn't have dental care for the children. We said that we could pay for the start-up (one hundred dollars). She checked around and found a dentist who would be willing to come out from the city as a volunteer; he just wanted his expenses paid. Okay, sounds good. We gave her the money. It took about a month to connect for various parts of this conversation. Finally we left the money for her with our trusted friend, Gloria. Now we are into October. The dentist suggested that the project wait until mid-November when school lets out so no one would have to miss classes because, of course, you would keep a child home from school to recuperate from any dental procedure. Okay, sounds good. And we had figured on a hundred dollars a month for several months until the backlog was cleared up.

November came and went. The dentist had a relapse. A relapse of what, we don't know, but it took him out of the picture. So another dentist was found. Same deal. She would come to evaluate the kids and prepare a plan of care. Sor was sure that she could write a UNICEF grant to pay for the dental work once it was clear what the cost would be. In January, the dentist came. Only the two kids whose toothaches brought the topic up needed dental work, so, no request for more money for dental care.

Finally, the public schools. We have spent hours in conversation about how to help improve public education. The information that I had obtained directly from teachers is now several years old. We want to help the most remote schools, thinking that they are likely to need help the most, but to visit them in order to learn the needs would be formidable. It would also be rather high profile. We do not want high profile. After all, we are a monastery, not an aid organization.

We had let this question wait for awhile since the school year ended in November. However, February is the start of their new year. We decided that Prairie and Autumn would visit the superintendent of public schools and ask what the needs were, thinking that notebooks and pencils would be the priority, since many people are too poor to even provide a forty-cent notebook and an eleven-cent pencil for their child. (Also, inflation is skyrocketing.) There was an article in the newspaper about the rising cost of school supplies. Details were given and there was no good news.

Prairie and Autumn were able to meet with the superintendent and arrange with Andrés (to order the notebooks and pencils.

Today, they went to the bank in Bonito to withdraw the money to pay for them. The school superintendent said that about seventy percent of the families with kids in elementary school are in financial need. There are about 2,500 students. Prairie ordered $1,000 worth of notebooks and pencils.

I am so grateful. My kids will have notebooks and pencils. And our budget is back in order.

Prairie—*Water, Garden, and a Campesino Family—March 8, 2008*

Water update: One evening at the end of February, I noticed that the winds had shifted from the standard southeast to coming from the north. That often signifies a cold front coming in. Sure enough, by morning the sky was heavy with dark clouds and the rains had begun. I attached the downspout, and by evening the water tank was full to overflowing—800 gallons of fresh rainwater! I couldn't help but smile; I hadn't been that grateful for rain (or any particular weather) in a long time.

We've had a few showers since then, so the tank has stayed topped off. However, we've continued to go to the creek to bathe and wash laundry, wanting to conserve water for the imminent dry season. (Summer here unofficially starts with Holy Week.) The overflowing tank seems like a symbol for my life these past six weeks while Autumn has been here with me: I feel like God has been showering me with blessings. It has been a good Lent, and I'm looking forward to Beth's return on Wednesday and celebrating the rest of Holy Week and Easter with her.

Garden update: First the heat and then the rain have been good for the garden as well. A tomato plant that had sprouted voluntarily near the orange tree seedling we'd planted (the seed must have been in the compost we used for fertilizer), grew at an amazing pace and is now bearing small, flavorful fruits. In January we'd planted some okra seeds, and the largest of those plants are also beginning to bear. I'm so excited to have fresh vegetables from our garden. The selection has been slim in town recently. Ten of the twelve original pineapple plants (May 2006) now have blossoms and fruit, which is encouraging. Sometimes I wonder if the slower-growing plants (like pineapple and banana) are really doing anything at all, and if our feeble efforts are enough, but patience pays off!

Visiting a campesino family: Every Monday while Autumn has been here, we've had someone to walk with us or give us a ride for at least part of the route to or from Limón. Three weeks in a row we have walked home with various members of a *campesino* (peasant-farming) family that lives further up the *desvío*, near the village of La Fortuna. The following week, Santos Emilia, the mother, sent us some tamalitos with one of her sons who was on his way to Limón that day. I was feeling a real connection with the family, so I suggested to him that Autumn and I would like to visit them sometime. That Friday, we did.

It was almost a two-hour walk up the desvio from the monastery to their home. I knew where the path toward their house was, but wasn't sure how far they lived off the road. The path impressed me: it was two tracks and had obviously been built by a bulldozer. After we'd walked a ways, a boy appeared at the top of a hill and called out. We realized he was telling us to come that way; the path we were on led to someone else's property. So we climbed up, and found a much humbler footpath which wound down the hillside to their house. To the north was a stunning view of the Caribbean and Limón. We could even make out the shiny rooftop of the monastery on its hill; La Fortuna is in a valley to the south from there.

The modest wood house is situated on a hillside with a fenced-in yard to keep out the cows. They have chickens and pigs running freely in the yard and are continuously shooing them out of the porch and kitchen. The only other room in the house had three or four twin-sized beds in it. Santos invited Autumn and I right in to the shaded porch area. With her were three of her daughters (ages approximately fourteen, ten, and five) and her youngest son and grandson, both toddlers. Her husband Francisco and the other four sons (sixteen, thirteen, nine, and eight) were out working in the field; the oldest daughter (eighteen) is going to school in Tocoa. They cultivate a variety of crops including corn, beans, plantains, yucca, and other root vegetables like melanga and sweet potato. Four of the kids currently attend the elementary school in La Fortuna. They have to walk or ride a horse an hour each way on the three days a week there are classes.

After we arrived, Santos invited us into the kitchen for a snack of corn flakes with fresh warm milk and sugar. There were two small tables, one on each wall, each with a chair, so we sat separately to eat. We chatted about various things and ended up staying till the afternoon. We were quite interested in seeing how they lived, going about the daily chores. Two middle daughters took laundry to wash in the creek. They pipe water to near the house for kitchen use. Santos reigned over the kitchen and spent much of the morning preparing a lunch, of rice, beans, corn flour tortillas, and a potato-like root vegetable called *yame*. She also fried fresh eggs for Autumn and me. The boys came in from the field for lunch, each being served, in turn, a bowl with food and then finding a place to perch and eat it. When the girls returned from washing, they served themselves.

Before we left, Santos gave us a few pounds of dried beans which they'd been sorting, as well as some elote, or young corn. She told us several recipes for using it, besides eating it as boiled corn-on-the-cob. So we had fun experimenting with that the next two days. One cuts the corn from the cob and grinds it in the mill; then there are various dishes that can be made: atol, a drink in which milk, sugar, cinnamon and vanilla are added; a type of tortilla cooked between banana leaves; fritters; and tamalitos, stuffed and boiled in the husk. She even gave us *cuajada*, a creamy soft cheese (technically curds) which she'd made from their milk. She said they get some ten liters (two-and-a-half gallons) a day from three cows, and easily use it all.

They seem to do pretty well with their little home farm, raising food for themselves as well as selling some of it, yucca and other root vegetables, in town. Unfortunately, after living there for eighteen years, they expect to have to move in April. The creek that runs near their house is considered pristine, since they are the only people that live along it, and the government in Limón plans to build a dam to collect the water and pipe it into town, as the current water source is contaminated from the many cattle upstream. Francisco has been visiting City Hall to try to get some recompense for their move; I'm not sure what's come of that.

In the end, it was certainly an interesting visit and well worth the walk!

Beth—Safe Arrival Home—March 20, 2008

I'm back in Honduras. All travel went smoothly all the way to San Pedro Sula. We ended up hitching a ride part of the way from the airport. It is Holy Week. Buses were so full that they didn't stop. Today we are on the road. Had to write because my Mom likes to know that her kids have arrived when they have arrived. Well, Mom, I have arrived.

Beth—The Fire and Miracles—April 18, 2008

We are now in the summer season—hot and dry. We walk to the stream to bathe and wash our laundry to conserve water. We will not likely get any rain until June. Last week most of our physical work was cutting firewood and gathering and putting down mulch for plants near the house. Saturday morning we finished up the mulch project with great satisfaction and moved on to our usual Saturday chores. It fell to me to burn the trash. There was a little more of it than usual. I lit the fire and returned to the house for other chores. Then we heard the crackling! The fire had escaped from the burning pit and was rapidly spreading in all directions!

We could control the line towards the buildings (using water, shovel, and hoe), but the strong wind took the flames up the mountain fast. We used the path as a firebreak to the south and just cut some of the vegetation and used the hoe to clean pine needles off the path. A little water here and there—about sixty yards. Prairie continued to cook, while also fighting the fire in the parts closest to the house. One arm of the fire went down the slope to the north into very steep terrain. It curved around back up hill and threatened the sanitario from the west. We got that taken care of—for awhile. Then it was back from the west again. Yet a third time the sanitario was threatened, this time from the north.

When Mateo built the structures of the monastery, he left

the branches of the pine trees and the useless upper trunks lying on the ground. There is one to the north, two to the south, one each to east and west. They are banked with leaves—lots of fuel.

The path-fire-line extended too far from the house to continue. The terrain just below is very steep, so the risk of the firefighter (me) being cut off from the house was genuine. We abandoned that fire line about the time the second fire threatened the sanitario. Then the blaze crossed the path and began back towards the house. The breeze was stiff.

This is what foresters call a cool fire. Even though we live in a forest, it is a grassfire, a brushfire. The large trees are not much involved. As the fire to the north of the house moved further east from the sanitario, it approached our terrace-line to the north and neared the large fuel supply of the downed pine. The fire to the south was returning fast, even lighting up trees as tall as twenty feet.

It was time to leave before the escape route was cut off. We quickly packed backpacks and hurried away, leaving the house in God's hands. We hastened down the path, through the garden to the stream and rested, ate our lunch and did afternoon prayers—with our feet in the cool water—lovely.

Prairie went up the path once to scout the fire. She could see the roof; the house was still standing, but seemed to be completely surrounded by flames. We walked in the stream back to the road. We had our boots, so that worked well—good protection from the rocks. The stream was often too deep for boots. No problem, more cooling water for the feet (I call this water socks).

We walked to the highway and hitched a ride to Limoncito, to Mateo's house. Margarita and Delmis (their oldest daughter) made us welcome. They had seen the smoke and had been concerned. We missed Mateo on the way (the stream route, remember) as he had gone to La Fortuna to take some lumber.

Soon their older son arrived with their second truck. A few

neighbor men, Delmis, Prairie and I piled in to see what we could see and to try to save what we could save. The truck bucked and heaved. When we were just a little over halfway there, the neighbor pulled off and we left the truck. The men and boys want ahead (machetes in hand) while we women followed, Delmis carrying my backpack.

The fire had passed. The house and sanitario were unscathed—completely unscathed! The fire had entirely surrounded them, in places coming to within a yard of the pine structure. But not even a scorch mark. Truly a miracle!

The firewood and mulch were all burned. (We store firewood under the water tank.) It had burned and the heat damaged the tank; water was till draining out, uncontrolled. There were still pockets of flame (even just to the east of the house where the building debris had been). We decided not to sleep there that night and returned to Mateo's house. There had been some stiff winds in the night lately. Another long walk to the truck, then the ride down. Margarita fed us and we were given a place to sleep. We were so grateful. Sunday morning, we had our sunrise prayers under their bougainvillea arbor. We were ready to return home.

Mateo cut some bougainvillea branches for us to plant. Margarita gave us two liters of fresh milk and a stalk of plátanos. Mateo gave us a ride as he was on his way to plant coconut trees on his property near the monastery. He gave us a sprouted coconut to plant. For everything, there is season, and after a fire and destruction, it is time to plant.

Mateo looked over the tank. He can't guarantee that any repair would last, but he is willing to try.

There was still water. We drained it into every bucket, pan, jug and bottle that we had. It is a long way down to the stream. We planted the bougainvillea in the planting holes that the fire had cleared of jackbeans and tomatoes and in two other spots where an arbor might be nice. They have a reputation of having a low percent of taking hold, so planting more than you want is highly recommended. It was not the very restful day of rest that we might have liked.

Monday morning we went to town as usual (so grateful that our legs could still carry us). No work in the clinic—national holiday, April fourteenth is Day of the Americas. That meant no mail either. I did one doctor visit on the porch of the clinic for a kid with an enlarged spleen—probably complicated malaria. I had no medicine to give him.[38] We visited friends.

When we returned to the monastery, we could see that Mateo had repaired the tank. We were so grateful. Tuesday, it rained. Wednesday, it rained. Not lots, but we now have water in our tank. We are very grateful. Remember, it is unseasonal rain!

Wednesday we visited the garden. We lost the cantaloupe, jackbeans, passionfruit vines, and one pineapple. The rest is all fine. Remember that the majority of the pineapples, bananas, plátanos, fruit trees, and pigeon peas are in the garden area.

Near the house, we lost the coconuts, tomatoes, plátanos, baby orange tree, compost pile, lime tree (ready to bear this year, sigh), pineapples, pigeon peas and chaya. We still have lemon grass. It looks as though some of the chaya may come back and one friend tells us that the coconuts could come back. We gratefully planted the new coconut in a planting hole that the fire had emptied for us.

Wednesday, we also went to cut wood. One has to eat, after all. A trunk that we had cut down last week was still there, ready to be carried home. So we carried it home.

While I was gone, Prairie and Autumn had constructed a rocket stove—a small stove used by campers, made with a large dried milk can and soda cans. We have been very grateful to have it as we can cook a one-dish meal with very little fuel. Very helpful when cooking wood is in short supply.

I really like miracles. They are just about my favorite. I am very grateful.

---

38 It turned out to be leukemia. No treatment. He died.

Immunization Programs—April 18, 2008

We got to Bonito a little earlier than we expected to arrive, so I can actually write to you again.

Next week is a huge immunization campaign. Each year the public health clinic is expected to do more and more with fewer and fewer people. This year when the auxiliary nurse (who is doing her required year of social service with the clinic) finishes, she will not be replaced. A physician has been hired for the clinic, but I have yet to lay eyes on him. Prairie saw him once. Juana Nidia is optimistic about him.

Every spring there is the big immunization campaign, but once every four years it is even bigger. Everyone between one and five years of age will get their measles, mumps, and rubella booster and an oral polio booster. Everyone between six months and five years of age will get a Vitamin A booster. Then of course, there are the standard immunizations that must be included as well.

This county did not meet their immunization goals last year. Part of that was bad weather (hence bad roads) during both major immunization campaigns of the year. Another part was one very weak worker (in her social service year) in an under-served part of the county. So, the catch-up is important and personnel are few.

Prairie and I will move into town for next week. We'll stay at Juana Nidia's house. The week of April twenty-first, we will focus on immunizing the town of Limón. The following week is outreach week. Juana Nidia will not be working with us; she will go to the under-served area to help their overworked nurse. Juana Nidia lives at the end of the street, past where the electrical service reaches. It won't be so much different from our home, but she does have a gas stove!

We have tentatively planned to work most of the second week of the immunization campaign, too. But this is Honduras. Advance planning is not part of the deal.

As we were walking to the road this morning, we were noticing how the green is coming back already. And how pretty the leaves are that fell from the fire-damaged trees (fall colors, even). We commented that now would be the time to work on our trails. We need more and better switchbacks, and now that the bushes are burned, we would actually be able to see to do that work. Well, it won't happen this month. Maybe next month.

If you have looked at the pictures that Prairie has posted, you may be curious about the picture of the dog. Well, we have been ready to accept a dog or dogs. One day we went over to visit our neighbors and they said, jokingly, "We have a dog for you if you want him." We said, "Yes, of course." Then we learned the details.

They had rescued this dog from starvation. He is only five months old and had been tied up, apparently to guard a cornfield—and not fed! He was skin and bones and walked with his tail curled under his belly. Very sad little guy. And perfect for us, of course. The fellows put together a leash for him, with a tie about his neck, then a wooden stick, and another tie at the other end. This way, he can't chew it off. We were told to keep him tied up for two weeks to be sure that he learns where home is.

Prairie has had some experience with dogs, which helped a lot. I had also picked up a dog training manual in Spanish when I was in the States. We fed him, but, at first, he ate very little. We got him on a Wednesday. By Sunday, he had doubled his intake and seemed eager to eat. We fed him tortillas for breakfast and lunch, then a balanced Honduran meal for dinner.

On Monday, we gave him a dried fish head after he had eaten his breakfast of two corn tortillas and left him tied up when we went off to Centro de Salud. When we arrived home, he was gone. The tie about his neck had come loose!

The next day we went to visit the neighbors, hoping that *Juguete* (means toy) had gone back to their place. They had cleared out! Their more permanent place is in Lauda. So, we don't know whether they have the dog or not.

We were so happy to take in this little guy. He was perfect for us. But, now he is gone. And it would have been tough to manage him with the immunization campaign. We take what comes.

Prairie—Prairie Looks at Postulancy—May 28, 2008

I'd been thinking for some months about whether I should be committing to another year here at the monastery. A part of me definitely had the sense that I would be here for a number of years more. But I also wanted to know what God is calling me to do with my life.

One Sunday in early April, during un-programmed worship, I felt a sense of contentment and joy in my life here in a way I hadn't before. I was happy to sit in contemplation and prayer, and grateful for a place where it is safe—and encouraged—to face the challenges of life and the spiritual journey. I also realized that I am eager to see things continue to develop at the monastery (garden production as well as the addition of sisters) and be a part of the communal discernment and planning.

So the idea came to me to ask Beth about becoming a postulant—one who is considering that the monastic life might be right for her and wants to continue her spiritual formation and discernment of God's call.

The next day, before I managed to get up the courage to ask Beth, she brought up the subject with me! She had been doing her own discernment about my call, and invited me to consider the postulancy. I was surprised and joyful.

So we talked some about it, and decided to have a clearness committee.[39] After two meetings considering questions of what it means to me to be a postulant, and possible reasons not

39 Quaker group discernment on an individual's calling or concern.

to do it, I felt clear that this is the next step for me. So, in our April monthly (business) meeting,[40] Beth and I confirmed our clarity, and made plans for an official ceremony.

In worship on Pentecost Sunday, May eleventh, we used the liturgy from the United Methodist Baptismal Covenant for me to reaffirm my faith and commit to spend the next year here at Amigas del Señor as a postulant. We read the Pentecost story from Acts, sang hymns about the Holy Spirit, read a couple of reflections on postulancy, and Beth invited me to remember my baptism with a sprinkling of water (particularly refreshing on that hot day!). It was a joyous celebration.

For me, becoming a postulant is a recognition and affirmation of God's call in my life, which seems to be leading me to the monastic life more permanently. Postulancy lasts at least a year, at the end of which I can consider becoming a novice. Sometimes monastic vows have been paralleled to getting married. Thus, the novitiate is like being engaged, and postulancy could be seen as serious dating, considering if this might be the one, the path for my life. I hope you will celebrate with me, and keep me in your prayers as I continue to try to discern and follow God's will for my life, every day and moment, in humility and love.

On the Road—May 30, 2008

We are on our way home after a brief stop in Tocoa (with a terrible keyboard on the computer—worse than usual, even).

Before we left home, we had met a new neighbor family. They have lived about a twenty minute min. walk from us for just over a year. I had heard of them, but thought they lived further away. On Wednesday, they just showed up and we all had a very friendly chat. On Friday, we went to visit them. We started talking about planting and about fertilizer. Well, one thing led to another and the next thing we knew we had made

40 Quaker Meeting for Worship Through Conduct of Business, the monthly gathering that distinguishes each worship community.

an agreement for him to carry six big sacks of cow manure from Mateo's corral to our place the next day.

And he did! We are very excited. Our agricultural efforts had come to a standstill for lack of organic fertilizer. Most of the potential mulch and compost got burned up in our fire. Jose, the neighbor man, is also interested in putting in a few days work with and for us. I am very hopeful that he'll be able to do that.

We are now down to less than ten gallons of water in the water tank. We have been carrying water up from the stream every time we went there to bathe and do laundry. The stream is lower, but still keeps flowing. Now is the time for the rain to start. We are ready. And we are likely to get quite a lot of rain soon. We may get wet walking home today. In spite of Prairie being a little sick with a virus, we managed to get most everything done that we wanted to in the city. We never get it all, so we are quite satisfied.

One of our city projects was buying blouse fabric. We are now two postulants. After a slightly more than one year clearness process (Quaker term for patient discernment) we decided on suitable blouses for postulants and novices. Since some of our blouses are falling apart, this was none too soon. We also bought a new belt for the treadle sewing machine. Fabric is not of much use if we can't sew it up.

Another item was a huge papaya. We shared it with our friends at El Pino and harvested seeds. We are thinking that the spot that used to have a lime tree might be good for papayas. And now we have manure, so our optimism on planting is high.

More news, or at least sort of news. Our attorney thinks that some progress has been made and that we will actually get our residency during our lifetime.[41] It's all about having realistic goals.

---

41 We received our legal residency June twenty-sixth, 2009!

Beth—Visit to Plan de Flores—June 24, 2008

In May of last year, a teenage girl and her mother came in for a consulta. The girl had finished elementary school, but did not attend junior high. Since Plan de Flores is a bus ride from the junior high, it is quite a financial investment to go to junior high. I mentioned the monastery and that we are looking for girls of good character. She was very interested. Her mother seemed interested, too. To put age in perspective, many girls are in a stable marriage-like arrangement and are mothers by age fourteen—the girl's age at that time. The girl's birthday is in July and she would be at a very crucial time for life-time decisions here in rural Honduras.

So, I let this season for a year. Last week, we went to Plan de Flores just to visit her. It was a very good day. We had no idea what to expect. We didn't know where she lived in this sprawling community, nor what may have transpired in her life since then. I also was pretty sure that I wouldn't recognize either of them. With these low expectations, it was pretty easy to put ourselves in God's hands for the day.

By the time we walked to the end of our path, we got a ride to the highway! Nice start to the outing. Then we walked to Rosa's place to wait for a bus or hitch a ride. Soon we caught a ride with two guys who work for the cell phone company. We rode in an air conditioned cab, with a CD player, a laptop computer and a few cell phones. They were checking the signal in the neighborhood. Interesting (a little cultural shock, too).

At what looked like a good starting point in Plan de Flores, we got out and asked for directions at pretty much every house and business establishment. The first few knew nothing. We visited with one woman who was sick and very sad. Her husband went north a few years ago and she has heard nothing. She thinks that he has abandoned the family, but others tell me that they always call to say that they arrived, even if they do abandon the family. Perhaps it is easier to face abandonment than widowhood, but it is a tough life.

We stopped at a shop that had *topogigios* (homemade popsicles). The scent got a little warmer. Each person we spoke to only gave us instructions for the equivalent of a half city block ahead, telling us to ask there. So we did.

We went to a house next to the elementary school and chatted for awhile with Doña María, who had been interested in hearing more about our life at the monastery. We gave her a postcard. She gave us banana soda pop (chilled, even), and instructions for the next leg of our treasure hunt.

The next house had two women watching soap operas. They could barely tear their eyes from the screen to give instructions. But one of them is the sister of Maylin, the adolescent in question. We, of course, have been asking after the Mom, but now, we ask about the girl, too. She is living at their aunt's house. Mom is doing laundry and isn't home. We get vague instructions to aunt's house.

On we go. We get a glimpse of folks doing laundry beside a little stream (much smaller than our stream, really a creek). So, we think, "Maybe Thelma (the mom) is one of those women." Down to the stream we go.

Not only is Thelma one of them, Maylin is also one of them. We were warmly welcomed. Maylin asked, "When can I visit?" We sat around for a long time in companionable silence. Hondurans are big on silent bonding.

Thelma was using something that looked like a potato in her scrubbing. I asked about it. It is homemade laundry soap, which can be purchased at one of the little shops in Plan de Flores. Hmm. We want some.

Then Maylin went to her aunt's house returning with soda pop (with ice) for us. We were very grateful. We think that it may be almost noon by now, but we don't wear watches, of course.

Maylin finished her part of the laundry and bathed, and then escorted us to her aunt's house. More hanging out. Aunt asked Maylin to go to the shop to buy tomatoes, onions and meat for lunch. They do a little cooking, saying nothing about it to us.

We sort of feel that we have accomplished our mission of the day, but sort of not. Maylin has not asked any questions. We still think more like foreigners than like monjas. We are still pretty new at this, you know, so we want to have more information exchange, but how?

Next Maylin took us to her grandmother's house. Grandmother asks the questions that any foreigner would have asked. Maylin listened, all ears. Another aunt brought us some Tang-like drink, chilled again. The luxury of a community with electricity!

It is now well past noon and we are very grateful for all of these calorie-containing drinks, but real food is feeling like a distant memory. Next, Maylin takes us back to Aunt's house and feeds us boiled green bananas and rice topped with sautéed beef with a tomato sauce and glasses of water. She apologizes that the water is warm. We are very grateful for the food and water.

Next, Maylin takes us to the shop where we buy a ball of homemade laundry soap (and a pineapple to take home). Lots of companiable silence. Well, it seems time to go home. We haven't seen the afternoon bus. Maylin says that it is already quarter to three and she doesn't think that there will be a bus. She would know. So we ask where is the best place to hitch a ride? At the restaurant. Okay, we confirm her visit for the first week in July, give her a proper monastic blessing, and off we go towards the restaurant. Before we get there, a very slow-moving pickup comes along. (When you ride in the back of a pickup, you want a slow driver—safety, you know.) The pickup dropped us off at our own road and we walked home. It was later than usual, so more shade and we didn't have backpacks full of groceries, hence, a pretty easy walk.

We arrive hot and sweaty, but not terribly tired. Afternoon

prayers, bathing, cooking dinner. A good day.

Beth—Agricultural Progress—June 16, 2008

While were gone to El Pino, the new neighbors moved away. We didn't know that and walked over to visit one afternoon. They were gone, but there were some other people there.

The new folks are making fences for the owner of the property, who hopes to use it for pasture. One is the brother to our friend, Francisco, who lives an hour closer to La Fortuna. The other is the ex-husband of the recent neighbor woman. It is a small world. We, of course, have heard her version of why she left him. An odd way to meet someone.

They were willing to do some work for us. We were thrilled. They have since worked with us two long mornings. A day's work is usually five hours for physical work here. We are pretty much caught up on our dry season gardening goals. It was hard work. We work with the men, of course. When we finished in the garden, they cut firewood while we made lunch for all of us. We are very grateful for the gardening progress.

Quaker unprogrammed worship. Drawing by Prairie

They built an arbor for the passionfruit vine (that has yet to give a fruit) and two primitive benches, one on each side of our back door. That's sort of our chapel and thus high priority for benches. Now we don't have to carry our little benches outside every morning and afternoon. We'll get spoiled, of course. The men also did some work with the terracing just south of the house.

Our friend, Daniel, who has some training in sustainable agriculture also has helped us a few days. He gave us some good seeds, too. Some are beach legumes that he says will produce a lot of foliage to use for mulch and fertilizer. The others are a legume whose leaves are eaten in soup around here.

So, within two weeks we had fourteen days of gardening work done. Very nice. The June rains have finally arrived, about three weeks late.

We have harvested a couple of pineapples and one dwarf plátanos has flowered. Pineapples, plátanos, and bananas share a lovely virtue. They produce even without any fertilizer. They take a lot longer and produce a lot less, but they do produce. Now, they have all received a nice manure meal and most have a nice layer of mulch. We are hoping that they don't need to revert to their slow production consistent with neglect. It is pretty nice to feel caught up on the gardening stuff.

Our Children—July 23, 2008

Last week, we worked the usual Monday morning at Centro de Salud. I gave thirty-five consultas and Prairie's pharmacy served even more. We were just leaving to run our other errands when we met up with Sor Leonarda and a group of children. She said that she was looking for me. She had thirteen kids who needed consultas.

We had seen a lot of people with high fevers. I suspected that we were having an influenza epidemic. It looks a lot like dengue, but the eyes don't hurt and, thank God, it doesn't last as long (two weeks). Well, of course, I couldn't turn down our children.

Sor Leonarda loaned Prairie a teenage girl to help her with errands. I reminded her that we go two by two after all. We figure if it was good enough for the Lord, sending out the disciples, it's good enough for us. Okay, easily done. I returned to Centro de Salud, figuring that if Sor doesn't count as a Sor to be my companion, who would? In a few minutes, she showed up with nineteen kids to be seen. I started registering them and then assigned that task to a bright fourteen-year-old boy while I began seeing children.

Sor brought a box of donated medicines. Since they all had English writing on them, they were of no use to her, but they were very useful to me. We had been all out of cough and runny nose medicines and most of her kids had coughs and runny noses. One had lobar pneumonia, one had asthma, but most had the crud. Half a dozen had vomiting and diarrhea. One was very sick without good explanation. We could treat them all with medicines from her box, medicines from our pharmacy, and two prescriptions that she would get filled the next day.

Sor has fifty children at the orphanage. The eighteen boys all sleep in the same room. Do we think that any of them will escape this respiratory crud? Sor knows almost nothing about children. She is eager to learn and demonstrated how well she listened in the last consult with her new plan to de-worm the kids every three months. She is a living, breathing example of the old adage: "God doesn't call the qualified; God qualifies the called."

One of the fabulous things that she does because of her ignorance about children is that she treats them like adults in some of the best ways, like assuming that they can remember something important, that their observations and opinions are important. Sor's training is in economics, and her spiritual formation, monastic. I am so grateful to get to work with her from time to time. She is an encouragement. She doesn't need to say or do anything to be an encouragement; her life is an encouragement.

It was a profound spiritual practice to do those few hours

of medical consults for her kids. Most are orphans, but some are abandoned. Many have had horrible experiences before coming to her. She talks about repairing the irreparable. Eyes wide open. I can't explain the powerful feelings that a pediatrician has while weighing a thirty-eight-pound eight-year-old child.

Prairie and her helper finished the errands and returned to Centro de Salud, filling prescriptions and administering nebulizer treatments to the asthmatic patients. We left about four PM. Just enough time to get home before dark. We caught a ride and there was still enough light for us to do afternoon prayers outside before making our dinner. A very successful day, we thought. I was tired.

Maybe you will say a little prayer for Sor Leonarda and our children this week.

Beth—Invitation to Amigas del Señor
February 23, 2007—Present

If you know someone who may be interested in spending time with us, please feel free to share this invitation with her.

Amigas del Señor is a monastery for women in Limón, Colón, Honduras. Our monastic calling is to a life of prayer, spiritual formation and voluntary poverty. A day in our life includes worship, gardening or sewing, housework, music and reading. Our spiritual practices are mostly in the United Methodist and Quaker traditions. We don't ask women who come to have particular religious beliefs or backgrounds. We ask that they be open and willing to participate fully in monastic life.

An aspirant is one who comes to the monastery suspecting that she has a long-term monastic call (several years or a lifetime). She makes a one-year commitment to begin to try out this call.

A sojourner is one who feels a call to invest time in her

spiritual growth and in service. She usually does not suspect a long-term monastic vocation. We accept sojourners for periods of one year or longer.

Discernment is a slow process. There is a lot of prayer involved. It is possible that one who is called to this monastery will not know whether she is a sojourner or an aspirant. Seeking God's will for each woman is part of the shared monastic work.

A woman who comes to us is at least eighteen years of age (twenty-one and over is preferred); there is no upper age limit. She is unmarried and without minor children. She has no medical conditions that would endanger her by living without electricity and remote from secondary health care.

An aspirant or sojourner is willing to live in a Spanish immersion household. She has the capacity to work alone and as part of a team. She enjoys learning. She knows how to laugh. She need not have specific vocational skills or minimum level of education. She understands that her job is whatever needs to be done, whether it uses her special training or gifts or not.

Aspirants and sojourners do not pay money for the privilege of living the monastic life. Neither do they receive financial recompense.

Interested women should contact me by mail:
Hermana Alegría (Beth Blodgett),
Amigas del Señor,
Limón, Colón,
Honduras.
By email: bethblodgettnow@yahoo.com

Information about Amigas del Señor is here: www.umoi. net/our-ministries/missions/amigas-del-senor.

The Sisters of Amigas del Señor

Amigas del Señor: Methodist Monastery

AFTERWORD

Novitiate—Prairie—A New Name

God called Abram and Sarai to leave their homeland and when they said yes, he gave them new names—Abraham and Sarah. After Jacob wrestled all night, God renamed him Israel. Jesus told Simon that he was to be called Peter (the rock), for the Church would be built on him. When Saul responded to Jesus' call to evangelize to the Gentiles, he began using the Greek version of his name, Paul. And, when a person enters the religious life, he or she may take a new name. It was a question for me to ponder during my postulancy: if I entered the novitiate, would I take a new name and what would it be?

I took that question seriously, and one of our Spiritual Formation courses helped me with it. The exercise was to consider what I saw or what I wanted in my relationship with God—like faith, hope, or patience. For me, it was trust and confidence (*confianza* in Spanish). I'd been discovering in the previous year that I can trust in God to provide for my needs, and I wanted to have more self confidence to be the me God created me to be. So, as I discerned that I am, in fact, called to the religious life, I decided that taking a new name would be an appropriate outward symbol of the inner change and my dedication to God. Therefore, during my Reception into the novitiate, I took the name Confianza.

In Honduran churches, people call each other *Hermana* (sister) and *Hermano* (brother), just as the early Christians did, for we are all children of God. Beth and I have decided to adopt this custom in the monastery, and are practicing calling each other Hermana. In town, children address us as *gringas*, many people call Beth *Doctora*, and I am sometimes *la muchacha* (the girl). In the weeks since my Reception, Beth, the staff at Centro de Salud, and our other friends are learning to use my new name, and I am learning to respond. But whatever title or name is used, we are committed to answering to what we are called.

Hermana Confianza—June 23, 2009

Pentecost Sunday, May thirty-first, was a very special day for me, as you can imagine. We had invited many of our friends from Limón to attend my reception into the novitiate, but as the hour approached and no one showed up, it was just as well That meant my sister was off the hook for translating! Instead, we had a beautiful intimate service with my family. My Mom April and Dad Craig, my sister Autumn, and my Aunt Becky were here and they all participated.

Each one did a scripture reading (see below) or prayer; my parents, who are United Methodist ministers, reaffirmed my baptism; and at the end, each of them, as well as Beth, gave me an individual blessing. My family and I sang two musical selections in full harmony, which was an extra-special treat for both Beth and me. Tears flowed freely throughout.

Beth, of course, was the emcee, and led us in worship as we sat in a circle on the porch. She even gave a sermon about wrestling with God—something I have demonstrated much skill at! It was a hot day. (My family's visit seemed to be during the hottest week we'd had in a year!) and we had a couple of stretch breaks during the service—I think it lasted close to three hours! The most formal moment was when Beth asked me the question of commitment (see below) and the most informal was as she gave me a haircut and everyone took photos. After the service, we celebrated by making and eating pastelitos and drinking limeade (Tang) plus some treats my family brought. It was so wonderful to have them here for five days.It was well worth the preparation ahead of time and the exhaustion afterward.

I'd like to thank everyone who has sent me encouraging words and gifts; it has made this time even more special, knowing there are so many people thinking about me. Novice means beginner and there is much to learn, but I go forward into the unknown, trusting that I am in God's strong hands and that He will guide and care for me.

Scripture selections included:
Psalm 84 (living in the house of God)
Jeremiah 9: 4–5, 7, 11–13 (God's promise to his exiled people)
Acts 2: 1–22, 36–42 (Pentecost)
Genesis 32: 24–31 (Jacob wrestles with God)
Colossians 3: 8–17 (Clothing ourselves in the good things of God)

We sang Jesus' Great Commandment (Matthew 22: 37–39) as well as many other wonderful songs—too many to name! This is the question Beth asked me:

¿Vivirá este año del noviciado dedicada a Dios y confiando en el proceso de este monasterio para discernir la voluntad divina, viviendo una vida profética de pobreza material y castidad en obediencia humilde?

"Will you live this year of the novitiate dedicated to God and trusting in the process of this monastery to discern the divine will, living a prophetic life of material poverty and chastity in humble obedience?" This was my answer:

Por la gracia de Dios quien me da las fuerzas para hacer todo, lo haré.
"By the grace of God who gives me the strength to do all, I will."

Peace and love,
Hermana Confianza

August, 2009 Profession—Beth

This month, I make my first Profession. It means that I move from being a Novice to being a Sister. It is one more official step in the process of no turning back. It is intensely personal and profound. This is one of those precious times when I am forcefully and graciously reminded that today truly is a new beginning, a reminder that all of the reign of God is there for me, all I need to do is to notice and accept it, again, today—and tomorrow.

One never makes an informed decision; the costs and the rewards reveal themselves along the way, just as in any vocation. It is a great privilege to live in the monastery and to become a Sister. I get to say with the Psalmist, "I will dwell in the house of the Lord for ever."

The name I have chosen to take is Sister Alegría (ah-leg-GREE-ah). It means happiness, joy. I seriously considered Sister Paciencia (Patience). I can certainly use more patience. But the name evoked a long-suffering, downtrodden sister; so Alegría moved into the lead. It is a name that I will be happy to live with. Of course, I will answer to what I am called. You are not obligated by my monastic decisions, only I am.

My Profession day is Saturday, August twenty-ninth, 2009. I wish that you could be here with us. Please hold us in your prayers that day. I pray for you as I hope you pray for me, that we can each say with our brother, "My meat is to do the will of him who sent me." [KJV]

Dios les bendiga,
Hermana Alegría

READING LIST

These are books that the authors have found very useful and/or were influential in the founding and early years of the monastery.

RADICAL CHRISTIAN LIVING

Claiborne, Shane, *The Irresistible Revolution: Living as an Ordinary Radical*, Grand Rapids, MI, Zondervan, 2006

Dubay, Fr. Thomas, *Happy are You Poor: The Simple Life and Spiritual Freedom*, Ft. Collins, CO, Ignatius Press, 2002

Jennings, Jr., Theodore W., *Good News to the Poor: John Wesley's Evangelical Economics*, Nashville, TN, Abingdon Press, 1990

SPIRITUAL PRACTICE AND PRAYER

La Nube del Desconocimiento: Orientacion Particular, (*The Cloud of Unknowing: Privy Counseling*, Spanish language edition) trans. Fr. Gabriel Ochoa Gomez, S.J., Mexico D.F., Mexico: *Obra Nacional de la Buena Prensa, A.C.*, 2004

The Cloud of Unknowing, New York, HarperCollins, 1981

Teresa of Avila, *The Way of Perfection*, trans. Otilio Rodriguez, O.C.D. and Kieran Kavanaugh, O.C.D.

Hermano Lorcenzo, *La Práctica de la Presencia de Dios*, Buenos Aires, Argentina, Editorial Peniel

Brother Lawrence, *The Practice of the Presence of God*, New Kensington, PA, Whitaker House, 1982

Douglas-Klotz, Neil, *Prayers of the Cosmos: Meditations on the Aramaic Words of Jesus*, New York, HarperCollins, 1990

Funk, Mary Margaret, *Thoughts Matter: The Practice of the Spiritual Life*, New York: Continuum, 1998

Justiniano, Raúl, *El Ayuno y la Oración*, Miami: Editorial Vida, 2001

Easwaran, Eknath, *The Mantram Handbook: What a Mantram is, How to Use it, What it can do for You*, Petaluma, CA, Nilgiri Press, 1977

Wilkinson, Bruce, *La Oración de Jabes*, trans. Pablo Barreto, M.D., Miami, FL, Editorial Unilit, 2001

Wilkinson, Bruce, *The Prayer of Jabez*, Sisters, OR, Multnomah Publishers, Inc. 2000

The Way of a Pilgrim, (fwd. Walter J. Ciszek), trans. Helen Bacovcin, New York: Image Books, 1978

Foster, Richard J., *Alabanza ala disciplina*, Eugene, OR., Wipf and Stock Publishers, 1986

Foster, Richard J., *Celebration of Discipline: The Path to Spiritual Growth*, New York, Harper and Row, 1978

FORMATIONAL COURSES

González, Justo L., *Tres theses en la Escuela del Espíritu: Estudios Sobre Hechos*, Nashville, TN, Abingdon Press, 1977

González, Justo L., *Tres theses en la Escuela de Juan: Estudios Sobre el Evangelio de Juan,* Nashville, TN, Abingdon Press, 1998

A Course in Miracles, Mid Valley, CA: Foundation for Inner Peace, 1976

Indermark, John, *Companions in Christ: The Way of Grace, A Small-Group Experience in Spiritual Formation, Participant's Book,* Nashville, TN, Upper Room Books, 2004

Thompson, Marjorie J. and Melissa Tidwell, *Companions in Christ: the Way of Grace Leader's Guide.* Nashville: Upper Room Books, 2004

Compañerismo en Cristo: Una Experiencia de Formación, Espiritual en Grupos Pequeños, Nashville TN, Upper Room Books, 2004, trans. Leticia Guacdiola Sáenz

Compañerismo en Cristo: Una Experiencia de Formación, Espiritual en Grupos Pequeños: Libro del Participante, Nashville TN, Upper Room Books, 2004, trans. Leticia Guacdiola-Sáenz

MONASTIC LIFE

Simpson, James B., Ed. Veil and Cowl: *Writings From the World of Monks and Nuns,* Chicago, Ivan R. Dee, 1994

Teresa of Avila, The Book of Her Life, in *Saint Teresa of Avila, Collected Works,* trans. Kieran Kavanaugh, O.C.D. and Otilio Rodriguez, O.C.D., Washington, D.C., ICS Publications, 1976

Santa Teresa de Jesús, *Historia de un alma: Autobiografía Espiritual,* adap. Fernando Onetto, Buenos Aires, Argentina, Editorial Bonum, 2000

Norris, Kathleen, *The Cloister Walk,* New York: Riverhead,

1996
Chittister, Joan, O.S.B., *The Rule of Benedict: Insights for the Ages*, New York, Crossroads, 1992

Benito de Nursia, *Tegla de los Monjes*, trans. Francisco Javier Molina de la Torre, Salamanca, España, Salamamnca, España, Ediciones Sígueme, 2006

BIOGRAPHIES AND AUTOBIOGRAPHIES

Woolman, John, *The Journal of John Woolman*, (Introduction by John Greenleaf Whittier), Glasgow, Scotland, Robert Smeal, Crosshill, 1883

Abbott, Margery Post, *A Certain Kind of Perfection: An Anthology of Evangelical and Liberal Quaker Writers*, Wallingford, PA, Pendle Hill, 1991

Spink, Kathryn, *Madre Teresa*, trans. Roser Berdagué, Barcelona, Spain: Random House Mondadori, 2003

Ellsberg, Robert, *Todos los santos: Reflexiones, diarias sobre santos, profetas, y testigos de nuestro tiempo*, Buenos Aires, Argentina, Editorial Lumen, 2001

Ellsberg, Robert, *All Saints*, New York, Crossroad, 1997

Moca, Pat, Una *Biblioteca para Juana*, Illus. Beatriz Vidal, New Yor, De Dragonfly Books, 2002

Teresa of Avila, The Book of Her Foundations in *Collected Works of St. Teresa of Avila, vol. 3*, trans. Kieran Kavanaugh, O.C.D. and Otilio Rodriguez, O.C.D., Washington, DC, ICS Publications, 1985

BIBLICAL

La Santa Biblia: Versión Popular, Segunda Edición, New York: Sociedades Bíblicas Unidas, 1983

Miller, Robert J., ed. *The Complete Gospels: Annotated Scholars' Version*, Sonoma, CA, Polebridge Press, 1994

Strange, John, *Atlas Bíblico*, Sociedades Bíblicas Unidas, 1999

Crossan, John Dominic, *The Historical Jesus: The Life of a Mediterranean Jewish Peasant*, New York, HarperCollins, 1991

Crossan, John Dominic and Jonathan L. Reed, *In Search of Paul: How Jesus's Apostle Opposed Rome's Empire with God's Kingdom*, New York, HarperCollins, 2004

THEOLOGY

Brown, Robert McAfee, *Unexpected News: Reading the Bible with Third World Eyes*, Philadelphia, Westminster Press, 1984

Cardenal, Ernesto, *El Evangelio en Solentiname*, Madrid, España, Editorial Trotta, 2006

Cardenal, Ernesto, *The Gospel in Soentiname*, Maryknoll, NY, Orbis Books

McNeill, Donald P., Douglas A. Morrison, and Henri J.M. Nouwen, *Compassion: A Reflection on the Christian Life*, Garden City, NY, Doubleday & Co., 1982

González, Justo L. *Breve Historia de los Doctrinas Cristianas*, Nashville, TN, Abingdon Press, 2007

TROPICAL

Burgess, Ann, Grace Maina, Philip Harris, Stephanie Harris, *How to Grow a Balanced Diet: A Handbook for Community Workers*, London, VSO Books, 1998

Mayhew, Susan and Anne Penny Macmillan, *Tropical and Sub-Tropical Foods*, Macmillan Education, Ltd, 1988

Strickland, G. Thomas, *Hunter's Tropical Medicine and Emerging Infectious Diseases*, 8th Ed., New York: W.B. Saunders Co., 2000

MISCELLANEOUS

Mil Voces Para Celebrar: Himnario Metodista, Nashville, The United Methodist Publishing House, 1996

Doce Pasos y Doce Tradiciones, New York, Alcoholics Anonymous World Services, Inc. 1981

Peck, M. Scott, *The Different Drum: Community Making and Peace*, New York, Simon and Schuster, 1987

Buber, Martin, *Tales of the Hasidim*, Schocken, 1991

Diamond, Jared, *Armas, gérmenes y acero: Breve historia de la humanidad en los ultimos trece mil años*, trans. Fabián Chueca, Barcelona, España, Debate, 2006

Diamond, Jared, *Guns, Germs and Steel: The Fates of Human Societies*, New York, W.W. Norton & Co., 1999

Diamond, Jared, *Collapse: How Societies Choose to Fail or Succeed*, New York, Penguin Group, 2005

Richardson, Jan L., *Sacred Journeys: A Woman's Book of Daily Prayer*, Nashville, Upper Room Books, 1996

Amigas del Senor Lyrics and Songs, a Gift to you from the Sisters.

FROM THE PUBLISHER

The letters in this collection have circulated "virally" from friend to friend, denomination to denomination. They describe the journey of two women desiring in all simplicity to live the life, do the deed, on a daily basis as monastics in the old tradition but with new knowledge of medicine, education, nutrition, cross-cultural communication and careful spiritual discernment. An Episcopalian friend sent me the first of Sister Alegria's letters from Honduras via email and I forwarded it and the others to Episcopalians and to Quakers and Celtic monastics. I met Prairie at Multnomah Meeting on Stark Street and when Beth came to Portland to speak, she came to Quaker Abbey, my home, to accept a donation for their work. This book grew out of our conversation at that time and our instant sympathy and understanding.

As the oldest graduate of Portland State's Publishing Program (2007) and as a member of the school's Ooligan Press community, I am indebted to those many friends from the program who have assisted with the editing and design of the books of Quaker Abbey Press, LLC. QA Press went global with this volume with authors in Honduras, Editor Tim Harnett in the Philippines and Book Designer Cliff Hansen in Korea.

Read current and archived letters at http://yahoogroup.com/group/amigasdelsenor or send a blank email to amigas-delsenor-subscribe@yahoo.com

Amigas del Senor Webpage: www.umoi.net/our-ministries/missions/amigas-del-senor

Rosalie V. Grafe
Quaker Abbey Press, LLC

MUSIC

The following songs are composed by the authors for voice and guitar. Some of the songs use the Methodist hymbook *Mil Voces* and provide original lyrics. In those cases, the references are given in a note printed on the scanned originals. These were mailed to the publisher in the spring of 2010. They are commended for worship in English and in Spanish speaking congregations.

Tune: *Lobe den Herren #29 Mil Voces*

Tune: *Blessings* (By Edwin O' Excell) #365 *Mil Voces*

BUSCANDO A DIOS

letra: Teresa de Ávila
musica: una hermana de Amigos del Señor, 2008

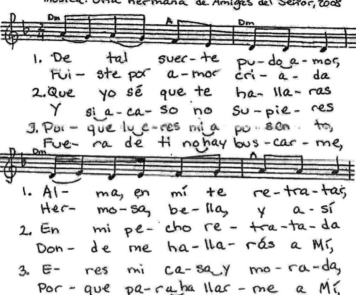

1. De tal suer-te pu-do a-mos,
   Fui-ste por a-mor cri-a-da

2. Que yo sé que te ha-lla-ras
   Y si a-ca-so no su-pie-res

3. Por-que tu e-res mi a po-son-to,
   Fue-ra de ti no hay bus-car-me,

1. Al-ma, en mí te re-tra-tas,
   Her-mo-sa, be-lla, y a-sí

2. En mi pe-cho re-tra-ta-da
   Don-de me ha-lla-rás a Mí,

3. E-res mi ca-sa y mo-ra-da,
   Por-que pa-ra ha-llar-me a Mí,

1. Que nin-gún sa-bio pin-tor
   En mis en-tra-ñas pin-ta-da,

2. Y tan al vi-vo sa-ca-da
   No an-des de a-quí pa-ra a-llí,

3. Y a-sí lla-mo en cual-quier tiem-po,
   Bas-ta-rá so-lo lla-mar-me,

EL REINO DE DIOS

13:33;

Letra: una hermana de Amigas del Señor, 2009 (Mat 13:44; Mar. 4:30-32;

música: "CORDERO" Raquel Mora Martínez, 1992 Luc 17:21, 7:16)

1. «El rei-no de Dios es co-mo le-va-du-
2. «El rei-no de Dios es co-mo un te-so-
3. «El rei-no de Dios es co-mo u-na se-mi-
4. «El rei-no de Dios se en-cuen-tra den-tro de

ra en la ma-sa que mez-cló y-na mu-
ro es-con-di-do que en-con-tró un
lla de mos-ta-za, es la más pe-que-ña
us-ted y de mí: no lo es-con-

cha-cha. fer-men-ta la ma-sa. El
hom-bre. ven-dió to-de y lo com-pró, El
que hay. que cre-ce has-ta un ar-bol. El.
da-mos. lo ha-ga-mos bri-llar. El

rei-no de Dios es co-mo le-va-du-
rei-no de Dios es co-mo un te-so-
rei-no de Dios es co-mo u-na se-mi-
rei-no de Dios se en-cuen-tra den-tro de

ra en la ma-sa.»
ro es-con di-do.»
lla de mos-ta-za.»
us-ted y de mí.»

Di-jo Je-sús.

EL PERDÓN

Letra: una hermana de Amigos del Señor (Mateo 6:14, 5:23-24, 18:22, Juan 20:23)

música de Ghana, adaptado por Tom Colvin

Coro: D

Je-sús, Je-sús, en-se-ña-me tu a per-do-nar, a-sí co-mo tu per-do-nas.

1. Tu nos en-se-ñas, Se-ñor,___
2. An-tes de a-cer-car___
3. He-mos de per-do-nar___
4. Pe-ca-dos que per-do-na-mos

que al per-do nar___
al al-tar de Dios___
no só-lo u-na vez,___
se-rán per-do-na-dos,___

Dios nos per-do-na-rá, tam-bién.
con o-tros he-mos de ha-cer la paz.
si-no se-ten-ta por sie-te más
pe-ro los que no, que-da-rán.

Tune: *Cheredoni* (Ghanaian Folk song) adapted by Tom Colvin #288 *Mil Voces*

Tune: *El Dios de Paz* (Hebrew melody) #79 *Mil Voces*

CPSIA information can be obtained at www.ICGtesting.com
Printed in the USA
BVOW03s2052240414

351512BV00002B/5/P